AF480909

COMPLEX ANALYSIS AND NUMERICAL METHODS

Useful for the students of Graduation and Post Graduation level

N.T. Katre

HOD and Asst. Professor ,

Department of Mathematics

Nabira Mahavidyalaya, Katol

A.D. Wagh

Assistant Professor

Department of Physics

Nabira Mahavidyalaya, Katol

L.D. Giradkar

Assistant Professor

Department of Physics

Nabira Mahavidyalaya, Katol

R. S. Goyte

Assistant Professor

Department of Physics

Govindrao Wanjari College of
Engineering and Technology, Nagpur

Dedication

To our beloved families and students,
whose unwavering support and enthusiasm
have been the driving force behind this work.

To our mentors and colleagues,
for their invaluable guidance and inspiration.

To all the learners, past, present, and future,
who seek knowledge and understanding
in the beautiful realms of complex analysis and numerical methods

Preface

This book, "**Complex Analysis and Numerical Methods,"** is designed to serve as a comprehensive guide for both Undergraduate and Postgraduate students. It aims to bridge the gap between theoretical concepts and practical applications, providing a solid foundation in these essential areas of mathematics.

Complex analysis is a cornerstone of mathematical theory, offering insights and solutions to many problems in engineering, physics, and other sciences. This book presents these concepts clearly and accessibly, ensuring students can grasp and apply them effectively.

Numerical methods provide powerful tools for solving mathematical problems that are difficult or impossible to address analytically. This book covers key numerical techniques essential for both theoretical analysis and practical problem-solving.

We blend theory with practice, offering numerous examples, exercises, and applications to illustrate the concepts discussed. Each chapter builds on the previous one, gradually increasing in complexity and depth.

We express our gratitude to everyone who contributed to this work, including colleagues, students, and reviewers, whose feedback has greatly enhanced the quality of the material presented.

We hope this book will serve as a useful textbook and a valuable reference for students and professionals alike. We encourage readers to approach the material with curiosity and an open mind, and we welcome feedback and suggestions for future editions.

Acknowledgement

We are deeply grateful to the many individuals and institutions that have supported the creation of this book, "**Complex Analysis and Numerical Methods**." This work would not have been possible without their encouragement, expertise, and assistance.

First and foremost, we would like to thank our students, whose curiosity and enthusiasm for learning have been a constant source of inspiration. Their questions and feedback have shaped the direction and content of this book, ensuring that it addresses the needs and challenges faced by learners at both the undergraduate and postgraduate levels.

We extend our sincere appreciation to our colleagues and peers for their invaluable insights and constructive critiques. Their expertise in complex analysis and numerical methods has been instrumental in refining the material presented in this book. Special thanks go to those who reviewed the manuscript and provided detailed feedback, helping us to improve clarity, accuracy, and pedagogical effectiveness.

We are also grateful to the academic institutions and libraries that provided the resources necessary for our research. Their extensive collections and supportive environments have facilitated our work and contributed significantly to the quality of this book.

A heartfelt thank you to our families and friends for their unwavering support and patience throughout the writing process. Their understanding and encouragement have been crucial in helping us to balance the demands of this project with our other professional and personal responsibilities.

Finally, we acknowledge the contributions of the many mathematicians and educators whose work has laid the foundation for the subjects covered in this book. Their pioneering research and dedication to teaching have provided us with the tools and inspiration to create this comprehensive guide.

We hope that this book will serve as a valuable resource for students and educators alike, and we welcome any feedback that can help us to improve future editions. It is our sincere wish that this work will contribute to a deeper understanding and appreciation of complex analysis and numerical methods, fostering a new generation of mathematicians and problem solvers.

.

Contents

UNIT I : COMPLEX ANALYSIS

INTRODUCTION:-

In this chapter, we will delve into the fundamental concepts of complex algebra, including addition, subtraction, multiplication, and division, as well as their geometrical representations in various systems. These topics are indispensable in both mathematical and physical sciences due to their wide range of applications. Complex algebra is instrumental in solving polynomial equations of different orders, from quadratic to nth-order equations, as well as hyperbolic equations. Furthermore, it offers significant advantages when working with complex exponentials and logarithmic functions. Mastering these concepts is essential for tackling advanced topics and solving practical problems in the physical sciences.

Origin of the Complex Number: In the 16th century, the Italian mathematician Gerolamo Cardano demonstrated that the square root of a negative number provides a solution to an equation, such as $-\sqrt{-2} = \sqrt{2}i$. He showed that to solve certain equations, it was necessary to consider numbers that included the square roots of negatives. This led to the development of the complex number system, where each number is expressed in the form $a + bi$with i being the imaginary unit defined by $i^2 = -1$ By using this system, mathematicians could extend their solutions to include these otherwise impossible cases, fundamentally expanding the scope of algebra.

Consider a quadratic equation, $ax^2 + bx + c = 0$

Whose roots are given by ,

$$x = \frac{-b \pm \sqrt{b^2 - 4ac}}{2a}$$

If $b^2 - 4ac > 0$ then $\sqrt{b^2 - 4ac} =$ Real and it is solvable

If $b^2 - 4ac < 0$ then $\sqrt{b^2 - 4ac} \neq$ Real and there is an existance of square root of negative number.

i,e., $\sqrt{-1} = i$, $\sqrt{-2} = \sqrt{2}i$, $\sqrt{-3} = \sqrt{3}i$, $i^2 = -1$, $i^3 = -i$, $i^4 = 1$, $i^5 = i$, ...

Complex Number: A number in the form of x +iy is called a complex number and it is denoted by z, i,e.,

$$z = x + iy \qquad \ldots (1)$$

where, x is a real part and y is a imaginary part of complex number z.

In short , $x = Rel(z)$ Real part of complex Number(z)

$y = Img(z)$ Imaginary part of complex Number (z)

In equation (1), If $y = 0$ then , $z = x$ purely real part of z

If $x = 0$, then $z = iy$ purely imaginary part of z

Complex number can be expressed in three different forms:

- Cartesian form : $z = x + iy$
- Polar form : $z = r\cos\theta + ir\sin\theta = r(\sin\theta + i\cos\theta)$

- Exponential form : $z = re^{i\theta}$

Mathematical representation of a complex number in a diagram is called as Argand Diagram (Given by Mathematician Argand)

Let the Cartesian form of complex number $z = x + iy$ is shown in fig (1), at point P(x, y) the distance

$r = \overline{OP}$ represent the length (modulus) of complex number

i,e. $r = |z| = \sqrt{x^2 + y^2} = \sqrt{(real\ part)^2 + (Img\ part)^2}$ and

θ is a angle between x-axis and $\overline{OP}$, represent the argument of complex number

$\arg(z) = \tan^{-1}\left(\frac{y}{x}\right) = \tan^{-1}\left(\frac{\text{Img part}}{\text{Real part}}\right)$

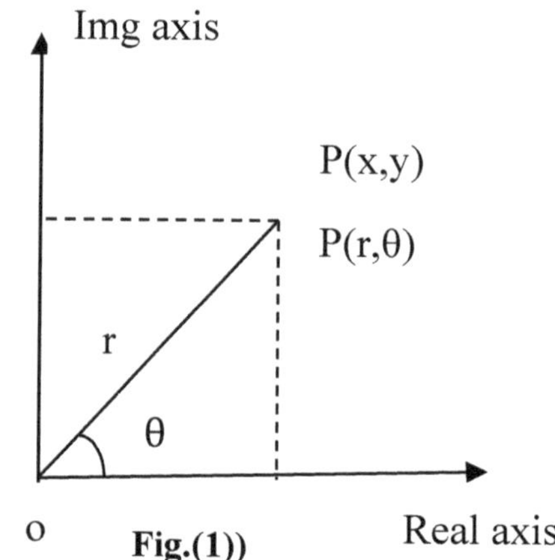

Fig.(1))

∴ (a) $\arg(z_1.z_2) = \arg(z_1) + \arg(z_2)$

(b) $\arg\left(\frac{z_1}{z_2}\right) = \arg(z_1) - \arg(z_2)$

(c) If both (x,y) are positive then $0 < \arg(z) < \frac{\pi}{2}$ and if both (x,y) are negative then $-\pi < \arg(z) < \frac{\pi}{2}$

<u>Properties</u> :-

1. $|z_1 . z_2| = |z_1|\,|z_2|$
2. $\left|\frac{z_1}{z_2}\right| = \frac{z_1}{z_2}$
3. $|z_1 + z_2| \leq |z_1| + |z_2|$
4. $|z_1 - z_2| \geq |z_1| - |z_2|$

Complex Conjugates :- It is the reflection of complex number(z) in the real axis of Argand diagram as shown in fig (2).

Consider the complex number, $z = x + iy$

Take the complex conjugate of a complex number(z)

(Means changing the negative sign of imaginary number) and it is represented by z^*(or $\bar{z}$). and given as $\bar{z} = x - iy$

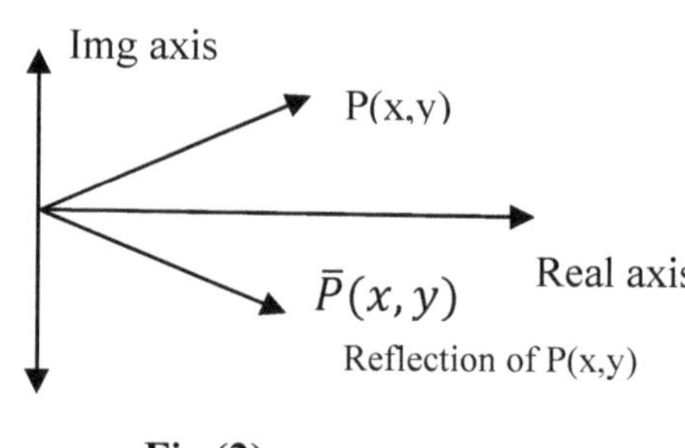

Fig.(2)

Properties of conjugate of a complex number :-

1. $\overline{z_1 + z_2} = \overline{z_1} + \overline{z_2}$
2. $\overline{z_1 - z_2} = \overline{z_1} - \overline{z_2}$
3. $\overline{z_1 . z_2} = \overline{z_1} . \overline{z_2}$

4. $\left|\frac{\overline{z_1}}{z_2}\right| = \frac{\overline{z_1}}{\overline{z_2}}$

Question: 1) Find the complex conjugate of a following complex numbers.

(1) $6 + 5i$ (2) $6 + 7i$ (3) $x - iy$

Solutions:- (1) Let $z = 6 + 5i$ (2) Let $z = 6 + 7i$ (3) Let $z = x - iy$

Complex conjugate of e.g (1), (2), (3) are given by

$\bar{z} = 6 - 5i$ $\bar{z} = 6 - 7i$ $\bar{z} = x + iy$

Question: 2) Find Complex Conjugate of $z = a + 3ib - 2i$.

Solution :- Let $z = a + 3ib - 2i$

$$z = a + i(3b-2)$$

$$\bar{z} = a - i(3b-2)$$

Question: 3) Find the complex conjugate of $W^{(3y+2ix)}$ where $W = x+5i$

Solution:- Let $z = W^{(3y+2ix)} = (x+5i)^{(3y+2ix)}$

$$\bar{z} = (x - 5i)^{(3y+2ix)}$$

Question: 4) Prove that (a) $|z_1 + z_2| \leq |z_1| + |z_2|$

(b) $|z_1 - z_2| \geq |z_1| - |z_2|$

Solution:- (a) Let $z = x + iy$

$$z_1 + z_2 = x_1 + iy_1 + x_2 + iy_2$$

$$= (x_1 + x_2) + i(y_1 + y_2)$$

$$|z_1 + z_2|^2 = (x_1 + x_2)^2 + (y_1 + y_2)^2$$

$$= (x_1^2 + y_1^2) + (x_2^2 + y_2^2) + 2(x_1x_2 + y_1y_2)$$

$$= (x_1^2 + y_1^2) + (x_2^2 + y_2^2) + 2\sqrt{(x_1x_2 + y_1y_2)^2}$$

$$= |z_1|^2 + |z_2|^2 + 2\sqrt{(x_1^2x_2^2 + y_1^2y_2^2 + 2x_1x_2y_1y_2)}$$

$$|z_1 + z_2|^2 \leq |z_1|^2 + |z_2|^2 + 2\sqrt{(x_1^2x_2^2 + y_1^2y_2^2 + x_1^2y_2^2 + x_2^2y_1^2)}$$

$$\leq |z_1|^2 + |z_2|^2 + 2\sqrt{(x_1^2 + y_1^2) + (x_2^2 + y_2^2)}$$

$$\leq |z_1|^2 + |z_2|^2 + 2|z_1||z_2|$$

$$\leq |z_1|^2 + |z_2|^2$$

$$|z_1 + z_2| \leq |z_1| + |z_2|$$

Hence proved.

(b) $|z_1| = |(z_1 - z_2) + z_2| \le |z_1 + z_2| + |z_2|$

$$|z_1| - |z_2| \le |z_1 - z_2|$$
$$|z_1 - z_2| \ge |z_1| - |z_2|$$

Hence proved.

Question: 5) Find the magnitude and argument of the given complex number $z = -4 + 7i$

Solution :- $|z| = \sqrt{(\text{real part})^2 + (\text{imaginary part})^2}$

$= \sqrt{(-4)^2 + (7)^2}$

$= \sqrt{16 + 49} = \sqrt{65} = 8.06$

$\arg(z) = \tan^{-1}\left(\frac{\text{Img part}}{\text{Real part}}\right) = \tan^{-1}\left(\frac{7}{-4}\right) = -60.25$

For magnitude of -4 -3i

Solution:- Let z = -4 -3i

$|z| = \sqrt{(-4)^2 + (7)^2}$

$= \sqrt{16 + 9} = \sqrt{25} = 5$

3) Find the magnitude of $|(2 + 3i)(-1 + 2i)|$

Solution:- Let $z = |(2 + 3i)(-1 + 2i)|$

$= \left|\sqrt{(2)^2 + (3)^2}\sqrt{(-1)^2 + (2)^2}\right| = \sqrt{13} * \sqrt{5} = \sqrt{65}$

4) Find the magnitude of $\left|\frac{1+2i}{1-2i}\right|$

Solution:- Let $z = \left|\frac{1+2i}{1-2i}\right| = \frac{|(1+2i)|}{|(1-2i)|} = \frac{\sqrt{(1)^2+(2)^2}}{\sqrt{(1)^2+(-2)^2}} = \frac{\sqrt{5}}{\sqrt{5}} = 1$

Note:

- It is clear that θ will have infinite number of values differing by multiplies of 2π
- If θ lies in the interval of [− π, π] then it is called as principal argument of complex number.

i.e. arg(Z)

$\therefore -\pi < arg\ (Z) < \pi$

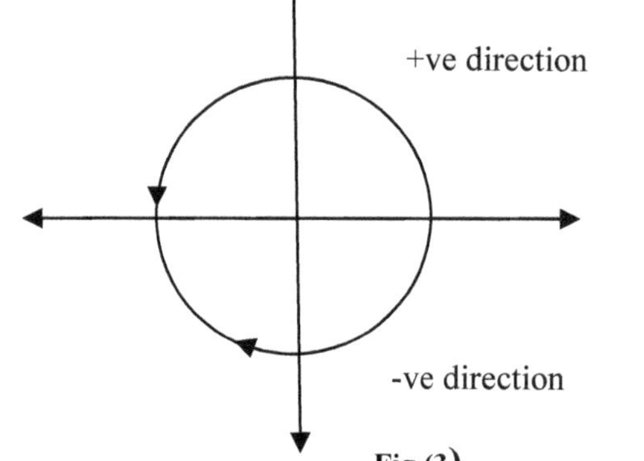

$0 < \theta < \pi$

Or $-\pi < \theta < 0$

Fig (3)

- **Steps to calculate principal argument:**

1. Let Z= x + iy, to find its θ values.

$$\theta = \arg(Z) = \tan^{-1}\left(\frac{\text{Img part}}{\text{Real part}}\right)$$

2. Determine the quadrant in which the x and y coordinates lie to identify the position of z within that quadrant.

If Z lies in 1st quadrant (+, +) then ,Arg(z) = θ

If Z lies in 2nd quadrant (-, +) then ,Arg(z) = $(\pi - \theta)$

If Z lies in 3rd quadrant (-, -) then ,Arg(z) = $-(\pi - \theta)$

If Z lies in 4th quadrant (+, -) then , Arg(z) = $-\theta$

Question: 6) Find the principal argument of complex number $-1+\sqrt{3}i$

Solution:- Let $Z = -1+\sqrt{3}\,i$

$$\theta = \tan^{-1}\left(\frac{\sqrt{3}}{-1}\right) = \frac{\pi}{3}$$

Given points of Z = (x, y) = $(-1,\sqrt{3})$

i.e. Z lies in 2nd quadrant.

∴ $\text{Arg}(z) = \pi - \theta = \pi - \frac{\pi}{3} = \frac{2\pi}{3}$

Question: 7) Find the modulus and principal argument of complex number $-\sqrt{3}- i$.

Soution:- Let $Z= -\sqrt{3} - i$

$$|Z| = \sqrt{(-\sqrt{3})^2 + (-1)^2} = \sqrt{3+1} = \sqrt{4} = 2$$

$$\theta = \tan^{-1}\left(\frac{-1}{-\sqrt{3}}\right) = \tan^{-1}\left(\frac{1}{\sqrt{3}}\right) = \frac{\pi}{6}$$

Given points of Z= (x,y) = $(-\sqrt{3},-1)$

i.e. Z lies in 3rd quadrant.

∴ $\text{Arg}(Z) = -(\pi - \theta) = -(\pi - \frac{\pi}{6}) = \frac{-5\pi}{6}$

∴ (Modulus and Argument) = $(2, \frac{-5\pi}{6})$.

Question: 8) Find the modulus and principal argument of complex number $\frac{(1+i)^2}{1-i}$.

Solution:- Let $Z = \frac{(1+i)^2}{1-i} = \frac{1+2i-1}{1-i} = \frac{2i}{1-i} = \frac{0+2i}{1-i}$

$|Z| = \frac{\sqrt{(0)^2+(2)^2}}{\sqrt{(1)^2+(-1)^2}} = \frac{2}{\sqrt{2}} = \sqrt{2}$

$\text{Arg}(Z) = \text{Arg}(\frac{2i}{1-i}) = \text{Arg}(2i) - \text{Arg}(1-i)$

$= \tan^{-1}(\frac{2}{0}) - \tan^{-1}(\frac{-1}{1})$

$= \tan^{-1}(0) - \tan^{-1}(1) = \frac{\pi}{2} - \frac{\pi}{4} = \frac{\pi}{4}$

Given points of Z = (x,y), the numerator (0 , 2) lies in 1st quadrant and the denominator (1 , -1) lies in 4th quadrant.

$\text{Arg}(z) = \text{Arg}(\frac{2i}{1-i}) = \text{Arg}(2i) - \text{Arg}(1-i)$

$= \tan^{-1}(\frac{2}{0}) - \tan^{-1}(\frac{-1}{1}) = \tan^{-1}(0) - \tan^{-1}(1)$

$= \frac{\pi}{2} - (-\frac{\pi}{4}) = \frac{3\pi}{4}$

$\therefore$(Modulus, Argument) = $(\sqrt{2}, \frac{3\pi}{4})$.

Question: 9) Find the modulus and principal argument of complex number $\frac{1+2i}{1-(1-i)^2}$.

Solution:- Let $Z = \frac{1+2i}{1-(1-i)^2} = \frac{1+2i}{1-(1+2i-1)} = \frac{1+2i}{1+2i} = 1$

$|Z| = \sqrt{1} = 1$

$\arg(Z) = \tan^{-1}(\frac{0}{1}) = 0$

Given points of Z= (x,y) = (1 , 0)

i.e. Z lies in 1st quadrant.

$\text{Arg}(Z) = \theta = 0$

$\therefore$ (Modulus , Argument) = (1 , 0)

EXERCISES :

1. Find the complex conjugate of

   1. $\frac{2+3i}{1-i}$ Ans: $\frac{-1}{2}$ - $\frac{-5i}{2}$

   2. $1 + i$ Ans: 1 - i

   3. $1 + 2i$ Ans: 1-2i

   4. $a + ib$ Ans: a - ib

2. Show that a) $\overline{z + 3i} = z - 3i$ b) $\overline{iz} = -i\bar{z}$

3. Find the modulus of the following complex number

   1. $(8 - i^3) - (7i^2 + 5) + (\overline{9 - i})$ Ans: $\sqrt{365}$

   2. $(7 + i^2) + (6 - i) - (4 - i^3)$ Ans: $4\sqrt{5}$

4. Find the principal argument of

   1. $Z = \frac{i}{-2-2i}$ Ans: $\frac{-3\pi}{5}$

   2. $Z =(\sqrt{3} - i)^6$ Ans: π

5. Find the modulus of the given complex number

   $\sqrt{\frac{1+i}{1-i}}$ Ans: $(1, \frac{\pi}{4})$

EQUALITY OF COMPLEX NUMBERS:-

If two complex numbers $x_1 + iy_1$ and $x_2 + iy_2$are said to be equal if $x_1 = x_2$ and $y_1 = y_2$.

Proof:- Consider two complex numbers

$$z_1 = x_1 + iy_1 \quad \text{and} \quad z_2 = x_2 + iy_2$$

If $z_1 = z_2$

$$x_1 + iy_1 = x_2 + iy_2$$

$$x_1 - x_2 = iy_2 - iy_1$$

$$x_1 - x_2 = i(y_2 - y_1)$$

$$(x_1 - x_2)^2 = -(y_2 - y_1)^2$$

$$(x_1 - x_2)^2 + (y_2 - y_1)^2 = 0$$

Here the sum of two numbers are zero, if and only if each numbers are zero.

i.e. $(x_1 - x_2)^2 = 0$ and $(y_2 - y_1)^2 = 0$

$x_1 - x_2 = 0$ and $(y_2 - y_1) = 0$

$\mathbf{x_1 = x_2}$ and $\mathbf{y_1 = y_2}$

ADDITION OF COMPLEX NUMBERS:-

The addition of two complex numbers $z_1 = x_1 + iy_1$ and $z_2 = x_2 + iy_2$ gives new complex number. This addition is similar to addition of real numbers. In complex addition, we add real part of two complex numbers separately and imaginary part of complex numbers separately.

i.e. $z = z_1 + z_2 = x_1 + iy_1 + x_2 + iy_2 = x_1 + x_2 + i(y_2 + y_1)$

ADDITION OF COMPLEX NUMBERS BY GEOMETRY:-s

Consider two complex numbers $z_1 = x_1 + iy_1$ and $z_2 = x_2 + iy_2$ represented by $A(x_1,y_1)$ and $B(x_2, y_2)$ respectively in below argand diagram fig(4).

Complete the parallelogram OACB.

Draw perpendicular lines BE, AF,

CG on Imaginary axis.

Also draw AD perpendicular to CG.

$OG = OE + OF = x_2 + x_1$

$CG = CD + (DG=AF) = y_1 + y_2$

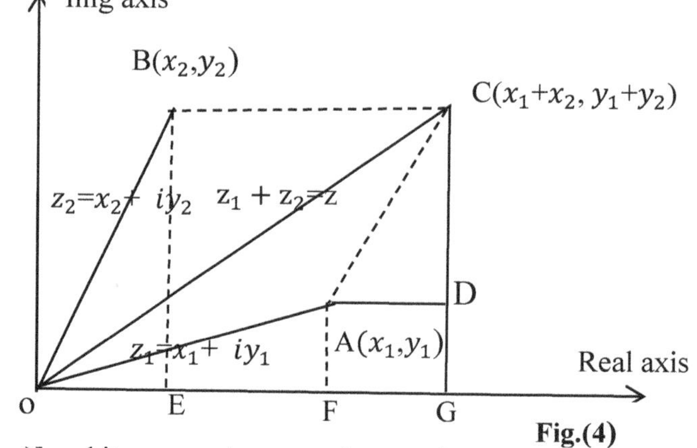

Fig.(4)

∴ The co-ordinate of point C [$(x_2 + x_1)$, $(y_1 + y_2)$] and it represents a complex number.

i.e. $z = x_1 + x_2 + i(y_2 + y_1) = (x_1 + iy_1) + (x_2 + iy_2) = z_1 + z_2$

SUBSTRACTION OF TWO COMPLEX NUMBERS:-

The substraction of two complex numbers $z_1 = x_1 + iy_1$ and $z_2 = x_2 + iy_2$ gives new complex number. This substraction is similar to substraction of real numbers. In complex substraction, we subtract real part of two complex numbers separately and imaginary part of complex numbers separately.

i.e. $z = z_1 - z_2 = (x_1 + iy_1) - (x_2 + iy_2) = (x_1 - x_2) + i(y_1 - y_2)$

SUBSTRACTION OF COMPLEX NUMBERS BY GEOMETRY:-

Consider two complex numbers $z_1 = x_1 + iy_1$ and $z_2 = x_2 + iy_2$ represented by $A(x_1,y_1)$ and $B(x_2,y_2)$ respectively in below diagram fig. (5)

i.e. $z_1 - z_2 = z_1 + (-z_2)$

It means that addition of z_1 and $-z_2$.

$-z_2$ is represented by OB^* form by producing OB to OB^*

such that $OB = OB^*$.Complete the parallelogram $OACB^*$.

Then the sum of z_1 and $-z_2$ (i.e. $z_1 + (-z_2)$) is represented

by OC.

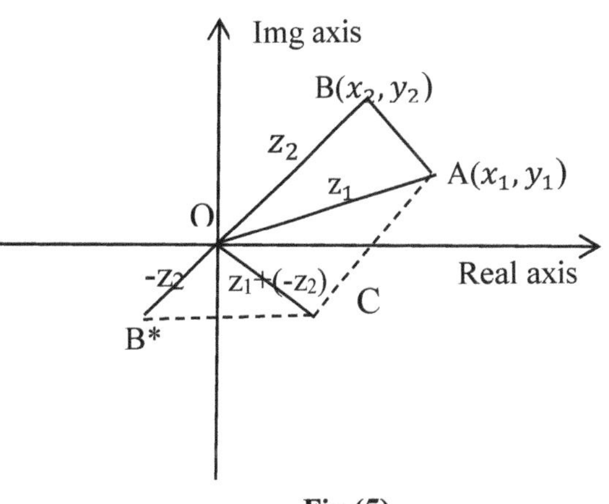

Fig.(5)

MULTIPLICATION OF TWO COMPLEX NUMBERS:-

The multiplication of two complex numbers $z_1 = x_1 + iy_1$ and $z_2 = x_2 + iy_2$ give new complex number. This is equivalent to the ordinary multiplication (like component wise).

i.e. $z = z_1 \times z_2 = (x_1 + iy_1) \times (x_2 + iy_2)$

$= x_1x_2 + i\,x_1y_2 + i\,x_2y_1 - y_1y_2$

$= (x_1x_2 - y_1y_2) + i(x_1y_2 - x_2y_1)$

MULTIPLICATION OF TWO COMPLEX NUMBERS BY GEOMETRY:-

Consider two complex number $z_1 = x_1 + iy_1$ and $z_2 = x_2 + iy_2$ represented by the point A (x_1,y_1) and B (x_2,y_2) respectively in argand di agram fig (6).

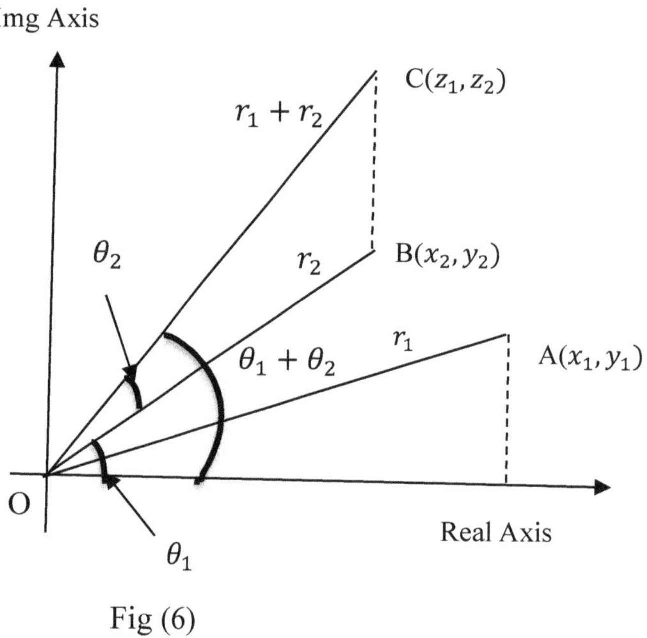

Fig (6)

The point z_1 and z_2 are written in polar form by considering $x = r\cos\theta$ and $y = r\sin\theta$

$\therefore z_1 = x_1 + iy_1 = r_1\cos\theta_1 + r_1\sin\theta_1 = r_1(\cos\theta_1 + i\sin\theta_1)$

Similarly, $z_2 = r_2(\cos\theta_2 + i\sin\theta_2)$

$$\therefore \quad z = z_1 \times z_2 = r_1.r_2(\cos\theta_1 + i\sin\theta_1)(\cos\theta_2 + i\sin\theta_2)$$

$$= r_1.r_2(\cos\theta_1\cos\theta_2 + i\cos\theta_1\sin\theta_2 + i\sin\theta_1\cos\theta_2 - \sin\theta_1\sin\theta_2)$$

$$= r_1.r_2(\cos\theta_1\cos\theta_2 - \sin\theta_1\sin\theta_2) + i(\cos\theta_1\sin\theta_2 + \sin\theta_1\cos\theta_2)$$

$$z = r_1.r_2[\cos(\theta_1 + \theta_2) + i\sin(\theta_1 + \theta_2)]$$

cut off OD = 1 along real axis. Construct $\triangle OBC$ on OB

Similarly for $\triangle ODA$,

$$\therefore \frac{OC}{OA} = \frac{OB}{OD}$$

$$\frac{OC}{OA} = \frac{OB}{1}$$

$$OC = OA.OB = r_{1.}r_2 = \angle DOB + \angle BOC$$

$$= \theta_2 + \theta_1$$

Hence the product of two complex numbers $z_1 and\ z_2$ are represented by the point

$$\therefore |z_1.z_2| = |z_1|.|z_2|$$

$Arg(z_1 . z_2) = Arg(z_1).Arg(z_2)$.

DIVISION OF COMPLEX NUMBER:-

The division of two complex numbers $z_1 = x_1 + iy_1$ and $z_2 = x_2 + iy_2$ gives new complex number.

i.e. $\frac{z_1}{z_2} = \frac{x_1 + iy_1}{x_2 + iy_2}$

In order to separate real and imaginary part of complex number, we multiply both numerator and denominator by the complex conjugate of the denominator.

$$\frac{z_1}{z_2} = \frac{(x_1 + iy_1)(x_1 - iy_1)}{(x_2 + iy_2)(x_2 - iy_2)}$$

$$= \frac{x_1 x_2 - i x_1 y_2 + iy_1 x_2 + y_1 y_2}{x_2^2 - (iy_2)^2}$$

$$= \frac{x_1 x_2 + y_1 y_2}{x_2^2 + y_2^2} + \frac{i(x_1 y_2 - y_1 x_2)}{x_2^2 + y_2^2}$$

DIVISION OF COMPLEX NUMBERS BY GEOMETRY:-

Consider two complex number $z_1 = x_1 + iy_1$ and $z_2 = x_2 + iy_2$ represented by the point $A(x_1, y_1)$ and $B(x_2, y_2)$ respectively in argand diagram fig (7).

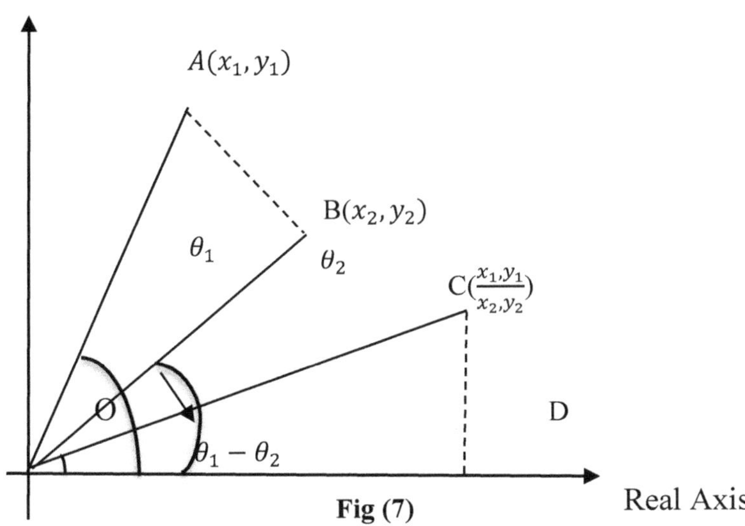

Fig (7)

The point z_1 and z_2 are written in polar form by considering $x = r\cos\theta$ and $y = r\sin\theta$

$$\therefore\ z_1 = x_1 + iy_1 = r_1 \cos\theta_1 + r_1 \sin\theta_1$$

$$z_1 = r_1 (\cos\theta_1 + i\sin\theta_1)$$

Similarly, $z_2 = r_2 (\cos\theta_2 + i\sin\theta_2)$

Let OD = 1 construct ΔODC on OD likewise ΔOBA on OB

$$\therefore \frac{OC}{OD} = \frac{OA}{OB}$$

$$\frac{OC}{1} = \frac{OA}{OB}$$

$$OC = \frac{OA}{OB} = \frac{r_1}{r_2}$$

∴ The division of two complex numbers $z_1(x_1,y_1)$ and $z_2(x_2,y_2)$ represented by point $C(\frac{z_1}{z_2})$.

$$\therefore \left|\frac{z_1}{z_2}\right| = \frac{|z_1|}{|z_2|}$$

$$Arg(\frac{z_1}{z_2}) = Arg(z_1) - Arg(z_2)$$

Question: 1) Add the following complex number.

a) $z_1 = \frac{3}{4} - \frac{7}{3}i$ and $z_2 = \frac{-5}{3} + \frac{11}{5}i$

Solution:- $z = z_1 + z_2 = \frac{-11}{12} + i\,(\frac{-2}{15}) = \frac{-11}{12} - \frac{2}{15}i$

b) 1+2i, 3 – 4i, -2 + i

Solution:- Let $z_1 = 1+2i$, $z_2 = 3 - 4i$ and $z_3 = -2 + i$

$$z = z_1 + z_2 + z_3 = (1 + 3 - 2) + i\,(2 - 4 + 1)$$

$$z = 2 - i$$

Question: 2) Substract the following complex number.

a) $2 + \frac{3}{2}i$ and $-5 + \frac{7}{4}i$

Solution:- Let $z_1 = 2 + \frac{3i}{2}$ and $z_2 = -5 + \frac{7i}{4}$

$$z = z_1 - z_2 = (2 + \frac{3}{2}i) - (-5 + \frac{7}{4}i) = (2 + 5) - i\,(\frac{3}{2} - \frac{7}{4})3$$

$$z = 7 + \frac{1}{4}i$$

b) $\frac{3}{4} - \frac{7}{3}i$ and $\frac{-5}{3} + \frac{11}{5}i$

Solution:- Let $z_1 = \frac{3}{4} - \frac{7i}{3}$ and $z_2 = \frac{-5}{3} + \frac{11i}{5}$

$$z = z_1 - z_2 = (\frac{3}{4} - \frac{7}{3}i) - (\frac{-5}{3} + \frac{11}{5}i)$$

$$z = (\frac{3}{4} + \frac{5}{3}) - i(\frac{-7}{3} - \frac{11}{5}) = \frac{29}{12} + \frac{68}{15}i$$

Question: 3) Multiply the following complex numbers.

a) 3 + 2i , -1 – 4i

Solution:- Let $z_1 = 3+2i$ and $z_2 = -1 -4i$

$$z = z_1 \times z_2 = (3 + 2i).(-1 - 4i) = -3 -12i -2i -8i^2$$

$$z = -3 -14i + 8 = 5 - 14i$$

b) 3 + 4i , 7 – 3i

Solution:- Let $z_1 = 3 + 4i$ and $z_2 = 7 - 3i$

$$z = z_1 \times z_2 = (3 + 4i).(7 - 3i) = 21 - 9i + 28i -12i^2$$

$$z = 21 + 19i + 12 = 33 + 19i$$

Question: 4) Find $z = \frac{3-2i}{-1+4i}$

Solution:- Given that $z = \frac{3-2i}{-1+4i}$

$$= \frac{3-2i}{-1+4i} \times \frac{-1-4i}{-1-4i} = \frac{-3-12i+2i+8i^2}{(-1)^2+(4i)^2} = \frac{-3-10i-8}{1+16}$$

$$z = \frac{-11}{17} - \frac{10}{17}i$$

Question: 5) Divide 1 + i by 8 + 4i .

Solution:- Let $z = \frac{1+i}{3+4i}$

$$Z = \frac{1+i}{3+4i} \times \frac{3-4i}{3-4i} = \frac{3-4i+3i-4i^2}{(3)^2-(4i)^2} = \frac{7-i}{9+16} = \frac{7}{25} - \frac{1}{25}i$$

Question: 6) Find $\frac{(6+i)(2-i)}{(4+3i)(1-2i)}$

Solution:- Let $z = \frac{(6+i)(2-i)}{(4+3i)(1-2i)} = \frac{12-6i+2i-i^2}{4-8i+3i-6i^2} = \frac{13-4i}{10-5i} = \frac{13-4i}{10-5i} \times \frac{10+5i}{10+5i}$

$$= \frac{130+65i-40i-20i^2}{(10)^2-(5i)^2} = \frac{150+25i}{100+25} = \frac{150+25i}{125}$$

$$z = \frac{6+i}{5} = \frac{6}{5} + \frac{1}{5}i$$

EXERCISES:-

Question: 1) Verify that

a) $(\sqrt{2} - i) - i(1 - \sqrt{2}i) = -2i$

b) $(2, -3)(-2, 1) = (-1, 8)$

Question: 2) Solve $\frac{4+i}{2-3i}$. Ans: $\frac{5}{13} + \frac{14}{13}i$

Question: 3) Add the given two numbers $z_1 = x_1 + iy_1$ and $z_2 = x_2 + iy_2$. Ans: $(x_1 + x_2) + i(y_1 + y_2)$

Question: 4) Substract the given two numbers 3 – 2i and 5 + 3i . Ans: -2 – 5i

Question: 5) Find the value of $\frac{(1+2i)^3}{(1+i)(2-i)}$. Ans: $\frac{-7}{2} + \frac{1}{2}i$

Continuity of the function:-

A function f(z) = u+iv is said to continuous at the point $z = z_0$, if f(z) is defined at $z = z_0$

$\lim_{z\to z_0} f(z)$ will exist (i.e, limiting value is path independent)

$\lim_{z\to z_0} f(z) = f(z = z_0)$

Differentiability of the function :-

Let f(z) be a single valued function of real variable z. Then the derivatives of f(z) is given by

$$f'(z) = \lim_{\delta z\to 0} \frac{f(z+\delta z)-f(z)}{\delta z} = \lim_{\delta z\to 0} \frac{f(z)}{\delta z}$$

Provided the limit exist and is independent of path along which $\delta z\to 0$.

Thus $f'(z)$ exist and the given function f(z) is differentiable at point z.

And $f'(z)$ is also called as 1st principal .

Let A be a fixed point and B be the neighbouring point. The point B

may approach P along any path as shown in fig (8).

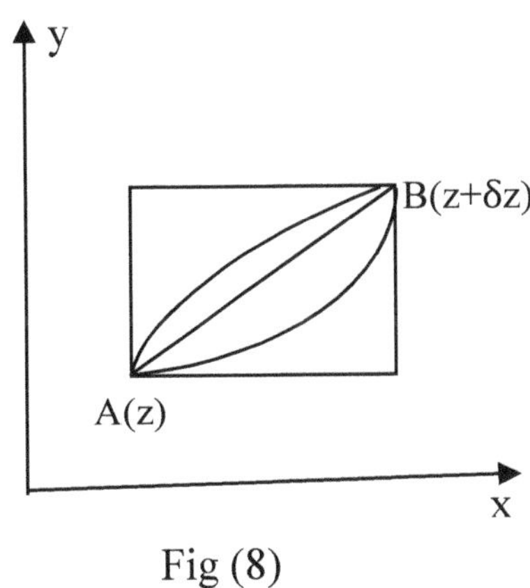

Fig (8)

ANALYTIC FUNCTION:-

A complex function f (z) is said to be analytic at a point $z = z_0$, if it is differentiable at $z = z_0$ as well as at each point in the same neighborhood of the point $z = z_0$.

A complex function f (z) is called analytic function in the region R, If it is analytic at every point in the region.

The point at which the function is not differentiable is called a singular point. Analyst function is also called as homomorphic / regular / monogenic function .

A complex function f (z) is analytic everywhere is called as Entire function.

Note: If the function f (z) contain $\bar{z}$, $|z|$, Rel(z) = $\frac{1}{2}(z+\bar{z})$ and Img(z) = $\frac{1}{2!}(z - \bar{z})$. Then f (z) is not analytic in nature.

CAUCHY-REIMANN EQUATION

Theorem:- Necessary condition for f (z) to be analytic.

A complex function f(z) = u(x, y) + iv(x, y) ...(1)

is to be analytic at all the point in the region R are

$$\frac{\partial u}{\partial x} = \frac{\partial v}{\partial y} \text{ and } \frac{\partial u}{\partial y} = -\frac{\partial v}{\partial x}, \text{ provided } \frac{\partial u}{\partial x}, \frac{\partial u}{\partial y}, \frac{\partial v}{\partial x} \, and \, \frac{\partial v}{\partial y} \text{ are exist.}$$

Proof:- Let f(z) = u(x, y) + iv(x, y) be an analytic function in region R , where u and v are the function of x and y.

Let u and v are the function of x and y having an small increment $\delta u, \delta v$ and $\delta x, \delta y$ respectively.

$$\therefore f(z+\delta z) = (u + \delta u) + i(v + \delta v) \quad ...(2)$$

Now

$$\frac{f(z+\delta z)-f(z)}{f(z)} = \frac{(u+\delta u)+i(v+\delta v)-(u+iv)}{\delta z} = \frac{(u+iv)+(\delta u+i\delta v)-(u+iv)}{\delta z} = \frac{(\delta u+i\delta v)}{\delta z}$$

$$= \frac{\delta u}{\delta z} + \frac{i\delta v}{\delta z}$$

$$\lim_{\delta z \to 0} \frac{f(z+\delta z)-f(z)}{\delta z} = \lim_{\delta z \to 0} \left(\frac{\delta u}{\delta z} + \frac{i\delta v}{\delta z}\right)$$

$$f'(z) = \lim_{\delta z \to 0} \left(\frac{\delta u}{\delta z} + \frac{i\delta v}{\delta z}\right) \quad ...(3)$$

Since δz can approach zero along any axis-

1. **Along real axis (x- axis)**

z = x+ iy

z = x $\because$ y = 0

$\delta z = \delta x$

Putting these value in equation (3) we get,

$$f'(z) = \lim_{\delta x \to 0} \left(\frac{\delta u}{\delta x} + \frac{i\delta v}{\delta x}\right) = \frac{\delta u}{\delta x} + \frac{i\delta v}{\delta x} \quad ...(4)$$

2. **Along Imaginary axis (y-axis)**

z = x+ iy

z = v $\because$ x = 0

$\delta z = \delta x$

Putting these value in equation (3) we get,

$$f'(z) = \lim_{\delta y \to 0}\left(\frac{\delta u}{i\delta y} + \frac{i\delta v}{i\delta y}\right) = \lim_{\delta y \to 0}\left(\frac{-i\delta u}{\delta y} + \frac{\delta v}{\delta y}\right) = \frac{\delta v}{\delta y} - \frac{i\delta u}{\delta y} \quad \ldots(5)$$

If f(z) is differentiable, then two values of $f'(z)$ must be same.

From equation (4) & (5) , we get

$$\frac{\delta u}{\delta x} + \frac{i\delta v}{\delta x} = \frac{\delta v}{\delta y} - \frac{i\delta u}{\delta y}$$

Equating real and imaginary part of above equations. We get,

$$\frac{\partial u}{\partial x} = \frac{\partial v}{\partial y} \text{ and } \frac{\partial u}{\partial y} = -\frac{\partial v}{\partial x}$$

Which are the required Cauchy- Riemann condition.

Theorem: Sufficient condition for f(z) to be analytic

A complex function f(z) = u(x,y) + iv(x,y) to be analytic at all the points in a region R are if,

1. $\frac{\partial u}{\partial x} = \frac{\partial v}{\partial y}$ and $\frac{\partial u}{\partial y} = -\frac{\partial v}{\partial x}$

2. $\frac{\partial u}{\partial x}, \frac{\partial v}{\partial x}, \frac{\partial u}{\partial y}, \frac{\partial v}{\partial y}$ are continuous function of x and y in region R.

Proof:- Let f(z) = u(x,y) + iv(x,y) be a single valued function having partial derivatives are $\frac{\partial u}{\partial x}, \frac{\partial v}{\partial x}, \frac{\partial u}{\partial y}, \frac{\partial v}{\partial y}$ are continuous in region R, hence the C-R equations are satisfied.

By Taylor's theorem,

$$f(z + \delta z) = u(x + \partial x, y + \partial y) + iv(x + \partial x, y + \partial y)$$

$$= u(x,y) + \left(\frac{\partial u}{\partial x}\delta x + \frac{\partial u}{\partial y}\delta y\right) + \cdots + i\left[v(x,y) + \left(\frac{\partial v}{\partial x}\delta x + \frac{\partial v}{\partial y}\delta y\right) + \cdots\right]$$

$$= [u(x,y) + iv(x,y)] + \left[\frac{\partial u}{\partial x}\delta x + \frac{\partial u}{\partial y}\delta y + \frac{i\,\partial v}{\partial x}\delta x + \frac{i\,\partial v}{\partial y}\delta y + \cdots\right]$$

$$= [u(x,y) + iv(x,y)] + \left(\frac{\partial u}{\partial x}\delta x + \frac{i\,\partial v}{\partial x}\delta x\right) + [\frac{\partial u}{\partial y}\,\delta y + i\frac{\partial v}{\partial y}\,\delta y] + \ldots$$

$$f(z + \delta z) = f(z) + \left(\frac{\partial u}{\partial x} + \frac{i\,\partial v}{\partial x}\right)\delta x + \left(\frac{\partial u}{\partial y} + \frac{i\,\partial v}{\partial y}\right)\delta y + \ldots$$

$$f(z + \delta z) - f(z) = \left(\frac{\partial u}{\partial x} + \frac{i\,\partial v}{\partial x}\right)\delta x + \left(\frac{\partial u}{\partial y} + \frac{i\,\partial v}{\partial y}\right)\delta y \quad \ldots(1)$$

Using Cauchy-Riemann equation i.e, $\frac{\partial u}{\partial x} = \frac{\partial v}{\partial y}$ and $\frac{\partial u}{\partial y} = -\frac{\partial v}{\partial x}$ in equation (1), we get

$$f(z+\delta z) - f(z) = \left(\frac{\partial u}{\partial x}+\frac{i\partial v}{\partial x}\right)\delta x + \left(-\frac{\partial v}{\partial x}+\frac{i\partial u}{\partial x}\right)\delta y = \left(\frac{\partial u}{\partial x}+\frac{i\partial v}{\partial x}\right)\delta x + \left(\frac{i\partial v}{\partial x}+\frac{\partial u}{\partial x}\right)i\delta y$$

$$= \left(\frac{\partial u}{\partial x}+\frac{i\partial v}{\partial x}\right)(\delta x + i\delta y) = \left(\frac{\partial u}{\partial x}+\frac{i\partial v}{\partial x}\right)(\delta z)$$

$$\frac{f(z+\delta z)-f(z)}{\delta z} = \frac{\partial u}{\partial x}+\frac{i\partial v}{\partial x}$$

$$\lim_{\delta z\to 0}\frac{f(z+\delta z)-f(z)}{\delta z} = \frac{\partial u}{\partial x}+\frac{i\partial v}{\partial x}$$

$$f'(z) = \frac{\partial u}{\partial x}+\frac{i\partial v}{\partial x} = \frac{\partial v}{\partial y}-\frac{i\partial u}{\partial y}$$

But $\frac{\partial u}{\partial x}, \frac{\partial v}{\partial x}$ exist, Hence $f'(z)$ exist.

Thus f(x) is analytic in the region R.

Cauchy- Riemann Equations in polar form :-

Statement:- A complex function f(z) = u(x, y) + iv(x, y) is to be analytic at all the points in the region R, then the Cauchy-Riemann equation in polar form are

$$\frac{\partial u}{\partial r} = \frac{1}{r}\frac{\partial v}{\partial \theta} \quad and \quad \frac{\partial v}{\partial r} = -\frac{1}{r}\frac{\partial u}{\partial \theta}$$

Proof:- Let f(z) = u(x, y) + iv(x, y) be an analytic function in region R where u and v are the functions of x and y. Also, we know that, $x = r\cos\theta \;\; and \;\; y = r\sin\theta$ ...(1)

$\therefore z = x + iy = r\cos\theta + ir\sin\theta = r(\cos\theta + i\sin\theta) = re^{i\theta}$

$f(z) = f(re^{i\theta}) = u(x, y) + iv(x, y) = u(r, \theta) + iv(r, \theta)$

i.e, $f(r.e^{i\theta}) = u(r, \theta) + iv(r, \theta)$ ...(2)

differentiating equation (2) partially with respect to r, we get

$$f'(r.e^{i\theta}).e^{i\theta} = \frac{\partial u}{\partial r}+\frac{i\partial v}{\partial r} \qquad ...(3)$$

differentiate equation (2) partially with respect to θ, we get

$$f'(re^{i\theta}).re^{i\theta}i = \frac{\partial u}{\partial \theta}+\frac{i\partial v}{\partial \theta} \qquad ..(4)$$

By using equation (3) in equation (4), we get

$$\frac{ir\partial u}{\partial r} - \frac{r\partial v}{\partial r} = \frac{\partial u}{\partial \theta}+\frac{i\partial v}{\partial \theta}$$

Comparing real and imaginary part of equation, we get

$$\frac{\partial u}{\partial \theta} = -\frac{r\partial v}{\partial r} \;\&\; \frac{r\partial u}{\partial r} = \frac{\partial v}{\partial \theta}$$

$$\therefore \frac{\partial v}{\partial r} = -\frac{1}{r}\frac{\partial u}{\partial \theta} \;\&\; \frac{\partial u}{\partial r} = \frac{1}{r}\frac{\partial v}{\partial \theta}$$ Hence proved

Question:1) identify the given below functions are analytic or not .

(1) $|z| = \sqrt{z\bar{z}}$ (2) Rel(z) = $x = \frac{1}{2}(z + \bar{z})$ (3) Img(z) = $y = \frac{1}{2i}(z - \bar{z})$

(4.) $f(z) = z^{20} + 4z^{12} + (\bar{z})^4$ (5) $(z-8)^3(4+z^2)^7$ (6) $z^7(1-z)^6$

(7) $(z^3 - 3)^5$ (8) $(1-\bar{z})^4(2+z)^6$

Solutions:- (1),(2),(3),(4) & (8) are not analytic functions,

and (5),(6),(7) are analytic functions.

Question: 2) If the function $e^x(\cos y + i\sin y)$ is analytic function . find the derivatives.

Solution:- Let u+iv = $e^x(\cos y + i\sin y)$

Here, $u = e^x\cos y$ and $v = e^x\sin y$

By using Cauchy- Riemann equations

$$\frac{\partial u}{\partial x} = \frac{\partial v}{\partial y} \text{ and } \frac{\partial u}{\partial y} = -\frac{\partial v}{\partial x}$$

$$\frac{\partial u}{\partial x} = e^x\cos y \quad \text{and} \quad \frac{\partial u}{\partial y} = -e^x\sin y$$

$$\frac{\partial v}{\partial y} = e^x\cos y \quad \text{and} \quad \frac{\partial v}{\partial x} = e^x\sin y$$

$$\frac{\partial u}{\partial x} = \frac{\partial v}{\partial y} \quad \text{and} \quad \frac{\partial u}{\partial y} = -\frac{\partial v}{\partial x}$$

Thus Cauchy-Riemann equations are satisfied.

Hence , the given function is analytic .

$$f'(z) = \frac{\partial u}{\partial x} + \frac{i\partial v}{\partial x} = e^x\cos y + ie^x\sin y = e^x(\cos y + i\sin y)$$

$$= e^x.e^{iy} = e^{x+iy} = e^z$$

Which is the required derivative.

Question: 3) Find the derivative of z^2 at any point of z.

Solution:- let $f(z) = z^2$

$$f'(z) = \lim_{\delta z \to 0}\frac{\delta f(z)}{\delta z} = \lim_{\delta z \to 0}\frac{(z+\delta z)^2 - z^2}{\delta z} = \lim_{\delta z \to 0}\frac{z^2 + (\delta z)^2 + 2z\delta z - z^2}{\delta z}$$

$$= \lim_{\delta z \to 0} 2z + \delta z$$

$$\lim_{\delta z\to 0}\frac{\delta f(z)}{\delta z} = 2z$$

Question: 4) If $f(z) = \begin{cases} \frac{x^3y(y-ix)}{x^6-y^2}, z \neq 0 \\ 0 \qquad\qquad , z = 0 \end{cases}$, then find $\frac{df}{dz}$ at z = 0.

Solution:- By the defination of differentiability

$$f'(z) = \lim_{\delta z\to 0}\frac{f(z+\delta z)-f(z)}{\delta z} = \lim_{\delta z\to 0}\frac{\delta f(z)}{\delta z}$$

The given path z = 0 along y axis i.e, y= mx

$$f'(z) = \lim_{z\to 0}\frac{f(z)-f(0)}{z} = \lim_{z\to 0}\frac{\frac{x^3y(y-ix)}{x^6+y^2}-0}{x+iy} = \lim_{z\to 0}\frac{-ix^3y(x+iy)}{(x^6+y^2)(x+iy)} = \lim_{z\to 0}\frac{-ix^3y}{x^6+y^2}$$

$$= \lim_{x\to 0}\frac{-ix^3}{x^6+(mx)^2} = \lim_{x\to 0}\frac{-im^2}{x^4+m^2} = 0$$

Again by using path, y = x^3

$$\lim_{z\to 0}\frac{f(z)-f(0)}{z} = \lim_{z\to 0}\frac{-ix^3y}{x^6+y^2} = \lim_{x\to 0}\frac{-ix^3(x^3)}{x^6+(x^3)^2} = \frac{-i}{2}$$

Thus, along different paths we get, different values

Hence, The given function f(z) is not derivable.

Question: 5) Check whether the function $\frac{1}{z}$ is analytic or not .

Solution :- Let f(z) = $\frac{1}{z} = \frac{1}{x+iy}$

$$u+iv = \frac{1}{x+iy} = \frac{1}{x+iy}\cdot\frac{x-iy}{x-iy}$$

$$u+iv = \frac{x-iy}{x^2+y^2}$$

On equating real and imaginary parts, we get

$$u = \frac{x}{x^2+y^2} \text{ and } v = \frac{-y}{x^2+y^2}$$

By using Cauchy-Riemann equations, we get

$$\frac{\partial u}{\partial x} = \frac{\partial v}{\partial y} \text{ and } \frac{\partial u}{\partial y} = -\frac{\partial v}{\partial x}$$

$$\frac{\partial u}{\partial x} = \frac{(x^2+y^2).1-x(2x)}{(x^2+y^2)^2} = \frac{y^2-x^2}{(x^2+y^2)^2}$$

$$\frac{\partial u}{\partial y} = \frac{(x^2+y^2).0-x(2y)}{(x^2+y^2)^2} = \frac{-2xy}{(x^2+y^2)^2}$$

$$\frac{\partial v}{\partial x} = \frac{(x^2+y^2).0-(-y)(2x)}{(x^2+y^2)^2} = \frac{2xy}{(x^2+y^2)^2}$$

$$\frac{\partial v}{\partial y} = \frac{(x^2+y^2).(-1)-(-y)(2y)}{(x^2+y^2)^2} = \frac{y^2-x^2}{(x^2+y^2)^2}$$

$$\therefore \frac{\partial u}{\partial x} = \frac{\partial v}{\partial y} \text{ and } \frac{\partial u}{\partial y} = -\frac{\partial v}{\partial x}$$

Thus C-R equations are satisfied.

Also f(z) is continuous except at (z= 0)

$\therefore$ f(z) = $\frac{1}{z}$ is analytic everywhere except at z=0.

Question: 6) Show that the function f(z) = xy +iy is continuous everywhere but not analytic.

Solution:- Given that

f(z) = xy +iy

u +iv = xy +iy

On equating real and imaginary parts,

$\therefore$ u = xy & v = y

Here u & v are the function of x & y so they are continuous everywhere

Thus f(z) is continuous everywhere

By using C-R equations

$$\frac{\partial u}{\partial x} = \frac{\partial v}{\partial y} \text{ and } \frac{\partial u}{\partial y} = -\frac{\partial v}{\partial x}$$

$$\frac{\partial u}{\partial x} = y \;\; and \;\; \frac{\partial v}{\partial x} = 0$$

$$\frac{\partial u}{\partial y} = x \; and \;\; \frac{\partial v}{\partial y} = 1$$

Hence C-R equations are not satisfied here.

i.e, $\frac{\partial u}{\partial x} \neq \frac{\partial v}{\partial y}$ and $\frac{\partial u}{\partial y} \neq -\frac{\partial v}{\partial x}$

Hence f(z) is not analytic function.

Question: 7) Find the value of a_1 and a_2 such that the function f(z) = $x^2 + a_1y^2 - 2xy + i(a_2x^2 - y^2 + 2xy)$ is analytic. Also find $f'(z)$.

Solution:- Let f(z) = $x^2 + a_1y^2 - 2xy + i(a_2x^2 - y^2 + 2xy)$ = u +iv

On equating real and imaginary parts,

u = $x^2 + a_1y^2 - 2xy$ and v = $a_2x^2 - y^2 + 2xy$

By using C-R Equations, we get

$\frac{\partial u}{\partial x} = \frac{\partial v}{\partial y}$ and $\frac{\partial u}{\partial y} = -\frac{\partial v}{\partial x}$

$\frac{\partial u}{\partial x} = 2x - 2y$ and $\frac{\partial v}{\partial x} = 2xa_2 + 2y$

$\frac{\partial u}{\partial y} = 2ya_1 - 2x$ and $\frac{\partial v}{\partial y} = -2y + 2x$

$\frac{\partial u}{\partial x} = \frac{\partial v}{\partial y}$ and $\frac{\partial u}{\partial y} = -\frac{\partial v}{\partial x}$

$2x - 2y = 2x - 2y$

$2ya_1 - 2x = -(2xa_2 + 2y)$

$2ya_1 - 2x = -2xa_2 - 2y$

Equating coefficient of x and y

$-2 = -2a_2$ and $-2 = 2a_1$

$\boxed{a_2 = 1}$ and $\boxed{a_1 = -1}$

putting value of $a_2 = 1$ in $\frac{\partial v}{\partial x}$ term, we get

$\frac{\partial v}{\partial x} = 2x + 2y$ and $\frac{\partial u}{\partial x} = 2x - 2y$

$f'(z) = \frac{\partial u}{\partial x} + i\frac{\partial v}{\partial x} = 2x - 2y + i(2x + 2y) = 2x(1+i) + i2y(1+i)$

$= 2(1+i)(x+iy) = 2z(1+i)$

Question: 8) Check f(z) = sin z is analytic and hence derive $\frac{d[f(z)]}{dz} = \cos z$.

Solution:- Let $f(z) = \sin z$ and $z = x+iy$

$u + iy = \sin(x + iy)$

$= \sin x \cos hy + \cos x \sin iy$ $\{\because \sin(A + B) = \sin A \cos B + \cos A \sin B\}$

$u + iy = \sin x \cos hy + i\cos x \sin hy$ $\{\because \sin iy = i\sin hy$ and $\cos iy = i\cos hy\}$

$\therefore$ $u = \sin x \cos hy$ and $v = \cos x \sin hy$

By using Cauchy Reimann Equations,

$\frac{\partial u}{\partial x} = \frac{\partial v}{\partial y}$ and $\frac{\partial u}{\partial y} = -\frac{\partial v}{\partial x}$

$\frac{\partial u}{\partial x} = \cos x \cos hy$ and $\frac{\partial v}{\partial x} = -\sin x \sin hy$

$\frac{\partial u}{\partial y} = \sin x \sin hy$ and $\frac{\partial v}{\partial y} = \cos x \cos hy$

$$\therefore \frac{\partial u}{\partial x} = \frac{\partial v}{\partial y} = \cos x \cosh y \quad \text{and} \quad \frac{\partial u}{\partial y} = -\frac{\partial v}{\partial x} = -\sin x \sinh y$$

Thus, Cauchy Reimann Equations are satisfied.

Hence f(z) = sin z is analytic.

$$\frac{d[f(z)]}{dz} = \frac{d}{dz}[\sin z] = \frac{d}{dz}[\sin(x+iy)]$$

$$= \frac{d}{dz}[\sin x \cosh y + i\cos x \sinh y]$$

$$= \frac{d}{dx}[\sin x \cosh y + i\cos x \sinh y]$$

$$= \cos x \cosh y - \sin x \sinh y$$

$$= \cos x \cos iy - \sin x \sin iy$$

$$\frac{d}{dz}[\sin z] = \cos(x+iy) \qquad \therefore \cos(A \pm B) = \cos A \cos B \mp \sin A \sin B$$

Question: 9) Discuss the analyticity of the function $f(z) = z \cdot \bar{z}$.

Solution:- Let $f(z) = u+iv = z \cdot \bar{z} = (x+iy)(x-iy) = x^2 - ixy + ixy + y^2$

$f(z) = u+iv = x^2 + y^2$

On equating real and imaginary parts , we get

$u = x^2 + y^2$ and $v = 0$

By using Cauchy Reimann Equations,

$$\frac{\partial u}{\partial x} = \frac{\partial v}{\partial y} \text{ and } \frac{\partial u}{\partial y} = -\frac{\partial v}{\partial x}$$

$2x = 0$ and $2y = 0$

i.e, $x=0$ and $y = 0$

$$\frac{\partial u}{\partial x} = \frac{\partial v}{\partial y} \quad \text{and} \quad \frac{\partial u}{\partial y} = -\frac{\partial v}{\partial x} \quad \text{at origin } (x,y = 0,0)$$

$\therefore$ f(z) is analytic at origin only.

Question: 10) State that the function $f(z) = \sqrt{|xy|}$ satisfies the C-R Equations at the origin, but is not analytic at that point.

Solution :- Given $f(z) = \sqrt{|xy|} = u + iv$

On equating real and imaginary parts, we get

$u = \sqrt{|xy|}$ and $v = 0$

At origin i.e, z(0,0)

$$\frac{\partial u}{\partial x} = \lim_{h\to 0} \frac{u(0+h,0)-u(0,0)}{h} = \lim_{h\to 0} \frac{0-0}{h} = 0$$

$$\frac{\partial u}{\partial y} = \lim_{k\to 0} \frac{u(0,0+k)-u(0,0)}{k} = \lim_{k\to 0} \frac{0-0}{k} = 0$$

$$\frac{\partial v}{\partial x} = \lim_{h\to 0} \frac{v(0+h,0)-v(0,0)}{h} = \lim_{h\to 0} \frac{0-0}{h} = 0$$

$$\frac{\partial v}{\partial y} = \lim_{k\to 0} \frac{v(0,0+k)-v(0,0)}{k} = \lim_{k\to 0} \frac{0-0}{k} = 0$$

Thus C-R Equations are satisfied

i.e, $\frac{\partial u}{\partial x} = \frac{\partial v}{\partial y}$ and $\frac{\partial u}{\partial y} = -\frac{\partial v}{\partial x}$

Hence C-R equations are satisfied at origin i.e, z=0

$$f'(z=0) = \lim_{z\to 0} \frac{f(z)-f(0)}{z} = \lim_{z\to 0} \frac{\sqrt{|xy|}-0}{x+iy}$$

Along y- axis y = mx

$$f'(0) = \lim_{x\to 0} \frac{\sqrt{m}\,x-0}{x+imx} = \lim_{z\to 0} \frac{\sqrt{m}}{1+im}$$

This limit is depend on the value of m

∴f"(0) is not unique

Hence f(z) is not analytic at z= 0 .

Question: 11) Show that the real and imaginary part of the function f(z) = $\log z$ satisfied the C-R equations when z is not zero, find its derivatives.

Solution:- Given f(z) = $\log z$

$$u + iv = \log(x + iy) = \log(r\cos\theta + ir\sin\theta) = \log r(\cos\theta + i\sin\theta)$$

$$= \log re^{i\theta} = \log r + \log e^{i\theta} = \log r + i\theta$$

$$u + iv = \log\sqrt{x^2 + y^2} + i\tan^{-1}\left(\frac{y}{x}\right)$$

On equating real and imaginary parts, we get

$$u = \log\sqrt{x^2 + y^2} \quad \text{and} \quad v = \tan^{-1}\left(\frac{y}{x}\right)$$

By using C-R equations, $\frac{\partial u}{\partial x} = \frac{\partial v}{\partial y}$ and $\frac{\partial u}{\partial y} = -\frac{\partial v}{\partial x}$

$$\frac{\partial u}{\partial x} = \frac{1}{\sqrt{x^2+y^2}} \cdot \frac{1}{2\sqrt{x^2+y^2}} \cdot 2x = \frac{x}{x^2+y^2}$$

$$\frac{\partial u}{\partial y} = \frac{1}{\sqrt{x^2+y^2}} \cdot \frac{1}{2\sqrt{x^2+y^2}} \cdot 2y = \frac{y}{x^2+y^2}$$

$$\frac{\partial v}{\partial x} = \frac{1}{1+\frac{y^2}{x^2}} \cdot \left(-\frac{y}{x^2}\right) = -\frac{y}{x^2+y^2}$$

$$\frac{\partial v}{\partial x} = \frac{1}{1+\frac{y^2}{x^2}} \cdot \left(\frac{1}{x}\right) = \frac{x}{x^2+y^2}$$

Thus C-R equations are satisfied.Hence, $f(z) = \log z$ is analytic function except $z = 0$.

If $x^2 + y^2 = 0 \Rightarrow x=y=0$

$x + iy = 0$ and $z = 0$

$f(z)= u + iv$

$$\frac{df'(z)}{dz} = \frac{\partial u}{\partial x} + i\frac{\partial v}{\partial x} = \frac{x}{x^2+y^2} - \frac{iy}{x^2+y^2} = \frac{x-iy}{x^2+y^2} = \frac{x-iy}{(x+iy)(x-iy)} = \frac{1}{(x+iy)} = \frac{1}{z}$$

Question: 12) The function $f(z) = u + iv$ Where, $f(z) = \frac{x^3(1+i)-y^3(1-i)}{x^2+y^2}$ $z\neq 0$

$= 0$ $z = 0$

Satisfy the C-R equations at $z = 0$. Is the function analytic at $z = 0$. Justify your answer.

Solution:- Given, $f(z) = u + iv = \frac{x^3(1+i)-y^3(1-i)}{x^2+y^2} = \frac{x^3-y^3+i(x^3+y^3)}{x^2+y^2}$

$$u + iv = \frac{x^3-y^3}{x^2+y^2} + i\frac{x^3+y^3}{x^2+y^2}$$

On equating real and imaginary parts, we get

$$u = \frac{x^3-y^3}{x^2+y^2} \quad \text{and} \quad v = \frac{x^3+y^3}{x^2+y^2}$$

After finding the partial derivatives, the values of $\frac{\partial u}{\partial x}, \frac{\partial v}{\partial y}, \frac{\partial u}{\partial y}, \frac{\partial v}{\partial x}$ at origin we get $\frac{0}{0}$ form. so we apply first principal method.

At origin,

$$\frac{\partial u}{\partial x} = \lim_{h\to 0} \frac{u(0+h,0)-u(0,0)}{h} = \lim_{h\to 0} \frac{\frac{h^3-0}{h^2+0} - \frac{0-0}{0+0}}{h} = \lim_{h\to 0} \frac{\frac{h^3}{h^2}}{h} = \lim_{h\to 0} \frac{h^3}{h^3} = 1$$

$$\frac{\partial u}{\partial y} = \lim_{k\to 0} \frac{u(0,0+k)-u(0,0)}{k} = \lim_{k\to 0} \frac{-k^3}{k} = -1$$

$$\frac{\partial v}{\partial x} = \lim_{h\to 0} \frac{v(0+h,0)-v(0,0)}{h} = \lim_{h\to 0} \frac{h^3}{h^3} = 1$$

$$\frac{\partial v}{\partial y} = \lim_{k\to 0}\frac{v(0,0+k) - v(0,0)}{k} = \lim_{k\to 0}\frac{k^3}{k} = 1$$

Thus $\frac{\partial u}{\partial x} = \frac{\partial v}{\partial y}$ and $\frac{\partial u}{\partial y} = -\frac{\partial v}{\partial x}$

Hence C-R equations satisfied at z = 0.

Again $f'(0) = \lim_{z\to 0}\frac{f(z)-f(0)}{z} = \lim_{z\to 0}\frac{\frac{x^3(1+i)-y^3(1-i)}{x^2+y^2}-0}{x+iy} = \lim_{z\to 0}\frac{x^3(1+i)-y^3(1-i)}{(x^2+y^2)\,(x+iy)}$

Along the path y = x ,

Then $f''(0) = \lim_{x\to 0}\frac{x^3-x^3+i(x^3+x^3)}{(x^2+x^2)\,(x+ix)} = \frac{2ix^3}{2x^2(x+ix)} = \frac{i}{1+i} = \frac{i(1-i)}{(1+i)(1+i)}$

$= \frac{1+i}{1+1} = \frac{1}{2}\,(1+i)$

Along the path y = 0,

Then $f''(0) = \lim_{x\to 0}\frac{x^3-y^3+i(x^3+y^3)}{(x^2+y^2)\,(x+iy)} = \frac{x^3+ix^3}{x^2}.\frac{1}{x} = (1+i)$

This shows that f'(0) is not equal along two different paths hence the function is not analytic at z = 0.

Question: 13) Examine the nature of the function $f(z) = \frac{x^2y^5(x+iy)}{x^4+y^{10}}$: $z \neq 0$

f(0) = 0 in the region including the origin.

Solution :- Given, $f(z) = u + iv = \frac{x^2y^5(x+iy)}{x^4+y^{10}} = \frac{x^3y^5+ix^2y^6}{x^4+y^{10}}$

$$u + iv = \frac{x^3y^5}{x^4+y^{10}} + i\,\frac{x^2y^6}{x^4+y^{10}}$$

On equating the real and imaginary parts , we get

$$u = \frac{x^3y^5}{x^4+y^{10}} \text{ and } v = \frac{x^2y^6}{x^4+y^{10}}$$

By using C-R equations ,$\frac{\partial u}{\partial x} = \frac{\partial v}{\partial y}$ & $\frac{\partial u}{\partial y} = -\frac{\partial v}{\partial x}$

$$\frac{\partial u}{\partial x} = \lim_{h\to 0}\frac{u(0+h,0) - u(0,0)}{h} = \lim_{h\to 0}\frac{\frac{(0+h)^3.0^5}{(0+h)^4+0^{10}}-(0)}{h} = \lim_{h\to 0}\frac{\frac{0}{h^4}}{h} = \frac{0}{h} = 0$$

$$\frac{\partial u}{\partial y} = \lim_{k\to 0}\frac{u(0,0+k) - u(0,0)}{k} = \lim_{k\to 0}\frac{\frac{0}{k^{10}}}{k} = 0$$

$$\frac{\partial v}{\partial x} = \lim_{h\to 0}\frac{v(0+h,0) - v(0,0)}{h} = \lim_{h\to 0}\frac{\frac{(0+h)^3.0^5}{(0+h)^4+0^{10}}-(0)}{h} = \lim_{h\to 0}\frac{\frac{0}{h^4}}{h} = \frac{0}{h} = 0$$

$$\frac{\partial v}{\partial y} = \lim_{k\to 0}\frac{v(0,0+k) - v(0,0)}{k} = \lim_{k\to 0}\frac{\frac{0}{k^{10}}}{k} = 0$$

Clearly C-R equations are satisfied at origin

Again , $f'(0) = \lim_{z\to 0}\frac{f(0+z)-f(0)}{z} = \lim_{z\to 0}\frac{\frac{x^3y^5+ix^2y^6}{x^4+y^{10}} - 0}{x+iy} = \lim_{z\to 0}\frac{x^2y^5}{x^4+y^{10}}$

Along the path y = mx , then

$$f'(0) = \lim_{x\to 0}\frac{x^2(mx)^5}{x^4+(mx)^{10}} = \lim_{x\to 0}\frac{x^7m^5}{x^4(1+m^{10}x^6)} = 0$$

Along the path $y^5 = x^2$, then

$$f'(0) = \lim_{x\to 0}\frac{x^2x^2}{x^4+x^4} = \frac{1}{2}$$

This shows that f'(0) is not equal along two different paths,

Hence the function is not analytic at z = 0.

Question: 14) If n is real number, Show that $r^n(\cos n\theta + i\sin n\theta)$ is analytic except possible when r = 0 and find its derivative.

Solution:- Given $f(z) = u+iv = r^n(\cos n\theta + i\sin n\theta)$

$$u+iv = r^n\cos n\theta + ir^n\sin n\theta$$

On equating real and imaginary parts,

$$u = r^n\cos n\theta \quad \text{and} \quad v = r^n\sin n\theta$$

By using C-R conditions in polar form,

$$\frac{\partial u}{\partial r} = \frac{1}{r}\frac{\partial v}{\partial \theta} \quad \text{and} \quad \frac{\partial v}{\partial r} = -\frac{1}{r}\frac{\partial u}{\partial \theta}$$

$$\frac{\partial u}{\partial r} = nr^{n-1}\cos n\theta \quad and \quad \frac{\partial v}{\partial r} = nr^{n-1}\sin n\theta$$

$$\frac{\partial u}{\partial \theta} = -nr^n\sin n\theta \quad \text{and} \quad \frac{\partial v}{\partial \theta} = nr^n\cos n\theta$$

$$\therefore \frac{\partial u}{\partial r} = \frac{1}{r}\frac{\partial v}{\partial \theta} = \frac{1}{r}nr^n\cos n\theta = nr^{n-1}\cos n\theta$$

$$\frac{\partial v}{\partial r} = -\frac{1}{r}\frac{\partial u}{\partial \theta} = \frac{-1}{r}nr^n\sin n\theta = nr^{n-1}\sin n\theta$$

Thus, C-R equations are satisfied.

Now, $\frac{d\,f(z)}{dz} = (\cos\theta - i\sin\theta)\frac{\partial f(z)}{\partial r} = (\cos\theta - i\sin\theta)(\frac{\partial u}{\partial r} + i\frac{\partial v}{\partial r})$

$$= (\cos\theta - i\sin\theta)\,(nr^{n-1}\cos n\theta + inr^{n-1}\sin n\theta)$$

$= nr^{n-1}(\cos\theta \cos n\theta + i\cos\theta \sin n\theta \;\; - i\sin\theta \cos n\theta + \sin\theta \sin n\theta)$

$= nr^{n-1}[(\cos\theta \cos n\theta + \sin\theta \sin n\theta) + i\,(\cos\theta \sin n\theta - i\sin\theta \cos n\theta)]$

$= nr^{n-1}\,[\cos(n-1) + i\sin(n-1)]$

This exist for all values of r except at r=0 and n≤1.

EXERCISES :

Question: 1) Determine the function is analytic or not analytic.

1. $\frac{x-iy}{x^2+y^2}$ Ans: Not analytic.

2. $2xy + i\,(x^2 + y^2)$ Ans: Not analytic.

3. $x^2 + iy^2$ Ans: Analytic.

Question: 2) If $\begin{cases} \frac{x^2y(y-ix)}{x^4+y^2} & \text{when } z \neq 0 \\ 0 & \text{when } z = 0 \end{cases}$

Prove that $\frac{f(z)-f(0)}{x}$ as z→0 along any radius vector but not z→0 in any manner.

Question: 3) Prove that the function $f(z) = |z|^2$ is differentiable at the origin.

Question: 4) Check the given function $f(z) = \frac{1}{z}$ is analytic or not analytic by using C-R equations in polar form.

Question: 5) Using the first principal find the derivative of $f(z) = z^3$.

HARMONIC FUNCTION:-

Any function which satisfies the laplace equation is called as harmonic function.

i.e. $\frac{\partial^2 u}{\partial x^2}+\frac{\partial^2 u}{\partial y^2}=0$ and $\frac{\partial^2 v}{\partial x^2}+\frac{\partial^2 v}{\partial y^2}=0$

Theorem:-If f(z) = u(x,y) + iv(x,y) is an analytic function, then u and v both are harmonic function.

Proof:- Let f(z) = u(x, y) + v(x, y) be an analytic function.

Also, we know that C-R equations are

$$\frac{\partial u}{\partial x}=\frac{\partial v}{\partial y} \quad \text{....(1)} \quad \text{and} \quad \frac{\partial u}{\partial y}=-\frac{\partial v}{\partial x} \quad \text{.....(2)}$$

Differentiating equation (1), with respect to x then, we will get $\frac{\partial^2 u}{\partial x^2}=\frac{\partial^2 v}{\partial x\,\partial y}$

Differentiating equation (2), with respect to y then,we will get $\frac{\partial^2 u}{\partial y^2}=-\frac{\partial^2 v}{\partial y\,\partial x}$

Add above two equation we will obtained,

$$\frac{\partial^2 u}{\partial x^2}+\frac{\partial^2 u}{\partial y^2}=\frac{\partial^2 v}{\partial x\,\partial y}-\frac{\partial^2 v}{\partial y\,\partial x}=0$$

Similarly, For v(x,y)

$$\frac{\partial^2 v}{\partial x^2}+\frac{\partial^2 v}{\partial y^2}=0$$

∴ Both u(x,y) and v(x,y) are harmonic functions.

Also u and v are called conjugate harmonic function, if u + iv is also analytic function.

Steps to find conjugate harmonic function:-

Case:- 1) If f(z) = u(x,y) + iv(x,y) is an analytic function and the real part u(x,y) is given, then to find its conjugate function v(x,y).

Solution:- we have, $dv=\frac{\partial v}{\partial x}dx+\frac{\partial v}{\partial y}dy$

By using C-R equations $\frac{\partial u}{\partial x}=\frac{\partial v}{\partial y}$ and $\frac{\partial u}{\partial y}=-\frac{\partial v}{\partial x}$ in above equation. we get,

$$dv=-\frac{\partial u}{\partial y}dx+\frac{\partial u}{\partial x}dy$$

$$\int dv=-\int\frac{\partial u}{\partial y}dx+\int\frac{\partial u}{\partial x}dy$$

$$\int dv=\int Mdx+\int Ndy \quad \text{.....(1)}$$

Where, $M = -\frac{\partial u}{\partial y}$ and $N = \frac{\partial u}{\partial x}$

$$\frac{\partial M}{\partial y} = -\frac{\partial^2 u}{\partial y^2} \quad \text{and} \quad \frac{\partial N}{\partial x} = -\frac{\partial^2 u}{\partial x^2} \qquad \ldots.(2)$$

Since **u** is conjugate harmonic function.

So, $$\frac{\partial^2 u}{\partial x^2} + \frac{\partial^2 u}{\partial y^2} = 0$$

$$\Rightarrow \quad \frac{\partial^2 u}{\partial x^2} = -\frac{\partial^2 u}{\partial y^2}$$

Putting above value in equation (2). we get,

$$\frac{\partial M}{\partial y} = \frac{\partial^2 u}{\partial x^2} = \frac{\partial N}{\partial x}$$

Thus equation (1) is exact differential equation.

Hence it is integrable. So solution of equation (1) is given by

$$v = \int_{\text{taking y constant}} Mdx + \int_{\text{excluding the terms of x}} Ndy + c$$

Thus, The conjugate function v(x,y) is determined.

Case:- 2) If f(z) = u(x,y) + iv(x,y) is an analytic function and the imaginary part v(x,y) is given then find to find its conjugate u(x,y).

Solution:- We have, $du = \frac{\partial u}{\partial x}dx + \frac{\partial u}{\partial y}dy$

By using C-R equations $\frac{\partial u}{\partial x} = \frac{\partial v}{\partial y}$ and $\frac{\partial u}{\partial y} = -\frac{\partial v}{\partial x}$ in above equations.

we get, $du = \frac{\partial v}{\partial y}dx - \frac{\partial v}{\partial x}dy$

$$\int du = \int \frac{\partial v}{\partial y}dx - \int \frac{\partial v}{\partial x}dy$$

$$u = \int \frac{\partial v}{\partial y}dx - \int \frac{\partial v}{\partial x}dy + c$$

$$\int du = \int Mdx + \int Ndy + c \qquad \ldots(1)$$

Where, $M = -\frac{\partial v}{\partial y}$ and $N = \frac{\partial v}{\partial x}$

$$\frac{\partial M}{\partial y} = -\frac{\partial^2 v}{\partial y^2} \quad \text{and} \quad \frac{\partial N}{\partial x} = -\frac{\partial^2 v}{\partial x^2} \qquad \ldots(2)$$

Since **v** is conjugate harmonic function.

So, $\frac{\partial^2 v}{\partial x^2} + \frac{\partial^2 v}{\partial y^2} = 0$

$\Rightarrow \quad \frac{\partial^2 v}{\partial x^2} = -\frac{\partial^2 v}{\partial y^2}$

Putting above value in equation (2) we get,

$$\frac{\partial M}{\partial y} = \frac{\partial^2 v}{\partial x^2} = \frac{\partial N}{\partial x}$$

Thus equation (1) is exact differentiable equation and it is integrable.

So solution of equation (2) is given by

$$v = \int_{\text{taking y constant}} M dx + \int_{\text{excluding the terms of x}} N dy + c$$

Thus conjugate function u(x,y) is determined. Consequently f(z) = u + iv also determined.

Question: 1) Find the harmonic conjugate of the given function u(x,y) = 2x(1-y).

Solution :- Given u = 2x(1-y)

To find v(x,y)

$$dv = \frac{\partial v}{\partial x}dx + \frac{\partial v}{\partial y}dy$$

By using C-R equations $\frac{\partial u}{\partial x} = \frac{\partial v}{\partial y}$ and $\frac{\partial u}{\partial y} = -\frac{\partial v}{\partial x}$

$$\frac{\partial u}{\partial x} = 2(1-y) = \frac{\partial v}{\partial y}$$

$$\frac{\partial u}{\partial y} = -2x = -\frac{\partial v}{\partial x}$$

$$\int dv = -\int \frac{\partial u}{\partial y}dx + \int \frac{\partial u}{\partial x}dy + c$$

$$v = -\int(-2x)dx + \int 2(1-y)dy$$

$$= \frac{2x^2}{2} + 2\left(y - \frac{y^2}{2}\right) + c$$

$$= x^2 + 2y - y^2 + c$$

Hence the harmonic conjugate of u(x,y) is $\mathbf{x^2 + 2y - y^2 + c}$.

Question: 2) State that the function $u(x,y) = \frac{1}{2}\log(x^2 + y^2)$ is harmonic. Find its harmonic conjugate.

Solution:- Given that, $u = \frac{1}{2}\log(x^2 + y^2)$

To Find v(x,y)

$$dv = \frac{\partial v}{\partial x}dx + \frac{\partial v}{\partial y}dy$$

By using C-R equations $\frac{\partial u}{\partial x} = \frac{\partial v}{\partial y}$ and $\frac{\partial u}{\partial y} = -\frac{\partial v}{\partial x}$

$$\frac{1}{2}\cdot\frac{2x}{x^2+y^2} = \frac{\partial v}{\partial y} \quad \text{and} \quad \frac{1}{2}\cdot\frac{2y}{x^2+y^2} = -\frac{\partial v}{\partial x}$$

$$\frac{x}{x^2+y^2} = \frac{\partial v}{\partial y} \quad \text{and} \quad \frac{2y}{x^2+y^2} = -\frac{\partial v}{\partial x}$$

$$\frac{\partial^2 u}{\partial x^2} = \frac{(x^2+y^2)\cdot 1 - x\cdot 2x}{(x^2+y^2)^2} = \frac{y^2-x^2}{(x^2+y^2)^2}$$

$$\frac{\partial^2 u}{\partial y^2} = \frac{(x^2+y^2)\cdot 1 - y\cdot 2y}{(x^2+y^2)^2} = \frac{x^2-y^2}{(x^2+y^2)^2}$$

$$\frac{\partial^2 u}{\partial x^2} + \frac{\partial^2 u}{\partial y^2} = \frac{y^2-x^2}{(x^2+y^2)^2} - \frac{x^2-y^2}{(x^2+y^2)^2} = 0$$

Thus the laplace equation was satisfied.

Hence the given function u is harmonic function.

Now, $dv = -\frac{\partial u}{\partial y}dx + \frac{\partial u}{\partial x}dy$ ∵ By C-R equations.

$$dv = \frac{-y}{x^2+y^2}dx + \frac{x}{x^2+y^2}dy$$

$$\int dv = -\int \frac{y}{x^2+y^2}\,dx + \int \frac{x}{x^2+y^2}\,dy$$

$$v = -y\cdot\frac{1}{y}\tan^{-1}\left(\frac{x}{y}\right) + 0 + c$$

$$v = \tan^{-1}\left(\frac{x}{y}\right) + c$$

Hence the harmonic conjugate of u(x,y) is $\tan^{-1}\left(\frac{x}{y}\right) + c$.

Question: 3) State that the function $x^2 - y^2 + 2y$ is a harmonic function.

Solution:- Given that, $u(x,y) = x^2 - y^2 + 2y$

To prove that, $u = x^2 - y^2 + 2y$ is harmonic. For that u must satisfies laplace equation.

$$\frac{\partial^2 u}{\partial x^2} + \frac{\partial^2 u}{\partial y^2} = 0 \qquad \ldots(1)$$

Now, $\frac{\partial u}{\partial x} = 2x$ and $\frac{\partial u}{\partial y} = -2y + 2$

$\frac{\partial^2 u}{\partial x^2} = 2$ and $\frac{\partial^2 u}{\partial y^2} = -2$

Equation (1) becomes, $\frac{\partial^2 u}{\partial x^2} + \frac{\partial^2 u}{\partial y^2} = 2 - 2 = 0$

Hence u is a harmonic function.

Question: 4) Find the value of A and B so that $f(x,y) = x^2 + Axy + By^2$ is harmonic.

Solution:- Given that, $f(x,y) = x^2 + Axy + By^2$

For harmonic function f(x,y) must satisfy the laplace equation.

$$\frac{\partial^2 f}{\partial x^2} + \frac{\partial^2 f}{\partial y^2} = 0$$

Now, $\frac{\partial f}{\partial x} = 2x + Ay$ and $\frac{\partial f}{\partial y} = Ax + 2By$

$\frac{\partial^2 f}{\partial x^2} = 2$ and $\frac{\partial^2 f}{\partial y^2} = 2B$

The laplace equation becomes,

$$\frac{\partial^2 u}{\partial x^2} + \frac{\partial^2 u}{\partial y^2} = 0$$

$$2 + 2B = 0$$

$$\mathbf{B = -1}$$

The required values of A and B are 0 and -1 respectively.

Question: 5) Let f(z) = u(x,y) + v(x,y) be an analytic function if u = 3x – 2xy then find v and f(z).

Solution:- Given that, $u = 3x - 2xy$

We have, $dv = \frac{\partial v}{\partial x}dx + \frac{\partial v}{\partial y}dy$

By using C-R equations $\frac{\partial u}{\partial x} = \frac{\partial v}{\partial y}$ and $\frac{\partial u}{\partial y} = -\frac{\partial v}{\partial x}$ in above equation. We get

$$dv = -\frac{\partial u}{\partial y}dx + \frac{\partial u}{\partial x}dy$$

$$dv = -(-2x)\,dx + (3-2y)\,dy$$

On integrating we get,

$$v = \int 2x\,dx + \int (3 - 2y)\,dy = 2\cdot\frac{x^2}{2} + 3y - 2\cdot\frac{y^2}{2} + c$$

$$v = x^2 - 2y^2 + 3y + c$$

Now, $f(z) = u + iv = (3x - 2xy) + i\,(x^2 - 2y^2 + 3y + c)$

$= (i\,x^2 - i\,y^2 - 2xy) + (3x + 3yi) + ic = i\,(x^2 - y^2 - 2ixy) + 3(x+iy) + ic$

$= i\,(x + iy)^2 + 3(x+iy) + ic$ $= \mathbf{i\,z^2 + 3z + ic}$

Which is the required the expression for f(z).

Question: 6) Prove that $u = x^2 - y^2 - 2xy - 2x + 3y$ is harmonic. Also find the function v.

State that f(z) = u+iv is analytic and express f(z) in terms of z.

Solution:- Given, $u = x^2 - y^2 - 2xy - 2x + 3y$

For harmonic function u satisfy the laplace equation.

$$\frac{\partial^2 u}{\partial x^2} + \frac{\partial^2 u}{\partial y^2} = (2x - 2y - z) + (-2y - 2z + 3) = 2 + (-2) = 0$$

Hence u is a harmonic function.

We have, $dv = \frac{\partial v}{\partial x}dx + \frac{\partial v}{\partial y}dy$

By using C-R equations $\frac{\partial u}{\partial x} = \frac{\partial v}{\partial y}$ and $\frac{\partial u}{\partial y} = -\frac{\partial v}{\partial x}$ in above equation. We get,

$$dv = -\frac{\partial u}{\partial y}dx + \frac{\partial u}{\partial x}dy$$

On integrating we get,

$$v = -\int(-2y - 2x + 3)\,dx + \int(2x - 2y - 2)\,dy$$

$$= \int(2y + 2x - 3)\,dx + \int(2x - 2y - 2)\,dy = 2xy + 2\cdot\frac{x^2}{2} - 3x + 2xy - 2\cdot\frac{y^2}{2} - 2y + c$$

$$v = x^2 - y^2 + 2xy - 3x - 2y + c$$

Now, $f(z) = u + iv$

$$= (x^2 - y^2 - 2xy - 2x + 3y) + i\,(x^2 - y^2 + 2xy - 3x - 2y + c)$$

$$= (x^2 - y^2 - 2ixy) + (ix^2 - iy^2 - 2xy) - x(2+3i) - iy(2+3i) + ic$$

$$= z^2 + iz^2 - (2+3i) + (x + iy) + ic$$

$$\mathbf{f(z) = (1+i)z^2 - (2+3i) + (x + iy) + ic}$$

Which is the required the expression for f(z).

Question: 7) If f(z)= u+iv represents the complex potential for an electric field and $v = x^2 - y^2(\frac{x}{x^2 + y^2})$ determine the function u.

Solution:- Given that, f(z)= u+iv and $v = x^2 - y^2(\frac{x}{x^2 + y^2})$

We have, $du = \frac{\partial u}{\partial x}dx + \frac{\partial u}{\partial y}dy$

By using C-R equations $\frac{\partial u}{\partial x} = \frac{\partial v}{\partial y}$ and $\frac{\partial u}{\partial y} = -\frac{\partial v}{\partial x}$ in above equation.

$$du = \frac{\partial v}{\partial y}dx - \frac{\partial v}{\partial x}dy = [2y + \frac{(x^2 + y^2)\cdot 0 - x\cdot 2y}{(x^2 + y^2)^2}]\,dx - [2x + \frac{(x^2 + y^2)\cdot 1 - x\cdot 2x}{(x^2 + y^2)^2}]\,dy$$

$$= [-2y - \frac{x\cdot 2y}{(x^2 + y^2)^2}]\,dx - [2x + \frac{y^2 - x^2}{(x^2 + y^2)^2}]\,dy$$

On integrating we get,

$$\mathbf{u = -2xy + \frac{y}{x^2 + y^2} + c}$$

Question: 8) Find the imaginary part of the analytic function whose real part is $x^3 - 3xy^2 + 3x^2 - 3y^2$.

Solution:- Let, $f(z) = u + iv$

Given that, $u = x^3 - 3xy^2 + 3x^2 - 3y^2$

We have, $dv = \frac{\partial v}{\partial x}dx + \frac{\partial v}{\partial y}dy$

By using C-R equations $\frac{\partial u}{\partial x} = \frac{\partial v}{\partial y}$ and $\frac{\partial u}{\partial y} = -\frac{\partial v}{\partial x}$ in above equation. We get,

$$dv = -\frac{\partial u}{\partial y}dx + \frac{\partial u}{\partial x}dy = -(-6xy - 6y)\, dx + (3x^2 - 3y^2 + 6x)\, dy$$

On integrating we get,

$$v = \int(6xy + 6x)\, dx + \int (3x^2 - 3y^2 + 6x)dy = 6\cdot\frac{x^2}{2}\, y + 6xy + 3x^2y - 3\cdot\frac{y^3}{3} + 6xy + c$$

$$= 3x^2y + 6xy + 3x^2y + 6xy - y^3 + c$$

$$\mathbf{v = 6x^2y + 12xy - y^3 + c}$$

Which is a required imaginary part of f(z).

Question: 9) If $u - v = (x-y)(x^2 + 4xy + y^2)$ and $f(z) = u + iv$ is an analytic function of $z = x + iy$. Find f(z) in terms of z.

Solution:- Given, $f(z) = u + iv$

$if(z) = iu - v$

Adding above both equation we get,

$(1+ i)\, f(z) = i(u+v) + (u - v)$

$(1+ i)\, f(z) = U + iV = F(Z)$

where $U = u - v$ and $V = u + v$

Here, $U = u - v = (x-y)(x^2 + 4xy + y^2) = x^3 + 4x^2y + xy^2 - yx^2 - 4xy^2 - y^3$

$$= x^3 + 3x^2y - 3xy^2 - y^3$$

We have, $dV = \frac{\partial V}{\partial x}dx + \frac{\partial V}{\partial y}dy$

By using C-R equations $\frac{\partial U}{\partial x} = \frac{\partial V}{\partial y}$ and $\frac{\partial U}{\partial y} = -\frac{\partial V}{\partial x}$ in above equation.

$$dV = -\frac{\partial U}{\partial y}dx + \frac{\partial U}{\partial x}dy = -(3x^2 + 6xy - 3y^2)dx + (3x^2 + 6xy - 3y^2)\, dy$$

On integrating we get,

$$V = -\int (3x^2 + 6xy - 3y^2)dx + \int(3x^2 + 6xy - 3y^2)\,dy$$

$$= -(3\cdot\frac{x^3}{3} + 6\frac{x^2}{2}y - 3xy^2) + 3x^2y + 6\frac{y^2}{2}x - 3\cdot\frac{y^3}{3} + c$$

$$= -x^3 - 3x^2y + 3xy^2 + 3x^2y + 3xy^2 - y^3 + c = -x^3 + 6xy^2 - y^3 + c$$

Now, $$F(Z) = U + iV = (x^3 + 3x^2y - 3xy^2 - y^3) + i(-x^3 + 6xy^2 - y^3 + c)$$

$$= (1-i)x^3 + (3+3i)x^2y + (-3+3i)xy^2 + (-1-i)y^3 + ic$$

$$= (1-i)x^3 + 3i(1-i)x^2y - 3(1-i)xy^2 - i(1-i)y^3 + ic$$

$$= (1-i)[x^3 + 3ix^2y - 3xy^2 - iy^3] + ic = (1-i)z^3 + ic$$

$$(1+i)f(z) = (1-i)z^3 + ic$$

$$f(z) = \frac{(1-i)z^3}{(1+i)} + \frac{ic}{(1+i)}$$

$$= \frac{(1-i)(1-i)}{(1+i)(1-i)}z^3 + \frac{i(1-i)}{(1+i)(1-i)}c$$

$$\mathbf{f(z) = \frac{-2i}{2}z^3 + \frac{1+i}{2}c}$$

Question: 10) If f(z) = u + iv is an analytic function of the complex variable z and

$u - v = e^x(\cos y - \sin y)$. Find f(z) in terms of z.

Solution :- Given, $f(z) = u + iv$

$if(z) = iu - v$

Adding above both equation we get,

$$(1+i)f(z) = i(u+v) + (u-v)$$

$$F(Z) = U + iV$$

Where, $U = u - v$ and $V = u + v$

Here, $U = u - v = e^x(\cos y - \sin y)$

We have, $$dV = \frac{\partial V}{\partial x}dx + \frac{\partial V}{\partial y}dy$$

By using C-R equations $\frac{\partial U}{\partial x} = \frac{\partial V}{\partial y}$ and $\frac{\partial U}{\partial y} = -\frac{\partial V}{\partial x}$ in above equation.

$$dV = -\frac{\partial U}{\partial y}dx + \frac{\partial U}{\partial x}dy = -e^x(-\sin y - \cos y)dx + e^x(\cos y - \sin y)dy$$

On integrating we get,

$$V = \int e^x (-\sin y - \cos y)\, dx + \int e^x (\cos y - \sin y)\, dy$$

$$= e^x (\sin y + \cos y) + c \quad \text{(using Exact Differential Equation)}$$

Now, $F(Z) = U + iV$

$$(1+i)\, f(z) = e^x (\cos y - \sin y) + ie^x (\sin y + \cos y) + ic$$

$$= e^x (\cos y + i\sin y) + ie^x (\cos y + i\sin y) + ic = e^x \cdot e^{iy} + ie^x \cdot e^{iy} + ic$$

$$= (1+i)\, e^{x+iy} + ic$$

$$(1+i)\, f(z) = (1+i)\, e^z + ic$$

$$\mathbf{f(z) = e^z + \frac{i}{1+i} c = e^z + c_1}$$

Question: 11) Let $f(z) = u(r, \theta) + iv(r, \theta)$ be an analytic function and $u = -r^3 \sin 3\theta$ then construct the corresponding analytic function f(z) in terms of z.

Solution:- Given $u = -r^3 \sin 3\theta$

We have, $dv = \frac{\partial v}{\partial r} dr + \frac{\partial v}{\partial \theta} d\theta$

By using C-R equations $\frac{\partial u}{\partial r} = \frac{1}{r}\frac{\partial v}{\partial \theta}$ and $\frac{\partial u}{\partial \theta} = -\frac{r\,\partial v}{\partial r}$ in above equation.

$$dv = \frac{-1}{r}\frac{\partial u}{\partial \theta} dr + \frac{r\,\partial u}{\partial r} d\theta = \frac{-1}{r}(-r^3 \cdot 3\cos 3\theta)dr + r(-3r^2 \sin 3\theta)d\theta$$

$$= 3r^2 \cdot \cos 3\theta dr - 3r^2 \sin 3\theta\, d\theta$$

On integrating , we get

$$v = \frac{3r^3}{3} \cos 3\theta + c = r^3 \cos 3\theta + C$$

Now, $f(z) = u + iv = -r^3 \sin 3\theta + ir^3 \cos 3\theta + ic = ir^3 (\cos 3\theta + i\sin 3\theta) + ic$

$$= ir^3 e^{3i\theta} + ic = i(re^{i\theta})^3 + ic$$

$$\mathbf{f(z) = i\, z^3 + ic}$$

This is a required analytic function.

Question: 12) Find the analytic function $f(z) = u(r, \theta) + iv(r, \theta)$. State that $v(r, \theta) = r^2 \cdot \cos 2\theta - r\cos\theta + 2$.

Solution:- Given, $v(r, \theta) = r^2 \cdot \cos 2\theta - r\cos 2\theta + 2$

We have, $du = \frac{\partial u}{\partial r} dr + \frac{\partial u}{\partial \theta} d\theta$

By using C-R equations $\frac{\partial u}{\partial r} = \frac{1}{r}\frac{\partial v}{\partial \theta}$ and $\frac{\partial u}{\partial \theta} = -\frac{r\,\partial v}{\partial r}$ in above equation.

$$du = \frac{1}{r}\frac{\partial v}{\partial \theta} dr - \frac{r\,\partial v}{\partial r} d\theta = \frac{-1}{r}(r^2 \cdot 2\sin 2\theta + r\sin\theta)dr - (2r^2 \cos 2\theta - r\cos\theta)d\theta$$

On integrating , we get,

$$du = \frac{-2\,r^2}{2}\sin 2\theta + r\sin\theta - 0 + c = -r^2 \cdot \sin 2\theta + r\sin\theta + c$$

$$\therefore f(z) = u + iv = (-r^2 \cdot \sin 2\theta + r\sin\theta + c) + i\,(r^2 \cdot \cos 2\theta - r\cos\theta + 2)$$

$$= ir^2 (\cos 2\theta + i \sin 2\theta) - ir (\cos\theta + i\sin\theta) + 2i + c$$

$$f(\mathbf{z}) = ir^2 e^{2i\theta} - ire^{i\theta} + 2i + c = \mathbf{i\,(z^2 - z) + 2i + c}$$

Which is a required analytic function.

MILNE – THOMSON METHOD (TO CONSTRUCT AN ANALYTIC FUNCTION):-

Method:(I) If real part u is given let f(z) = u + iv.

1. Find $\frac{\partial u}{\partial x} = \varphi_1(x, y)$ and $\frac{\partial u}{\partial y} = \varphi_2(x, y)$

2. Write $f'(z) = \varphi_1(x, y) - i\varphi_2(x, y)$

3. Replace by z and y by 0

i.e. x = z and y = 0 and integrating.

4. $f(z) = \int[\varphi_1(z, 0) - i\varphi_2(z, 0)]dz + c$

Method:(II) If imaginary part v is given let f(z) = u + iv.

1) Find $\frac{\partial u}{\partial x} = \Psi_1(x, y)$ and $\frac{\partial u}{\partial y} = \Psi_2(x, y)$

2) Write $f'(z) = \Psi_1(x, y) - i\Psi_2(x, y)$

3) Replace x by z and y by 0

i.e. x=z and y = 0 and integrating

4) $f(z) = \int[\Psi_1(z, 0) - i\Psi_2(z, 0)]dz + c$

Method:(III) If u – v is given

Let f(z) = u + iv

if(z) = iu – v

Adding we get,

(1 + i)f(z) = (u – v) + i(u + v)

F(z) = U + iV

Method:(IV) If u + v is given

Let f(z) = u + iv

if(z) = iu – v

Adding we get,

(1 + i)f(z) = (u – v) + i(u + v)

F(z) = U + iV

Where $U = u - v$ and $V = u + v$

$F(z) = (1 + i)f(z)$

$U = u - v$ is given

$f(z) = \frac{F(z)}{1+i}$ Apply Method 1 to find F(z)

Where $U = u - v$ and $V = u + v$

$F(z) = (1 + i)f(z)$

$U = u - v$ is given

$f(z) = \frac{F(z)}{1+i}$ Apply Method 2 to find F(z)

Question: 1) If $u = x^2 - y^2$ find the corresponding analytic function.

Solution :- Given that, $u = x^2 - y^2$

$$\varphi_1(x, y) = \frac{\partial u}{\partial x} = 2x$$

$$\varphi_2(x, y) = \frac{\partial u}{\partial y} = -2y$$

$$f(z) = \int[\varphi_1(x, y) - i\varphi_2(x, y)]dz = \int[\varphi_1(z, 0) - i\varphi_2(z, 0)]dz$$

$$f(z) = \int[2z - i(0)]dz = 2\cdot\frac{z^2}{2} + c = z^2 + c$$

Which is a required analytic function.

Question: 2) Find the analytic function $f(z) = u + iv$ when imaginary part id given $v = e^x(x\sin y + y\cos y)$.

Solution:- Given, $f(z) = u + iv$

$$\Psi_2(x, y) = \frac{\partial v}{\partial x} = e^x(\sin y) + e^x(x\sin y + y\cos y)$$

$$\Psi_1(x, y) = \frac{\partial v}{\partial y} = e^x(x\cos y + \cos y - y\sin y)$$

$$\therefore f(z) = \int[\Psi_1(x, y) - i\Psi_2(x, y)]dz = \int[\Psi_1(z, 0) - i\Psi_2(z, 0)]dz$$

$$= \int[e^z(z + 1) + i(0)]dz = \int[e^z(z + 1)dz = e^z(z + 1) - \int e^z dz + c$$

$$= e^z(z + 1) - e^z + c = \mathbf{ze^z + c}$$

Which is required function.

Question: 3) State that $v = e^x(x\cos y - y\sin y)$ is an harmonic function and also find analytic function.

Solution:- Given, $v = e^x(x\cos y - y\sin y)$

For Harmonic function, v satisfy the laplace equation

$$\frac{\partial^2 u}{\partial x^2} + \frac{\partial^2 u}{\partial y^2} = 0$$

Now, $\frac{\partial v}{\partial x} = e^x(x\cos y) + e^x(x\cos y - y\sin y) = \Psi_2(x, y)$

$$\Psi_2(z,0) = e^z(z\cos(0)) + e^z = e^z(z+1) \quad \ldots(1)$$

$$\frac{\partial v}{\partial y} = e^x(-x\sin y) - y\cos y - \sin y) = \Psi_1(x,y)$$

$$\Psi_1(z,0) = e^z(-z(0) - 0 - 0) = 0 \quad \ldots(2)$$

$$\frac{\partial^2 v}{\partial x^2} = e^x(x\cos y - y\sin y) + 2e^x(\cos y) = e^x(x\cos y - y\sin y + 2\cos y) \quad \ldots(3)$$

$$\frac{\partial^2 v}{\partial y^2} = e^x(-x\cos y + y\sin y + 2\cos y) \quad \ldots(4)$$

Adding equation (3) and (4), we get

$$\frac{\partial^2 v}{\partial x^2} + \frac{\partial^2 v}{\partial y^2} = e^x(x\cos y - y\sin y + 2\cos y) + e^x(-x\cos y + y\sin y + 2\cos y) = 0$$

Thus v is a harmonic function.

By Using Milne Thomson's method, We Have

$$f(z) = \int[\Psi_1(x,y) - i\Psi_2(x,y)]dz = \int[\Psi_1(z,0) - i\Psi_2(z,0)]dz$$

$$= \int[(0) - i(e^z(z+1))]\,dz = -i(z e^z - e^z + e^z) + c$$

$f(z) = zi\,e^z + c$

which is required analytic function.

Question: 4) If $u - v = (x-y)(x^2 + 4xy + y^2)$ and $f(z) = u + iv$ is an analytic function of $z = x + iy$.

Find f(z) in terms of z.

Solution:- Given, $f(z) = u + iv$

$if(z) = iu - v$

Adding above both equation we get,

$(1+i)\,f(z) = i(u+v) + (u-v)$

$(1+i)\,f(z) = U + iV = F(Z)$

Where, $U = u - v$ and $V = u + v$

Here, $U = u - v = (x-y)(x^2 + 4xy + y^2)$

Real part is given hence apply method (III).

$$\frac{\partial U}{\partial x} = (x^2 + 4xy + y^2) + (x-y)(2x+4y) = \varphi_1(x,y)$$

$\varphi_1(z,0) = [(z^2 + 4z(0) + (0)^2)] + (z-0)(2z) = z^2 + 2z^2 = 3z^2$

$\frac{\partial U}{\partial y} = -(x^2 + 4xy + y^2) + (x - y)(2y + 4x) = \varphi_2(x,y)$

$\varphi_2(z,0) = [-(z^2 + 4z(0) + (0)^2)] + (z-0)(4z) = -z^2 + 4z^2 = 3z^2$

Now, $F(z) = \int[\varphi_1(x,y) - i\varphi_2(x,y)]dz = \int[\varphi_1(z,0) - i\varphi_2(z,0)]dz$

$= \int(3z^2 - 3iz^2) = 3\cdot\frac{z^3}{3} - 3i\cdot\frac{z^3}{3} + c$

$F(z) = z^3(1 - i) + c$

$(1+i) f(z) = z^3(1 - i) + c$

$f(z) = \frac{z^3(1-i)}{(1+i)} + \frac{c}{(1+i)} = \frac{z^3(1-i)(1-i)}{(1+i)(1-i)} + \frac{c}{(1+i)}$

$f(z) = -iz^3 + c$

which is a required analytic function.

Question: 5) Prove that $4\cdot\frac{\partial^2}{\partial z\cdot\partial\bar{z}} = [\frac{\partial^2}{\partial x^2} + \frac{\partial^2}{\partial y^2}]$.

Solution:- we know that, $z = x + iy$ and $\bar{z} = x - iy$

$z + \bar{z} = 2x$ and $z - \bar{z} = 2iy$

$x = \frac{1}{2}(z + \bar{z})$ and $y = \frac{1}{2i}(z - \bar{z}) = \frac{-i}{2}(z - \bar{z})$

$\frac{\partial x}{\partial z} = \frac{1}{2}$ and $\frac{\partial x}{\partial z} = \frac{i}{2}$

$\frac{\partial x}{\partial \bar{z}} = \frac{1}{2}$ and $\frac{\partial x}{\partial \bar{z}} = \frac{-i}{2}$

Also, $\frac{\partial}{\partial z} = \frac{\partial}{\partial x}(\frac{\partial x}{\partial z}) + \frac{\partial}{\partial y}(\frac{\partial y}{\partial z}) = \frac{\partial}{\partial x}(\frac{1}{2}) + \frac{\partial}{\partial x}(\frac{-i}{2}) = \frac{1}{2}(\frac{\partial}{\partial x} - i\frac{\partial}{\partial y})$

$\frac{\partial}{\partial \bar{z}} = \frac{\partial}{\partial x}(\frac{\partial x}{\partial \bar{z}}) + \frac{\partial}{\partial y}(\frac{\partial y}{\partial \bar{z}}) = \frac{\partial}{\partial x}(\frac{1}{2}) + \frac{\partial}{\partial x}(\frac{i}{2}) = \frac{1}{2}(\frac{\partial}{\partial x} + i\frac{\partial}{\partial y})$

$\frac{\partial^2}{\partial z\cdot\partial\bar{z}} = \frac{\partial}{\partial z}(\frac{\partial}{\partial \bar{z}}) = \frac{1}{4}(\frac{\partial}{\partial x} - i\frac{\partial}{\partial y})(\frac{\partial}{\partial x} + i\frac{\partial}{\partial y}) = \frac{1}{4}(\frac{\partial^2}{\partial x^2} + \frac{\partial^2}{\partial y^2})$

$\mathbf{4\cdot\frac{\partial^2 u}{\partial z\cdot\partial\bar{z}} = [\frac{\partial^2}{\partial x^2} + \frac{\partial^2}{\partial y^2}]}$

Question: 6) Prove that $\{\frac{\partial}{\partial x}|f(z)|\}^2 + \{\frac{\partial}{\partial y}|f(z)|\}^2 = |f(z)|^2$.

Solution:- Let $f(z) = u(x, y) + iv(x, y)$

$$|f(z)| = \sqrt{u^2+v^2}$$

Differentiating above equation w.r.t. x. Then we will get,

$$\frac{\partial}{\partial x}|f(z)| = \frac{1}{2\sqrt{u^2+v^2}}(2u\frac{\partial u}{\partial x} + 2v\frac{\partial v}{\partial x}) = \frac{u\frac{\partial u}{\partial x} + v\frac{\partial v}{\partial x}}{\sqrt{u^2+v^2}} = \frac{u\frac{\partial u}{\partial x} + v\frac{\partial v}{\partial x}}{|f(z)|} \qquad \ldots(1)$$

Similarly, $$\frac{\partial}{\partial y}|f(z)| = \frac{u\frac{\partial u}{\partial y} + v\frac{\partial v}{\partial y}}{|f(z)|} \qquad \ldots(2)$$

On squaring and adding equation (1) and (2), We obtained,

$$\{\frac{\partial}{\partial x}|f(z)|\}^2 + \{\frac{\partial}{\partial x}|f(z)|\}^2 = \frac{\left(u\frac{\partial u}{\partial x} + v\frac{\partial v}{\partial x}\right)^2 + \left(u\frac{\partial u}{\partial y} + v\frac{\partial v}{\partial y}\right)^2}{|f(z)|^2}$$

$$= \frac{[\left(u\frac{\partial u}{\partial x}\right)^2 + \left(v\frac{\partial v}{\partial x}\right)^2 + 2uv(\frac{\partial u}{\partial x})(\frac{\partial v}{\partial x})] + [\left(u\frac{\partial u}{\partial y}\right)^2 + \left(v\frac{\partial v}{\partial y}\right)^2 + 2uv(\frac{\partial u}{\partial y})(\frac{\partial v}{\partial y})]}{|f(z)|^2} \qquad \ldots(3)$$

By used C-R equations $\frac{\partial u}{\partial x} = \frac{\partial v}{\partial y}$ and $\frac{\partial u}{\partial y} = -\frac{\partial v}{\partial x}$.

Now, $2uv(\frac{\partial u}{\partial x})(\frac{\partial v}{\partial x}) = 2uv(\frac{\partial v}{\partial y})(-\frac{\partial u}{\partial xy})$ putting in above equation (3), we get

$$= \frac{[u^2\left(\frac{\partial u}{\partial x}\right)^2 + v^2\left(\frac{\partial v}{\partial x}\right)^2] + [u^2\left(\frac{\partial u}{\partial y}\right)^2 + v^2\left(\frac{\partial v}{\partial y}\right)^2]}{|f(z)|^2}$$

$$= \frac{[u^2\left(\frac{\partial u}{\partial x}\right)^2 + v^2\left(-\frac{\partial v}{\partial y}\right)^2] + [u^2\left(\frac{\partial u}{\partial y}\right)^2 + v^2\left(\frac{\partial u}{\partial x}\right)^2]}{|f(z)|^2} \qquad (\because \text{By C-R equation})$$

$$= \frac{(u^2+v^2)[\left(\frac{\partial u}{\partial x}\right)^2 + \left(\frac{\partial v}{\partial x}\right)^2]}{|f(z)|^2} = \frac{|f(z)|^2[\left(\frac{\partial u}{\partial x}\right)^2 + \left(\frac{\partial v}{\partial x}\right)^2]}{|f(z)|^2}$$

$$= [\left(\frac{\partial u}{\partial x}\right)^2 + \left(\frac{\partial v}{\partial x}\right)^2] = f'(z)$$

Question:7) Prove that $(\frac{\partial^2}{\partial x^2} + \frac{\partial^2}{\partial y^2})\log|f'(z)| = 0$.

Solution:- We know that, $4\cdot\frac{\partial^2}{\partial z\cdot\partial \bar{z}} = [\frac{\partial^2}{\partial x^2} + \frac{\partial^2}{\partial y^2}]$ (From question(5))

Consider,

$$(\frac{\partial^2}{\partial x^2} + \frac{\partial^2}{\partial y^2})\log|f'(z)| = 4\cdot\frac{\partial^2}{\partial z\cdot\partial \bar{z}}\log|f'(z)|$$

$$= 4\cdot\frac{\partial^2}{\partial z\cdot\partial \bar{z}}\frac{1}{2}\{\log|f'(z)|\}^2 = 2\cdot\frac{\partial^2}{\partial z\cdot\partial \bar{z}}\log(f'(z)\cdot f'(\bar{z}))$$

$$= 2\cdot\frac{\partial^2}{\partial z\cdot\partial \bar{z}}\log\{f'(z) + f'(\bar{z})\} = 2\cdot\frac{\partial}{\partial z}\{0 + \frac{1}{f'(\bar{z})}f''(\bar{z})\}$$

$$(\frac{\partial^2}{\partial x^2}+\frac{\partial^2}{\partial y^2})\log|f'(z)| = 2\cdot\frac{\partial}{\partial z}\{0+\frac{f''(\bar{z})}{f'(\bar{z})}\} = 0$$

Question: 8) $(\frac{\partial^2}{\partial x^2}+\frac{\partial^2}{\partial y^2})|R+iz|^2 = 2|f'(\bar{z})|^2$

Solution:- Let f(z) = u + iv

Where, u = real part and v= imaginary part

$$\frac{\partial}{\partial x}u^2 = 2u\frac{\partial u}{\partial x} = 2u\frac{\partial^2 u}{\partial x^2}+2\cdot\frac{\partial u}{\partial x}\cdot\frac{\partial u}{\partial x} = 2u\frac{\partial^2 u}{\partial x^2}+2\cdot(\frac{\partial u}{\partial x})^2$$

Similarly, $\frac{\partial^2}{\partial y^2}u^2 \quad = 2u\frac{\partial^2 u}{\partial y^2}+2\cdot(\frac{\partial u}{\partial y})^2$

Adding above two equation, we get

$$(\frac{\partial^2}{\partial x^2}+\frac{\partial^2}{\partial y^2})u^2 = 2\,[(\frac{\partial u}{\partial x})^2+(\frac{\partial u}{\partial y})^2]+2u\,[\frac{\partial^2 u}{\partial x^2}+\frac{\partial^2 u}{\partial y^2}]$$

Using C-R equations $\frac{\partial u}{\partial x} = \frac{\partial v}{\partial y}$ and $\frac{\partial u}{\partial y} = -\frac{\partial v}{\partial x}$

$$= 2\,[(\frac{\partial u}{\partial x})^2+(\frac{\partial u}{\partial y})^2] = 2\,[(\frac{\partial u}{\partial x})^2+(-\frac{\partial v}{\partial x})^2] = 2|f'(\bar{z})|^2$$

$$(\frac{\partial^2}{\partial x^2}+\frac{\partial^2}{\partial y^2})|R+iz|^2 = 2|f'(\bar{z})|^2$$

Question: 9) Prove that $(\frac{\partial^2}{\partial x^2}+\frac{\partial^2}{\partial y^2})|f(z)|^2 = 4|f'(z)|^2$.

Solution:- Let, f(z) = u + iv

$$|f(z)|^2 = u^2+v^2 = \varphi$$

Differentiate above equation with respect to x we get,

$$\frac{\partial\varphi}{\partial x} = 2u\frac{\partial u}{\partial x}+2v\frac{\partial v}{\partial x}$$

$$\frac{\partial^2\varphi}{\partial x^2} = 2\,[u\cdot\frac{\partial^2 u}{\partial x^2}+(\frac{\partial u}{\partial x})^2+v\cdot\frac{\partial^2 v}{\partial x^2}+(\frac{\partial v}{\partial x})^2]$$

Similarly, $\frac{\partial^2\varphi}{\partial y^2} = 2\,[u\cdot\frac{\partial^2 u}{\partial y^2}+(\frac{\partial u}{\partial y})^2+v\cdot\frac{\partial^2 v}{\partial y^2}+(\frac{\partial v}{\partial y})^2]$

Adding above two equation, we get

$$\frac{\partial^2\varphi}{\partial x^2}+\frac{\partial^2\varphi}{\partial y^2} = 2\,[u\cdot\frac{\partial^2 u}{\partial x^2}+(\frac{\partial u}{\partial x})^2+v\cdot\frac{\partial^2 v}{\partial x^2}+(\frac{\partial v}{\partial x})^2+u\cdot\frac{\partial^2 u}{\partial y^2}+(\frac{\partial u}{\partial y})^2+v\cdot\frac{\partial^2 v}{\partial y^2}+(\frac{\partial v}{\partial y})^2]$$

By using C-R equation and laplace equation, we get

$$= 2\,[\,2(\frac{\partial u}{\partial x})^2+2(\frac{\partial v}{\partial y})^2\,]$$

$$= 4\,[(\frac{\partial u}{\partial x})^2 + (\frac{\partial v}{\partial y})^2\,] = 4\,[\frac{\partial u}{\partial x} + i\frac{\partial v}{\partial x}]^2$$

$$\mathbf{[\frac{\partial^2}{\partial x^2} + \frac{\partial^2}{\partial y^2}]\,\varphi = (\frac{\partial^2}{\partial x^2} + \frac{\partial^2}{\partial y^2})|f(z)|^2 = 4|f'(z)|^2}$$

Question: 10) If $|f(z)|$ is constant, prove that f(z) is also constant.

Solution:- Let, $f(z) = u + iv$

$$|f(z)|^2 = u^2 + v^2$$

$$|f(z)| = \text{constant} = C$$

$$u^2 + v^2 = C^2$$

Differentiate above equation with respect to x and y respectively, we get

$$2u\frac{\partial u}{\partial x} + 2v\frac{\partial v}{\partial x} = 0 \qquad \text{and} \qquad 2u\frac{\partial u}{\partial y} + 2v\frac{\partial v}{\partial y} = 0$$

$$u\frac{\partial u}{\partial x} + v\frac{\partial v}{\partial x} = 0 \qquad \text{...(1)}$$

And $$-u\frac{\partial v}{\partial x} + v\frac{\partial u}{\partial x} = 0 \qquad \text{...(2)}$$

(Since, by using C-R equations)

On squaring and adding equation (1) and (2), we get

$$u^2(\frac{\partial u}{\partial x})^2 + v^2(\frac{\partial v}{\partial x})^2 + u^2(\frac{\partial v}{\partial x})^2 + v^2(\frac{\partial u}{\partial x})^2 = 0$$

$$(u^2 + v^2)\,[\left(\frac{\partial u}{\partial x}\right)^2 + \left(\frac{\partial v}{\partial x}\right)^2] = 0$$

$$\left(\frac{\partial u}{\partial x}\right)^2 + \left(\frac{\partial v}{\partial x}\right)^2 = 0$$

Now, $f(z) = u + iv$

$$f'(z) = \frac{\partial u}{\partial x} + i\frac{\partial v}{\partial x}$$

$$\overline{f'(z)} = \frac{\partial u}{\partial x} - i\frac{\partial v}{\partial x}$$

$$(f'(z))^2 = \left(\frac{\partial u}{\partial x}\right)^2 + i\left(\frac{\partial v}{\partial x}\right)^2 = 0$$

Hence, f(z) is also a constant.

Exercise:-

1. Prove that $\left(\frac{\partial^2}{\partial x^2}+\frac{\partial^2}{\partial y^2}\right)|u)^p$ = p(p-1) $|u)^{p-2}$|f'(z) $|^2$.

2. Prove that $\left(\frac{\partial\psi}{\partial x}\right)^2+\left(\frac{\partial\psi}{\partial x}\right)^2 = \left[\left(\frac{\partial\psi}{\partial u}\right)^2+\left(\frac{\partial\psi}{\partial v}\right)^2\right]$|f'(z) $|^2$.

3. Prove that $\frac{\partial^2\psi}{\partial x^2}+\frac{\partial^2\psi}{\partial y^2} = \left(\frac{\partial^2\psi}{\partial x^2}+\frac{\partial^2\psi}{\partial y^2}\right)$|f'(z) $|^2$.

4. If f(z) = u + iv is an analytic function of z and u –v = $\frac{\cos x+\sin x- e^{-y}}{2cosx-2coshy}$ prove that

f(z) = $\frac{1}{2}\left(1-\cot\frac{z}{2}\right)$ when f$\left(\frac{\pi}{2}\right)$ = 0.

5. If u = $\frac{\sin 2x}{cosh2y+cos2x}$, find f(z). Ans: tanz +c

6. Determine analytic function whose real part is

(a) U = $\log\sqrt{x^2+y^2}$ Ans: logz +c

(b) cosx coshy Ans: cosz +c

7. Determine analytic function whose real part is

(a) U = log($\sqrt{x^2+y^2}$) + x-2y. Ans: logz +c

(b) sinhx cosy Ans siniz +c

8. If f(z) = u + iv is an analytic function of z = x + iy and

u – v = $e^x[(x-y)siny-(x+y)cosy]$ find f(z). Ans: i$(z+1)e^{-z}+c$

9. Prove that u = x^2+y^2& $v=\frac{y}{x^2+y^2}$ are harmonic function f(x.y) but are not harmonic conjugate.

10. If u & v are harmonic function in region R . prove that the function $\left\{\left[\frac{\partial u}{\partial y}-\frac{\partial v}{\partial x}\right]+i\left[\frac{\partial u}{\partial x}+\frac{\partial v}{\partial y}\right]\right\}$ is an analytic function z = x +iy.

SIMPLY CONNECTED REGION

All the interior points of a closed curve drawn within region D are considered points of the region D. This curve is continuous and does not intersect or cross itself at any point, ensuring it encloses a distinct, well-defined area within region D as show in fig.(9)

Fig.(9)

MULTIPLY CONNECTED REGION

A region bounded by more than one curve is called a multiply connected region. We can transform this multiply connected region into a simply connected region by making one or more cuts. In doing so, the curves may intersect or cross each other. This is illustrated in Figure (10).

Fig.(10)

Contour: An arc whose starting point is the same as its endpoint is called a contour

CAUCHY'S INTEGRAL THEOREM

Statement:- If f(z) is analytic function and its derivatives f(z) is continuous at each points inside and on a simple closed curve C.

then $\int_c f(z)dz = 0$.

Proof: - Given, f(z) be an analytic function.

f(z) = u(x,y) +iv(x,y) and z = x + iy

i.e. dz = dx + idy

Let R be the region enclosed by the curve c.

$$\int f(z)dz = \int_c (u+iv)(dx+idy) = \int_c [udx + iudy + ivdx - vdy]$$

$$= \int_c (udx - vdy) + i\int_c (vdx + udy)$$

$$= \iint_R \left(-\frac{\partial v}{\partial x} - \frac{\partial u}{\partial y}\right) dxdy + i\int_R \left(\frac{\partial u}{\partial x} - \frac{\partial v}{\partial y}\right) dxdy \qquad (\because \text{By Green theorem})$$

By using C-R equations, $\frac{\partial u}{\partial x} = \frac{\partial v}{\partial y}$ and $\frac{\partial u}{\partial y} = -\frac{\partial v}{\partial x}$, we get

$$= \iint_R \left(\frac{\partial u}{\partial x} - \frac{\partial u}{\partial y}\right) dxdy + i\iint_R \left(\frac{\partial u}{\partial x} - \frac{\partial u}{\partial y}\right) dxdy$$

$$\int f(z)dz = 0$$

Note:– if there is no pole inside and on the closed curve then the value of the integral is zero.

Extension for Cauchy's theorem for multiply connected region:-

Statement:– If f(z) is analytic in the region R, between two simple closed curve C_1& C_2 then

$$\int_{C_1} f(z)dz = \int_{C_2} f(z)dz$$

Proof:– We know that, $\int f(z)dz = 0$

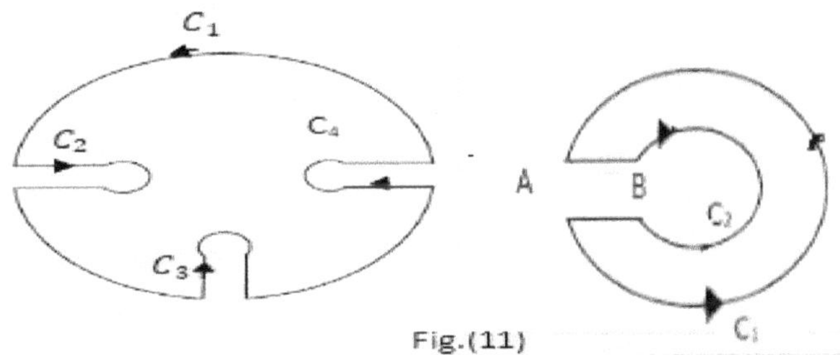

Fig.(11)

Where, The path of integration is along AB , and curves C_2 in clockwise direction and along C_1 in anticlockwise direction.

$$\int_{AB} f(z)dz - \int_{C_2} f(z)dz + \int_{BA} f(z)dz + \int_{C_1} f(z)dz = 0$$

Since, $\int_{AB} f(z)dz = -\int_{BA} f(z)dz$

$\therefore$ $\quad -\int_{C_2} f(z)dz + \int_{C_1} f(z)dz = 0$

$$\Rightarrow \int_{C_1} f(z)dz = \int_{C_2} f(z)dz$$

In general closed curve C contain non-intersecting curves $C_1, C_2, C_3, \ldots\ldots C_n$.

Then, $\int_C f(z)dz = \int_{C_1} f(z)dz + \int_{C_2} f(z)dz + \int_{C_3} f(z)dz + \ldots\ldots + \int_{C_n} f(z)dz$

CAUCHY INTEGRAL FORMULA

Statement:- If f(z) is an analytic within and on a simple closed curve C and if O is any point within C then

$$f(a) = \frac{1}{2\pi i}\int_C \frac{f(z)}{(z-a)}\,dz \qquad \text{or} \qquad \int_C \frac{f(z)}{(z-a)}\,dz = 2\pi i\, f(a)$$

Proof:- Let f(z) be an analytic function at all points within C except at z = a. Draw a semi-circle C_1 lying within circle C with its centre **a** and radius **r**.

Also $\frac{f(z)}{(z-a)}$ is an analytic function in region between C and C_1 and Cauchy integral theorem for multiple connected region.

Then ,
$$\int_C \frac{f(z)}{z-a}dz = \int_{C_1}\frac{f(z)}{z-a}dz = \int_{C_1}\frac{f(z)-f(a)+f(a)}{(z-a)}dz$$

$$= \int_{C_1}\frac{f(z)-f(a)}{(z-a)}dz + f(a)\int_{C_1}\frac{dz}{(z-a)} \qquad \ldots(1)$$

For circle C_1, $|z-a| = r$ or $|z-a| = re^{i\theta}$ $\qquad dz = ire^{i\theta}d\theta \qquad (\because 0 \le \theta \le 2\pi)$

Now,
$$\int_{C_1}\frac{f(z)-f(a)}{(z-a)}dz = \int_0^{2\pi}\frac{f(a+re^{i\theta})-f(a)}{(z-a)}ire^{i\theta}d\theta = \int_0^{2\pi}[f(a+re^{i\theta})-f(a)]id\theta = 0 \qquad \ldots(2)$$

And
$$\int_{C_1}\frac{dz}{(z-a)} = \int_0^{2\pi}\frac{ire^{i\theta}d\theta}{re^{i\theta}} = \int_0^{2\pi} id\theta = 2\pi i \qquad \ldots(3)$$

From equation (1) (2) and (3), We get

$$\int_C \frac{f(z)}{(z-a)}dz = 2\pi i\, f(a) + 0$$

$$\therefore \quad f(a) = \frac{1}{2\pi i}\int_C \frac{f(z)}{(z-a)}dz$$

CAUCHY INTEGRAL FORMULA FOR THE DERIVATIVE OF AN ANALYTIC FUNCTION

Statement:- If a function is an analytic function in region R then its derivative at any point z = a of R is also analytic in R and is given by,

$f'(a) = \frac{1}{2\pi i}\int_C \frac{f(z)}{(z-a)}dz$, Where C is the contour in R surrounding at the point z = a.

Proof:- We know that, the Cauchy integral formula and its given by,

$$f(a) = \frac{1}{2\pi i}\int_C \frac{f(z)}{(z-a)}dz \qquad \text{or} \qquad 2\pi i\, f(a) = \int_C \frac{f(z)}{(z-a)}dz$$

Differentiating the above equation with respect to. a we get,

$$f'(a) = \frac{1}{2\pi i}\int_C \frac{\partial}{\partial z}\left[\frac{f(z)}{(z-a)}\right]dz = \frac{1}{2\pi i}\int_C f(z)\frac{-1}{(z-a)^2}(-1)\,dz = \frac{1}{2\pi i}\int_C \frac{f(z)}{(z-a)^2}dz$$

Again, Differentiating with respect to. a we get,

$$f''(a) = \frac{2}{2\pi i}\int_C \frac{f(z)}{(z-a)^3}dz$$

In general, (or derivative of f(a) w. r. t. a upto n times)

$$f^n(a) = \frac{n!}{2\pi i}\int_C \frac{f(z)}{(z-a)^{n+1}}\,dz .$$

Hence proved.

Question: 1) Find the integral $\oint \frac{3z^2+7z+1}{z+1}dz$, where C is the center $|z| = \frac{1}{2}$.

Solution:- Given $|z| = \frac{1}{2}$. Draw a circle having center (0, 0) and radius $(r = \frac{1}{2})$.

The pole of the given integrand is given by

$z + 1 = 0$

$z = -1$

The pole outside the circle $|z| = \frac{1}{2}$

Hence by Cauchy's Integral theorem

$$\oint \frac{3z^2+7z+1}{z+1}dz = 0.$$

Question: 2) Find the value of $\oint \frac{z+4}{z^2+2z+5}dz$, if C is the circle $|z + 1| = 1$.

Solution:- Given $|z + 1| = 1$, Draw a circle having radius r = 1 and center (-1, 0) .

The pole of the given integral is given by

$z^2 + 2z + 5 = 0$

$z = \frac{-2 \pm \sqrt{4-20}}{2} = \frac{-2 \pm 4i}{2} = -1 \pm 2i$

The pole lies outside the circle $|z + 1| = 1$

Hence by Cauchy's Integral theorem,

$$\oint \frac{z+4}{z^2+2z+5}dz = 0$$

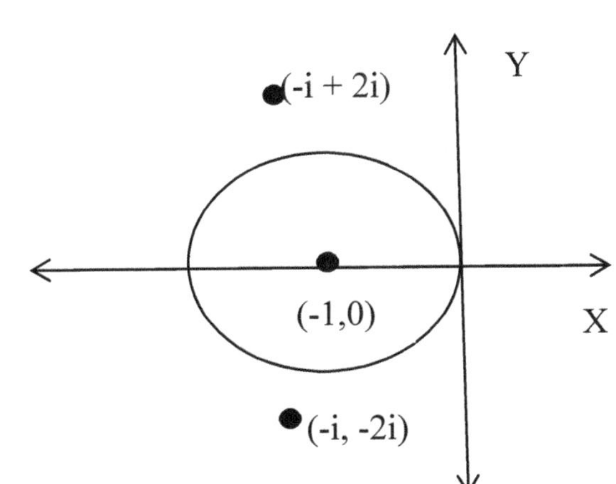

Question: 3) Find the $\oint \frac{e^{-z}}{z+1}dz$, where C is the circle $|z| = \frac{1}{2}$.

Solution:- Given $|z| = \frac{1}{2}$, Draw a circle having center (0, 0) and radius $(r = \frac{1}{2})$.
The pole of the given integrand is given by,

$z + 1 = 0$

$z = -1$

The pole outside the circle $|z| = \frac{1}{2}$

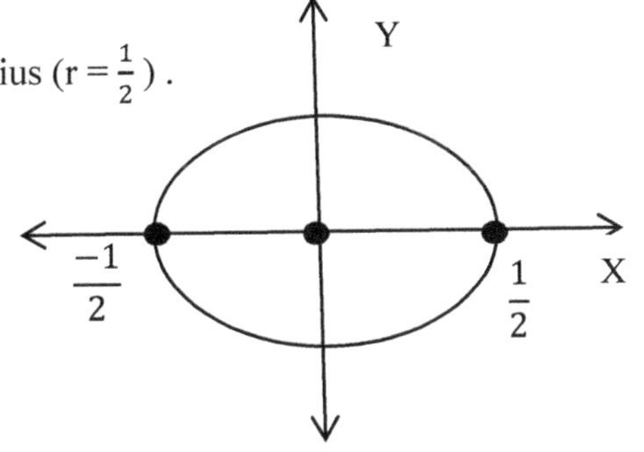

Hence by Cauchy's Integral theorem

$$\oint \frac{e^{-z}}{z+1}\, dz = 0$$

Question: 4) Find $\oint \frac{2z^2+5}{(z+2)^3\,(z^2+4)}\, dz$, where C is the square with the vertices at $1+i$, $2+i$, $2+2i$, $1+2i$.

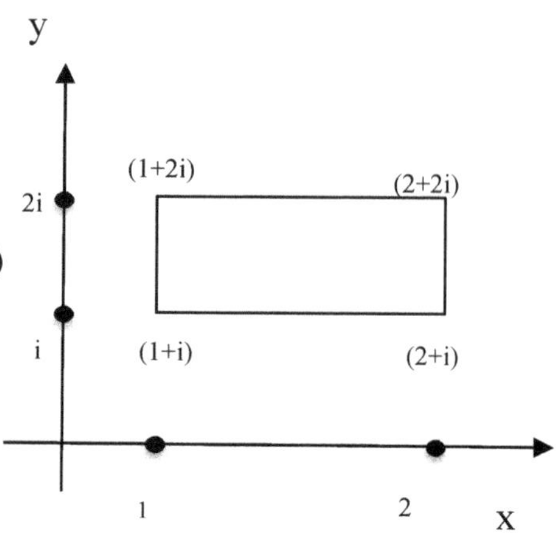

Solution:- Draw a square by taking the parts $(1+i)$, $(2+i)$, $(2+2i)$ and $(1+2i)$.

The pole of the given integrand is given by,

$(z+2)^3\,(z^2+4) = 0$

$(z+2)^3 = 0$ and $(z^2+4) = 0$

$z = -2$ and $z^2 = -4$

(pole of order 3) and $z = \pm 2i$ (simple pole)

The poles lies outside the square (contour) .

Hence by Cauchy's Integral theorem,

$$\oint \frac{2z^2+5}{(z+2)^3\,(z^2+4)}\, dz = 0$$

Question: 5) State that $\int_C \frac{1}{z-a}\, dz = 2\pi i$, where C is the circle $|z-a| = r$

Solution:- Given that, $\int_C \frac{1}{z-a}\, dz$, Where, C is the circle $(z-a) = r$ with center $(a, 0)$ and Radius $(r = r)$.

Draw a circle having center $(a, 0)$ and radius $(r = r)$.

By using Cauchy's integral theorem,

$$\int_C \frac{1}{z-a}\, dz = 2\pi i\, f(a)$$

$$\int_C \frac{1}{z-a}\, dz = 2\pi i\,(1)$$

$$\int_C \frac{1}{z-a}\, dz = 2\pi i$$

Question: 6) Evaluate the integral $\int_C \frac{1}{z}\cos z\, dz$ where C is the ellipse $9x^2 + 4y^2 = 1$.

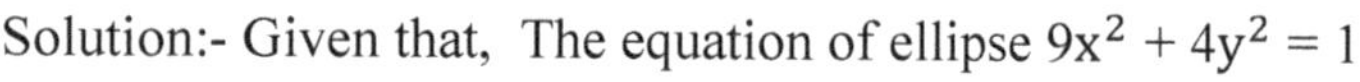
Solution:- Given that, The equation of ellipse $9x^2 + 4y^2 = 1$

Pole of the given integrand is given by,

$z = 0$

Draw a ellipse that encloses the pole $z = 0$.

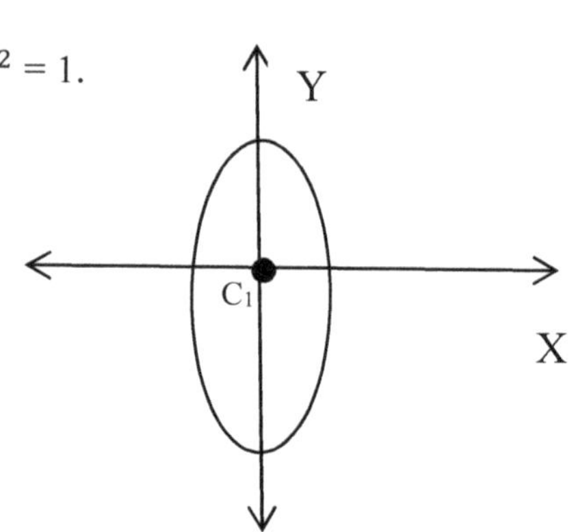

By Cauchy's Integral formula,

$$\int_C \frac{1}{z}\cos z\, dz = (2\pi i \cos z)_{z=0} = 2\pi i$$

Question: 7) Find $\int_C \frac{z}{z^2 - 3z+2}\, dz$ by using Cauchy,s integral formula with C is a circle $|z - 2| = \frac{1}{2}$

Solution:- Given that, $|z - 2| = \frac{1}{2}$.

Draw a circle having center (2,0) and radius ($r = \frac{1}{2}$).

\ The pole of the integrand is given by,

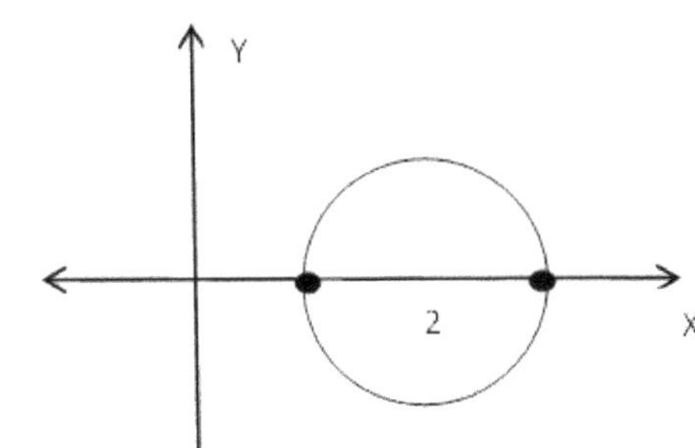

$$z^2 - 3z + 2 = 0$$

$$(z-1)(z-2) = 0$$

$$z = 1, 2$$

There is only one pole at $z = 2$ which lies inside the given circle

Apply Cauchy's integral formula

$$\int_C \frac{z}{z^2 - 3z+2}\, dz = \int_C \frac{z}{(z-1)(z-2)}\, dz$$

$$= \int_C \frac{\frac{z}{(z-1)}}{(z-2)}\, dz = 2\pi i \left(\frac{z}{(z-1)}\right)_{z=2} = 2\pi i \left(\frac{2}{(2-1)}\right) = 4\pi i .$$

Question: 8) Use Cauchy's integral formula to calculate $\int_C \frac{2z+1}{z^2+z}\, dz$, where C is $|z| = \frac{1}{2}$.

Solution:- Given that, $|z| = \frac{1}{2}$, Draw a circle having center (0, 0) and radius ($r = \frac{1}{2}$) .

The pole of the given integrand is given by,

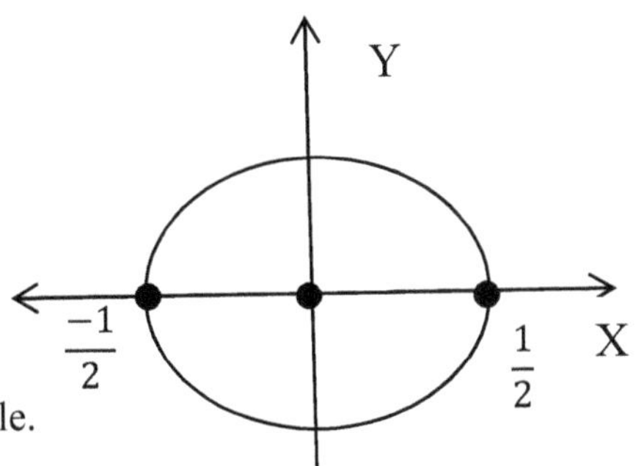

$$z^2 + z = 0$$

$$z(z + 1) = 0$$

$$z = 0, 1$$

There are only one pole at $z = 0$ lies inside the given circle.

Apply Cauchy's integral formula.

$$\int_C \frac{2z+1}{z^2+z}\, dz = \int_C \frac{2z+1}{z(z+1)}\, dz = \int_C \frac{\frac{2z+1}{(z+1)}}{z}\, dz$$

$$= 2\pi i \left(\frac{2z+1}{(z+1)}\right)_{z=0}$$

$$\int_C \frac{2z+1}{z^2+z}\, dz = \mathbf{2\pi i}$$

Question: 9) Evaluate the complex integral $\int_C \tan z\, dz$, where C is $|z| = 2$

Solution:- Given that, $|z| = 2$, Draw a circle having center (0, 0) and radius (r = 2) .

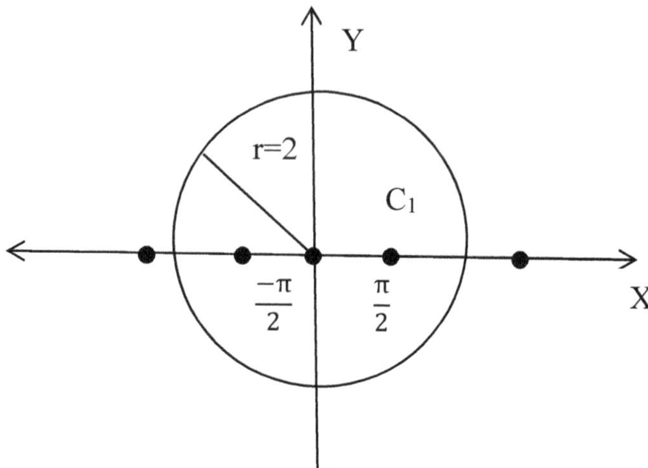

$$\int_C \tan z\, dz = \int_C \frac{\sin z}{\cos z} dz$$

The pole of the given integrand is given by

$$\cos z = 0$$

$$z = \pm\frac{\pi}{2}$$

By using Cauchy's integral formula,

$$\int_C \frac{\sin z}{\cos z} dz = \int_{C_1} \frac{\sin z}{\cos z} dz + \int_{C_2} \frac{\sin z}{\cos z} dz$$

$$= 2\pi i(\cos z)_{z=\frac{\pi}{2}} + 2\pi i(\cos z)_{z=\frac{-\pi}{2}}$$

$$= 2\pi i\,(1) + 2\pi i\,(-1) = 0$$

Question: 10) Evaluate $\int_C \frac{e^{-z}}{z+1} dz$, where C is the circle $|z| = 2$.

Solution:- Given $|z| = 2$. Draw a circle having center (0, 0) and radius (r=2).

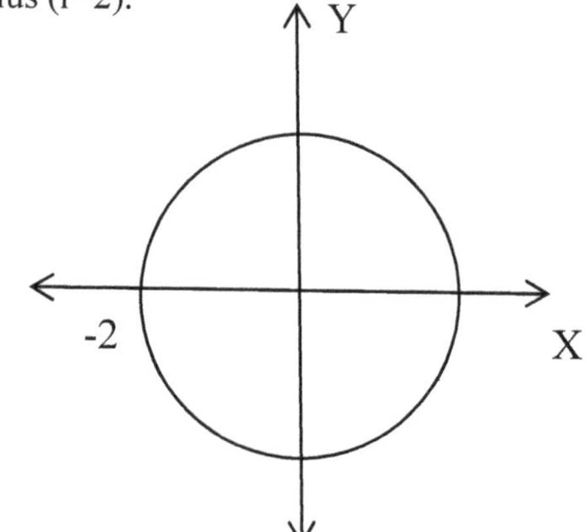

The pole of the given integrand is given by,

$$z + 1 = 0$$

$$z = -1$$

The pole $z = -1$ lies inside the circle $|z| = 2$.

By Cauchy's integral formula ,

$$\int_C \frac{e^{-z}}{z+1} dz = 2\pi i(e^{-z})_{z=-1} = 2\pi i e$$

$$\int_C \frac{e^{-z}}{z+1} dz = 2\pi i e$$

Question: 11) Evaluate $\int_C \frac{e^{z}}{z^2+1} dz$, over the circular path $|z| = 2$.

Solution:- Given $|z| = 2$ .Draw a circle having center (0, 0) and radius (r = 2) .

The pole of the given integrand is given by,

$$z^2 + 1 = 0$$

$$z^2 = -1 = i^2$$

$$z = \pm I$$

There are two poles at z = i and z = - I .

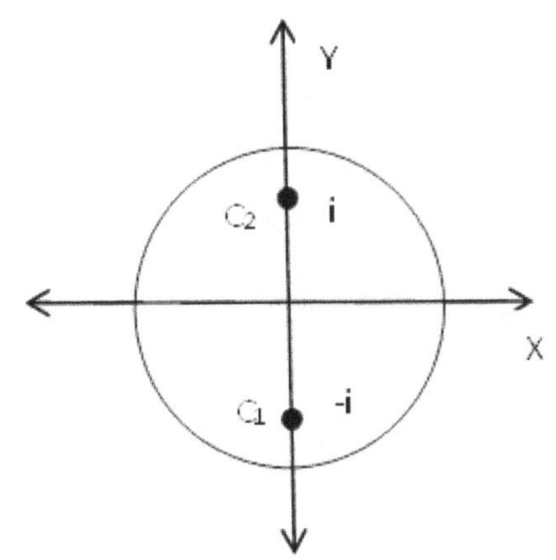

Apply Cauchy's integral formula.

$$\int_C \frac{e^z}{z^2+1} dz = \int_C \frac{e^z}{(z+i)(z-i)} dz$$

$$= \int_{C_1} \frac{\frac{e^z}{(z-i)}}{(z+i)} dz + \int_{C_2} \frac{\frac{e^z}{(z+i)}}{(z-i)} dz$$

$$= 2\pi i\left(\frac{e^z}{(z-i)}\right)_{z=-i} + 2\pi i\left(\frac{e^z}{(z+i)}\right)_{z=i}$$

$$= 2\pi i\left[\frac{e^{-i}}{-2i} + \frac{e^{i}}{2i}\right] = 2\pi i\left(\frac{e^{i} - e^{-i}}{2i}\right)$$

$$\int_C \frac{e^z}{z^2+1} dz = 2\pi i \sin(i) .$$

Question: 12) Use Cauchy's integral formula to evaluate $\int_C \frac{\sin \pi z^2 + \cos \pi z^2}{(z-1)(z-2)} dz$ where C is the circle $|z| = 3$.

Solution:-Given that, $|z| = 3$. Draw a circle having center (0,0) and radius (r = 3).

The pole of the given integrand is given by,

$$(z - 1)(z - 2) = 0$$

$$z = 1, 2$$

There are two poles at z = 1 and z =2 .

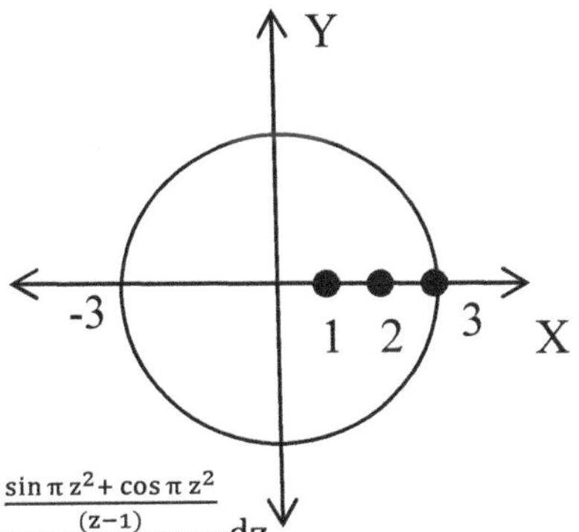

Apply Cauchy's integral formula,

$$\int_C \frac{\sin \pi z^2 + \cos \pi z^2}{(z-1)(z-2)} dz = \int_{C_1} \frac{\frac{\sin \pi z^2 + \cos \pi z^2}{(z-2)}}{(z-1)} dz + \int_{C_2} \frac{\frac{\sin \pi z^2 + \cos \pi z^2}{(z-1)}}{(z-2)} dz$$

$$= 2\pi i \left\{\left(\frac{\sin \pi z^2 + \cos \pi z^2}{(z-2)}\right)_{z=1} + \left(\frac{\sin \pi z^2 + \cos \pi z^2}{(z-1)}\right)_{z=2}\right\}$$

$$= 2\pi i \left\{\left(\frac{\sin \pi + \cos \pi}{(1-2)}\right) + \left(\frac{\sin 4\pi + \cos 4\pi}{(2-1)}\right)\right\}$$

$$= 2\pi i \left\{\left(\frac{-1}{-1}\right) + \left(\frac{1}{1}\right)\right\}$$

$$= 2\pi i (1+1)$$

$$\int_C \frac{\sin \pi z^2 + \cos \pi z^2}{(z-1)(z-2)} dz = 4\pi i$$

Question: 13) Using Cauchy's integral formula evaluate $\frac{1}{2\pi i}\int_C \frac{ze^z}{(z-a)^3}dz$, where the point a lies within the closed curve C.

Solution:- Used Cauchy's integral formula of the derivatives

$$f''(a) = \frac{n!}{2\pi i}\int_C \frac{f(z)}{(z-a)^{n+1}}\,dz$$

Now, $\int_C \frac{f(z)}{(z-a)^{n+1}}\,dz = \int \frac{ze^z}{(z-a)^{2+1}}\,dz = \frac{2\pi i}{2!}\left[\frac{d^2}{dz^2}(ze^z)\right]_{z=a}$

$$= \frac{2\pi i}{2!}\left[\frac{d}{dz}(ze^z + e^z)\right]_{z=a} = \frac{2\pi i}{2!}\left[(ze^z + e^z + e^z)\right]_{z=a}$$

$$= \frac{2\pi i}{2!}\left[e^z(z+2)\right]_{z=a} \quad = \pi i\,(a+2)\,e^a$$

$$\frac{1}{2\pi i}\int_C \frac{f(z)}{(z-a)^{n+1}}\,dz = \frac{1}{2\pi i}\pi i\,(a+2)\,e^a$$

$$\frac{1}{2\pi i}\int_C \frac{f(z)}{(z-a)^{n+1}}\,dz = \frac{1}{2}(a+2)\,e^a$$

EXERCISES:-

1) Evaluate the following complex integration using Cauchy's integral formula $\oint \frac{3z^2+z+1}{(z^2-1)(z+3)}dz$, where C is a circle $|z| = 2$.

Ans : $\frac{\pi i}{4}$

2) Verify the Cauchy's theorem by integrating e^{iz} along the boundary of the triangle with the vertices at the point 1 +i, -1+i, and -1+i.

Ans : 0

3) Evaluate the following complex integration by Cauchy's integral formula.

1. $\int_C \frac{e^{3iz}}{(z+a)^3}dz$, where C is the circle $|z-\pi| = 3$

2. $\oint \frac{3z^2+z}{(z^2-1)}dz$, where C is the circle $|z-1| = 1$

3. $\oint \frac{4-3z}{z(z-1)(z-2)}dz$, where C is the circle $|z| = \frac{3}{2}$

4. $\oint \frac{1}{(z^2-1)}dz$, where C is the circle $x^2+y^2 = 4$

5. $\oint \frac{z^2-2z}{(z+1)^2(z^2+4)}dz$, where C is the circle $|z| = 10$

6. $\int_C \frac{e^z}{(z-1)(z-4)}dz$, where C is the circle $|z| = 2$

7. $\int_C \frac{1}{z(z+\pi i)}dz$, where C is $|z+3i| = 1$

UNIT II : SINGULARITIES

INTRODUCTION

The theory of complex variables is extensively used to address a wide range of problems in engineering, technology, and applied sciences. In this chapter, we will delve into various techniques for evaluating complex integrals when the function in question is not analytic. Contour integration, a powerful method within the field of complex analysis, is employed to evaluate certain integrals by integrating along a specified path in the complex plane. This approach is particularly useful for functions that exhibit singularities, allowing for the calculation of integrals that would otherwise be challenging or impossible to solve using traditional real-variable methods. By understanding and applying these techniques, one can effectively tackle complex integrals in practical applications.

PRELIMINARY

1. **Power series of complex function:-**

If a complex function f(z) is analytic at point z = z_0, then f(z) can be expanded into power series about z = z_0. The power series expansion of f(z) z = z_0 will be

$$f(z) = \sum_{n=0}^{\infty} C_n(z-z_0)^n = C_0 + C_1(z-z_0) + C_2(z-z_0)^2 + \cdots$$

Where, z_0 is a centre of power series expansion.

C_0 is a constant term of related to $f^n(z_0)$.

2. **Taylor's series expansion of complex function:–**

A complex function f(z) is analytic at all point inside the circle C: $(z - z_0)$ = R in fig(1) .

Here, The point inside the circle the taylor's series expansion of f(z) about the point z = z_0 will be given by

$$f(z) = \sum_{n=0}^{\infty} C_n(z-z_0)^n = \sum_{n=0}^{\infty} \frac{f^n(z_0)}{n!}(z-z_0)^n = f(z_0) + f'(z-z_0) + \frac{f''(z_0)}{2!}(z-z_0)^2 + \ldots$$

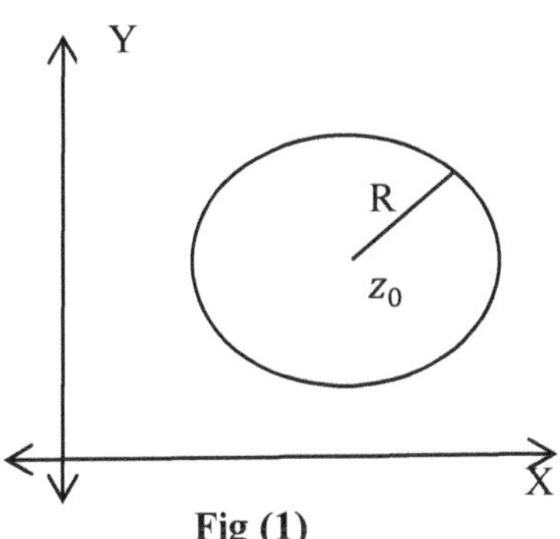

Fig (1)

3.Laurentz series expansion of complex function:-

A complex function f(z) is analytic at all points in the ring shaped region or circular annulus

$r_1 < |z - z_0| < r_2$. in the below fig(2), Then all points are in the region The Lorentz series expansion about $z = z_0$ will be,

$$f(z) = \sum_{n=0}^{\infty} a_n(z - z_0)^n + \sum_{n=1}^{\infty} \frac{b_n}{(z-z_0)^n}$$

The region of the convergence $R_1 < |z - z_0| < R$.

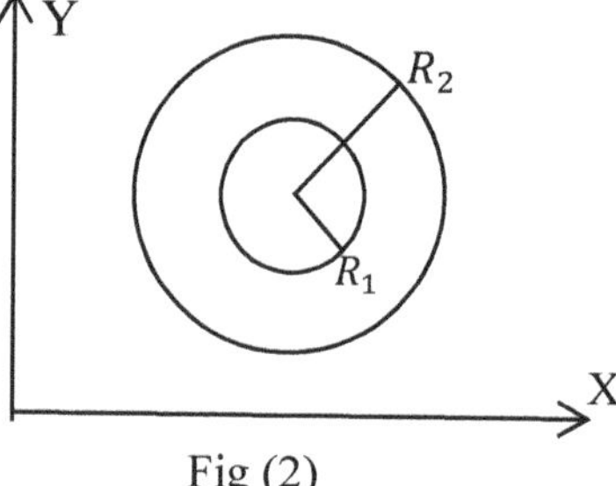

Fig (2)

SINGULAR POINTS

1. A point at which function f(z) is fails to be analytic is called a singular point or singularity of the function f(z). e.g. The function $f(z) = \frac{1}{z-2}$ then z = 2 is a singularity of f(z).

2. Isolated Singular points:- If $z = z_0$ is a simple pole of complex function f(z) then there exists a small neighborhood about $z = z_0$, then $z = z_0$ is an isolated singular point of function f(z).

3. Non-isolated Singular point:- If $z = z_0$ is a simple pole of complex function f(z) then there is no existence of small neighborhood about $z = z_0$ then $z = z_0$ is a non-isolated singular point of the complex function f(z).

e.g.(a) The function $f(z) = \frac{1}{(z-1)(z-3)}$ has two isolated singular points at z = 1 and z = 2.

(b) The function $f(z) = \frac{1}{2}$ has one singular point at z = 0.

(c) The function $f(z) = \frac{5z^2+4}{(z+1)^2\,(z^2+12)}$ has an isolated singular point at z = -2, $2\sqrt{3}$i and -$2\sqrt{3}$i.

(d) The function $f(z) = \frac{1}{\sin\frac{\pi}{2}}$ is not analytic at the point where $\sin\frac{\pi}{2} = 0$ is at point $\frac{\pi}{2} = n\pi$ i.e. the point

$z = \frac{1}{n}$ (n = 1,2,3…). Thus $z = 1, \frac{1}{2}, \frac{1}{3}$ …… z = 0 are the points of singularity. z = 0 is the

non-isolated singularity of the function $\frac{1}{\sin\frac{\pi}{2}}$.

POLE

The Laurent's series of the function f(z) at $z = z_0$ is given by

$$f(z) = \sum_{n=0}^{\infty} a_n(z - z_0)^n + \sum_{n=1}^{\infty} \frac{b_n}{(z-z_0)^n}.$$

where the first part of Laurent's series expansion represents the (regular) analytic point and the second part of Laurent's series expansion represents the singular (principal) part of the function f(z).

The power of principal part of Laurent's series expansion at $z = z_0$ is called the pole of order n.

The principal part is used to decide the nature of the isolated singular points.

e.g. (1) $f(z) = \frac{1}{(z-2)^3}$ the function f(z) has the poles of order 3 at z = 2.

(2) $f(z) = \frac{3z-2}{(z-1)^3\,(z-1)\,(z+4)}$ The function f(z) has pole of order 3 at z = 1 and simple pole at z = 1 and z = -4.

Removable Singular Points:-

If $z = z_0$ is an singular point of the complex function f(z) and the principal part of the Laurent's series expansion at $z = z_0$ does not contain negative power of $z = z_0$ (i.e. principal part is zero). Then $z = z_0$ is a removable singular point of the complex function f(z). Or simply analytic part exists.

i.e. $f(z) = \sum_{n=0}^{\infty} a_n (z - z_0)^n \neq 0$.

Non-essential Singular Points:-

If $z = z_0$ is a singular point of a complex function f(z) and the principal part of the Laurent's series expansion at $z = z_0$ contain finite number of negative power of $z = z_0$ is called Non-essential singular points of the complex function f(z).
i.e. $f(z) = \sum_{n=0}^{\infty} a_n (z - z_0)^n + \sum_{n=1}^{\infty} \frac{b_n}{(z-z_0)^n}$.

where, The term $\frac{b_n}{(z-z_0)^n}$, the value of n is finite quantity.

Essential Singular points:-

If $z = z_0$ is a singular point of a complex function f(z) and the principal part of the Laurent's series expansion at $z = z_0$ contain infinite number of negative power of $z = z_0$ is called Non-essential singular points of the complex function f(z).

i.e. $f(z) = \sum_{n=0}^{\infty} a_n (z - z_0)^n + \sum_{n=1}^{\infty} \frac{b_n}{(z-z_0)^n}$

where, $\frac{b_n}{(z-z_0)^n}$ the value of n is infinite quantity.

Question: 1) Discuss the nature and singularity of the following functions.

(I). $f(z) = \frac{1}{z(1-z^2)}$.

Solution:- Let $f(z) = \frac{1}{z(1-z^2)}$

Pole of f(z) are given by

$z(1 - z^2) = 0$

$z = 0, -1, 1$

Which are the simple pole.

(II). $f(z) = \frac{1}{1-e^z}$.

Solution:- Let $f(z) = \frac{1}{1-e^z}$

Pole of f(z) are given by

$1 - e^z = 0$

$e^z = 1 = e^{2n\pi i}$

$z = 2n\pi i$

which is the simple pole.

(III). $f(z) = \frac{1}{\sin z - \cos z}$.

Solution:- Let $f(z) = \frac{1}{\sin z - \cos z}$

pole of f(z) are given by,

$\sin z - \cos z = 0$

$\frac{\sin z}{\cos z} = \tan z = 1$

$z = n\pi + \frac{\pi}{4}$ where $n = 0, \pm 1, \pm 2.....$

clearly, $z = \frac{\pi}{4}$ is a simple pole.

(IV). $f(z) = \tan z$.

Solution:- Let $f(z) = \frac{1}{\sin z - \cos z}$

pole of the f(z) are given by

$\tan z = \frac{\sin z}{\cos z}$

$\cos z = 0$

$z = \frac{\pi}{2}$

clearly, $z = \frac{\pi}{2}$ is a simple pole.

(V). $f(z) = \frac{e^z}{z^2+4}$.

Solution:- Let $f(z) = \frac{e^z}{z^2+4}$

pole of f(z) are given by $z^2 + 4 = 0$

$z = \pm 2i$

which are the simple pole.

Question: 2) Identify the type of singularity for the following function.

(I). $f(z) = \sin\frac{1}{z}$.

Solution:- Let $f(z) = \sin\frac{1}{z}$

$$f(z) = \sin\frac{1}{z} = \frac{1}{z} - \frac{1}{3!\,z^3} + \frac{1}{5!z^5} - \frac{1}{7!z^7} + \ldots..$$

Here, there are no of singularity

$\sin\frac{1}{z}$ is not analytic at $z = 0$

Hence, $\sin\frac{1}{z}$ has singularity at $z = 0$.

(II). $f(z) = \frac{e^{\frac{1}{z}}}{z^2}$.

Solution:- Let $f(z) = \frac{e^{\frac{1}{z}}}{z^2}$

$$f(z) = \frac{e^{\frac{1}{z}}}{z^2} = \frac{1}{z^2}\left(1 + \frac{1}{z} + \frac{1}{2!\,z^2} + \frac{1}{3!z^3} \ldots\ldots + \frac{1}{n!\,z^n} + \ldots.\right)$$

$$= \frac{1}{z^2} + \frac{1}{z^3} + \frac{1}{2!\,z^4} + \frac{1}{3!z^6} \ldots\ldots + \frac{1}{n!\,z^n} + \ldots.)$$

Here f(z) contains infinite number of positive power of z.

Thus, f(z) has essential singularity at $z = 0$.

Question: 3) Find the pole of the following function.

(I). $f(z) = \frac{e^{z-a}}{(z-a)^2}$.

Solution:- Let $f(z) = \frac{e^{z-a}}{(z-a)^2}$

$$f(z) = \frac{e^{z-a}}{(z-a)^2} = \frac{1}{(z-a)^2}\left(1 + (z-a) + \frac{(z-a)^2}{2!} + \frac{(z-a)^3}{3!} + \ldots\ldots\right)$$

Here, given function has –ve power of z at (z-a).

Hence the given function has a pole at $z = a$ of order 2.

(II). $f(z) = \frac{\sin(z-a)}{(z-a)^4}$.

Solution:- Let $f(z) = \frac{\sin(z-a)}{(z-a)^4}$

$$f(z) = \frac{\sin(z-a)}{(z-a)^4} = \frac{1}{(z-a)^4}\left[(z-a) + \frac{(z-a)^3}{3!} + \frac{(z-a)^5}{5!} - \ldots..\right]$$

$$= \frac{1}{(z-a)^3}\left[1 + \frac{(z-a)^2}{3!} + \frac{(z-a)^4}{5!} - \ldots\ldots\right]$$

Thus, f(z) has 3 pole at z = a.

Question: 4) Identify the singularity of the given function.

f(z) = Sin($\frac{1}{z}$).

Solution:- Let f(z) = Sin($\frac{1}{z}$)

$$= \frac{1}{Z-a} - \frac{1}{3!(Z-a)^3} + \frac{1}{5!(Z-a)^5} - \ldots\ldots .$$

The given function f(z) has infinite number of negative power of (z - a).

Thus, f(z) has essential singularity at z = a .

Question: 5) Find the kind of singularity of the following function.

(I). f(z) = cos$\frac{1}{z}$ at z = 0 .

Solution:- f(z) = cos$\frac{1}{z}$

Pole of f(z) are given by

$\cos\frac{1}{z} = 0$

$\frac{1}{z} = \frac{\pi}{2} = 2n + \frac{\pi}{2}$ where, n = ±1, ±2 .....

$z = \frac{1}{2n + \frac{\pi}{2}}$

Clearly, z = 0 is the limit of these pole.

Thus z = 0 is non-isolated essential singularity.

(II). f(z) = sin($\frac{1}{1-z}$) .

Solution:- Let f(z) = sin($\frac{1}{1-z}$)

Pole of f(z) are given by

$\sin(\frac{1}{1-z}) = 0$

$(\frac{1}{1-z}) = n\pi$

$z = 1 - \frac{1}{n\pi}$ where, n = ±1, ±2 ....

Clearly, z = 1 is the limit of poles.

Hence z = 1 is isolated essential singularity.

(III). $f(z) = \operatorname{cosec}\frac{1}{z}$.

Solution:- Let $f(z) = \operatorname{cosec}\frac{1}{z}$

The pole of f(z) is given by,

$\operatorname{cosec}\frac{1}{z} = 0$

$\sin(\frac{1}{z}) = 0$

$(\frac{1}{z}) = n\pi$

$z = \frac{1}{n\pi}$ where, $n = \pm 1, \pm 2 \ldots.$

Hence z = 0 is the limit of these poles at z = 0.

f(z) shows non-isolated singularity.

Question: 6) Specify the nature of singularity at z = -2 of $f(z) = (z-3)(\sin(\frac{1}{z+2}))$.

Solution:- The given function is $f(z) = (z-3)(\sin(\frac{1}{z+2}))$.

i.e. $(z-3)(\sin(\frac{1}{z+2})) = 0$

$(z-3) = 0$ and $(\sin(\frac{1}{z+2})) = 0$

$z = 3$ and $\frac{1}{z+2} = n\pi$

$z = -2 + \frac{1}{n\pi}$ where, n= 1,2,3, …

Limit point of the pole is z = -2 .

Hence, f(z) shows isolated essential singularity of f(z) at z = -2.

EXERCISE:-

1. Find the kind of singularities for $f(z) = \frac{\cot \pi z}{(z-a)^2}$ at z = a and z = 0. Ans: Non essential singularity .
2. Find the pole of $(\frac{z+1}{z^2+1})^2$. Ans: $\pm$ i .
3. Discuss the singularities of $f(z) = z \csc z$ at $z = n\pi$ Ans: Non essential singularity .
4. Show that the function has $e^{\frac{-1}{z^2}}$ has no singularities.
5. Discuss the nature of singularity following functions.

   1. $\frac{\sin(z)}{(z-\pi)^2}$. 2. $\frac{z^8 + z^4 + 2}{(z-1)^3 + (3z+2)^2}$

BRANCH POINTS

The branch point of multiple valued functions are the singular points .

e.g. (1) f(z) = $(z-3)^{\frac{1}{2}}$ has the branch point z = 3 .

(2) f(z) = $\log(z^2+z-2)$ has the branch points where $z^2+z-2=0$, i.e, at z =1 and z = 2.

RESIDUE AT A POLE

Let f(z) be the angle valued function has a pole of order n at point z = z_0 and C_1 is the circle at z = z_0, which do not contain any other singularities except at z = z_0. Then f(z) be analytic within the circular annulus $R_1 < z - z_0 < R_2$ can be expanded within the annulus .(by fig(3)).

Then Laurent's series expansion is given by,

$$f(z) = \sum_{n=0}^{\infty} a_n(z-z_0)^n + \sum_{n=1}^{\infty} \frac{b_n}{(z-z_0)^n}$$

Where, $a_n = \frac{1}{2\pi i}\int_C \frac{f(z)dz}{(z-z_0)^{n+1}}$ and $b_n = \frac{1}{2\pi i}\int_C \frac{f(z)dz}{(z-z_0)^{-n+1}}$

$|z-z_0| = R_1$ being the circle C_1

Particularly , $b_1 = \frac{1}{2\pi i}\int_{C_1} f(z)dz$

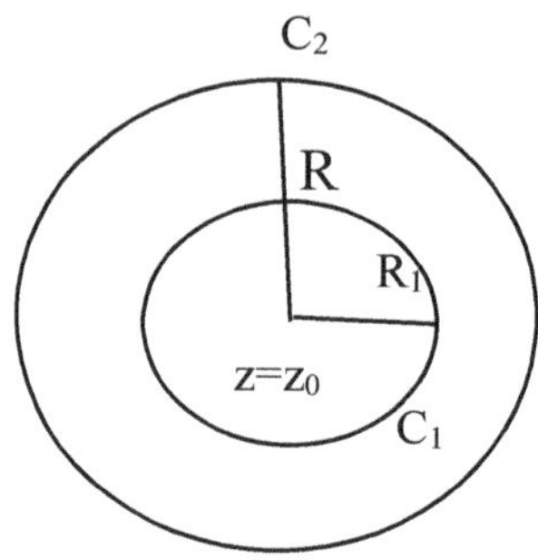

Fig (3)

The coefficient of b_1 is called the residue of f(z) of the point z= a. it is denoted by the symbol

Res(z = z_0) = b_1 .

Residue at a z = ∞:-

Let f(z) has an isolated singularity at z = 0, then the residue at z = ∞ is defined as $\frac{-1}{2\pi i}\int_{C_1} f(z)dz$, Where C is the closed countour taken in anticlockwise direction and it also contain an infinite singularities of f(z).

METHOD OF FINDING THE RESIDUE AT INFINTE POLE

1. **Residue at simple pole:-**

1. Let z = z_0 be a simple pole of f(z) then, Res(z = z_0) = $\lim_{z\to z_0}(z-z_0)$ f(z) .

Proof:- Let z = z_0 be a simple pole of f(z). then

$$f(z) = z_0 + a_1(z-z_0) + a_2(z-z_0)^2 + \ldots\ldots + \frac{b_1}{(z-z_0)}$$

$$(z-z_0)f(z) = z_0(z-z_0) + a_1(z-z_0)^2 + a_2(z-z_0)^3 + \ldots\ldots + b_1$$

$$b_1 = (z-z_0)f(z) - [z_0(z-z_0) + a_1(z-z_0)^2 + a_2(z-z_0)^3 + \ldots\ldots]$$

taking limit as $z \to z_0$ we have, $b_1 = \lim_{z\to z_0}(z-z_0)$ f(z)

Res(z = z_0) = $\lim_{z\to z_0}(z-z_0)$ f(z) .

2. Let $z = z_0$ be the simple pole of f(z) = $\frac{\varphi(z)}{\psi(z)}$. where, $\psi(z) = 0$ but $\varphi(z) \neq 0$ then

$$\text{Res}(z = z_0) = \frac{\varphi(z_0)}{\psi'(z_0)}.$$

Proof:- Let $z = z_0$ be the simple pole of f(z) $\frac{\varphi(z)}{\psi(z)}$.

$$\psi(z) = 0$$

then $\text{Res}(z = z_0) = \lim_{z \to z_0} (z - z_0)\, f(z) = \lim_{z \to z_0} (z - z_0) \frac{\varphi(z)}{\psi(z)}$ $\quad (\frac{0}{0}$ form)

By using Taylor's theorem,

$$= \lim_{z \to z_0} \frac{(z - z_0)\,[\,\varphi(z_0) + (z - z_0)\,\varphi'(z_0) + \frac{(z-z_0)^2}{2!}\varphi''(z_0) + \cdots\ldots\,]}{\psi(z_0) + (z - z_0)\,\psi'(z_0) + \frac{(z-z_0)^2}{2!}\psi''(z_0) + \cdots\ldots}$$

$$= \lim_{z \to z_0} \frac{\varphi(z_0) + (z - z_0)\,\varphi'(z_0) + \frac{(z-z_0)^2}{2!}\varphi''(z_0) + \cdots\ldots}{\psi'(z_0) + \frac{(z-z_0)}{2!}\psi''(z_0) + \cdots\ldots} \qquad [\because \psi(z_0) = 0\,]$$

$$\text{Res}(z = z_0) = \frac{\varphi(z_0)}{\psi'(z_0)}$$

3. Residue at a pole of order n:-

Let f(z) be the nth order pole at $z = z_0$. then $\text{Res}(z = z_0) = \frac{1}{(n-1)!}\{\frac{d^{n-1}}{dz^{n-1}}(z - z_0)^n f(z)\}_{z = z_0}$.

Proof :- Let f(z) be the nth order pole of function f(z) then by Laurent'z series expansion is given by

$$f(z) = \sum_{n=0}^{\infty} a_n (z - z_0)^n + \sum_{n=1}^{\infty} \frac{b_n}{(z-z_0)^n}$$

$$= a_0 + a_1(z - z_0) + a_2(z - z_0)^2 + \ldots\ldots + \frac{b_1}{(z-z_0)} + \frac{b_2}{(z-z_0)^2} + \ldots\ldots + \frac{b_n}{(z-z_0)^n}$$

Multiplying by $(z - z_0)^n$ we get,

$$(z - z_0)^n f(z) = a_0\,(z - z_0)^n + a_1(z - z_0)^{n+1} + a_2(z - z_0)^{n+2} + \ldots\ldots + b_1(z - z_0)^{n-1} + b_2(z - z_0)^{n-2} + \ldots\ldots + b_n$$

Differentiating above equation with respect to a_2, (n-1)! times and putting $z = z_0$, we get

$$\{\frac{d^{n-1}}{dz^{n-1}}(z - z_0)^n f(z)\}_{z = z_0} = (n-1)!\, b_1,$$

$$b_1 = \frac{1}{(n-1)!}\{\frac{d^{n-1}}{dz^{n-1}}(z - z_0)^n f(z)\}_{z = z_0}$$

$$\therefore \quad \text{Res}(z = z_0) = \frac{1}{(n-1)!}\{\frac{d^{n-1}}{dz^{n-1}}(z - z_0)^n f(z)\}_{z = z_0}.$$

4. Residue at $z = z_0$ for any order (n^{th} order or simple pole).

$\operatorname{Res}(z = z_0)$ = coefficient of $\frac{1}{t}$.

Let f(z) be a any order pole at $z = z_0$ then, $\operatorname{Res}(z = z_0)$ = coefficient of $(\frac{1}{t})$.

Proof:- If f(z) be a nth order pole at $z = z_0$. then Laurent'z series expansion is given by

$$f(z) = a_0 + a_1(z - z_0) + a_2(z - z_0)^2 + \ldots\ldots + \frac{b_1}{(z-z_0)} + \frac{b_2}{(z-z_0)^2} + \ldots\ldots + \frac{b_n}{(z-z_0)^n}$$

putting $z - z_0 = t \quad \Rightarrow z = z_0 + t$ then we get,

$$f(z_0 + t) = a_0 + a_1(t) + a_2(t)^2 + \ldots\ldots + \frac{b_1}{(t)} + \frac{b_1}{(t)^2} + \ldots\ldots + \frac{b_n}{(t)^n}$$

$\operatorname{Res}(z = z_0) = b_1$

$\operatorname{Res}(z = z_0)$ = coefficient of $(\frac{1}{t})$.

Question: 1) Find the residue at z = 0 at $z\cos\frac{1}{z}$.

Solution:- Let $f(z) = z\cos\frac{1}{z}$

$$= z\left[1 - + \frac{1}{2!\,z^2} + \frac{1}{4!z^4} \ldots\ldots\right] = z - \frac{1}{2z} + \frac{1}{4!z^3} + \ldots\ldots$$

This is the Laurent'z series Expansion about z = 0 .

Then, Res(z=0) = coefficient of $\frac{1}{z}$ in Laurent'z series Expansion = $-\frac{1}{2}$.

Question: 2) Find the residue of $f(z) = z^2 \sin h(\frac{1}{z})$.

Solution:- Given $f(z) = z^2 \sin h(\frac{1}{z}) = z^2 \left[\frac{1}{z} + \frac{1}{3!z^3} + \frac{1}{5!z^5} + \ldots\right]$

$$f(z) = z + \frac{1}{3!z} + \frac{1}{5!z^3} + \ldots\ldots$$

This is the Laurent'z series Expansion about z = 0 .

Then, Res(z = 0) = coefficient of $\frac{1}{z}$ in Laurent's series Expansion

Res(z=0) = $\frac{1}{3!} = \frac{1}{6}$.

Question: 3) Find the residue of f(z) = $\frac{z^3}{z^2-1}$ at z = ∞ .

Solution:- Given f(z) = $\frac{z^3}{z^2-1}$

$$= \frac{z^3}{z^2(1-\frac{1}{z^2})} = z\,(1-\frac{1}{z^2})^{-1} = z\,(\,1+\frac{1}{z^2}+\frac{1}{z^4}+\ldots.) = z+\frac{1}{z}+\frac{1}{z^3}+\ldots.$$

This is the Laurent′z series Expansion about z = ∞ .

Then, Res(z = ∞) = coefficient of $\frac{1}{z}$ in Laurent′z series Expansion = 1.

Question: 4) Determine the order of pole and values of residues of the function $\frac{z+3}{z^2-2z}$.

Solution:- Let f(z) = $\frac{z+3}{z^2-2z}$

The pole of the f(z) are given by

$z^2 - 2z = 0$

z = 0, 2

The given function f(z) has the pole at z = 0 and z = 2.

$$\therefore\ \text{Res}(z=0) = \lim_{z\to z_0}(z-0)\,f(z) = \lim_{z\to z_0}\frac{(z-0)(z+3)}{z\,(z-2)}$$

$$= \lim_{z\to z_0}\frac{(z+3)}{(z-2)} = \frac{-3}{2}$$

$$\text{Res}(z=2) = \lim_{z\to z_0}(z-2)\,f(z) = \lim_{z\to z_0}\frac{(z-2)(z+3)}{z\,(z-2)} = \lim_{z\to z_0}\frac{(z+3)}{z} = \frac{5}{2}.$$

Question: 5) Find the residues of $\frac{z^2}{(z-1)\,(z-2)\,(z-3)}$ at z = 1, 2, 3 and identify and prove that sum is zero.

Solution:- Let f(z) = $\frac{z^2}{(z-1)\,(z-2)\,(z-3)}$

The pole of the function f(z) is given by,

(z – 1) (z – 2) (z – 3) = 0

z = 1, 2, 3

$$\text{Res}(z=1) = \lim_{z\to 1}(z-1)\,f(z) = \lim_{z\to 1}\frac{z^2}{(z-2)\,(z-3)} = \frac{1}{2}.$$

$$\text{Res}(z=2) = \lim_{z\to 2}(z-2)\,f(z) = \lim_{z\to 2}\frac{z^2}{(z-1)\,(z-3)} = -4\,.$$

$$\text{Res}(z=3) = \lim_{z\to 3}(z-3)\,f(z) = \lim_{z\to 3}\frac{z^2}{(z-2)\,(z-1)} = \frac{9}{2}.$$

$$\text{Res}(z=\infty) = \lim_{z\to\infty}(-z)\,f(z) = \lim_{z\to\infty}\frac{-z\text{-}\,z^2}{(z-1)(z-2)\,(z-3)} = \lim_{z\to\infty}\frac{-1}{(1-\frac{1}{z})(1-\frac{1}{2})\,(1-\frac{1}{2})} = -1\,.$$

The sum of the residues is given by,

$$= \text{Res}(z = 1) + \text{Res}(z = 2) + \text{Res}(z = 3) + \text{Res}(z = \infty) = \frac{1}{2} - 4 + \frac{9}{2} - 1$$

$$= 0$$

∴ Hence residues are zero.

Question: 6) Determine the pole and residues at the pole of the function $f(z) = \frac{z}{(z-1)}$.

Solution:- Given, $f(z) = \frac{z}{(z-1)}$

The pole of f(z) given by

$$z - 1 = 0$$

$$z = 1$$

$$\text{Res}(z = 1) = \lim_{z \to 1}(z - 1)\, f(z) = \lim_{z \to 1}(z - 1)\frac{z}{(z-1)} = \lim_{z \to 1} z = 1$$

Hence f(z) has a simple pole at z = 1 and its residues at pole z = 1 is found to be 1.

Question: 7) Find the pole and residues at simple pole of the function $f(z) = \frac{z^2}{(z-1)^2(z+2)}$.

Solution:- Given, $f(z) = \frac{z^2}{(z-1)^2(z+2)}$

The pole of the function is given by,

$$(z - 1)^2(z + 2) = 0$$

$$z = 1, 1, -2$$

The function f(z) has a single pole at z = 2 and at z = 1 is 2nd order pole.

$$\text{Res}(z = -2) = \lim_{z \to -2}(z + 2)\, f(z) = \lim_{z \to -2}(z + 2)\frac{z^2}{(z-1)^2(z+2)}$$

$$= \lim_{z \to -2}\frac{z^2}{(z-1)^2} = \frac{4}{9}$$

Hence the residue at simple pole z = -2 is $\frac{4}{9}$.

Question: 8) Find the residue of $f(z) = \frac{z^3}{(z-1)^4(z-2)(z-3)}$ at its simple pole.

Solution:- Given, $f(z) = \frac{z^3}{(z-1)^4(z-2)(z-3)}$

The pole of f(z) are given by,

$$(z - 1)^4(z - 2)(z - 3) = 0$$

$$(z - 1)^4 = 0, \quad (z - 2) = 0, \quad (z - 3) = 0$$

z = 1, 1, 1, 1, 2, 3

The given function f(z) has the simple pole at z = 2 and z = 3.

$$\text{Res}(z=2) = \lim_{z\to 2}(z-2)\, f(z) = \lim_{z\to 2}(z-2)\frac{z^3}{(z-1)^4(z-2)(z-3)}$$

$$= \lim_{z\to 2}\frac{z^3}{(z-1)^4(z-3)} = -8$$

$$\text{Res}(z=3) = \lim_{z\to 3}(z-3)\, f(z) = \lim_{z\to 3}(z-3)\frac{z^3}{(z-1)^4(z-2)(z-3)}$$

$$= \lim_{z\to 3}\frac{z^3}{(z-1)^4(z-2)} = \frac{27}{16}$$

∴ Hence the residues at z = 2 and z = 3 are -8 and $\frac{27}{16}$ respectively .

Question: 9) Find the order of pole and values of residues of the function cosec z .

Solution:- Let $f(z) = \operatorname{cosec} z = \frac{1}{\sin z}$

The pole of the function is given by,

$\sin z = 0$

$z = n\pi$ where, $n = 0, \pm1, \pm2, \ldots..$

The function has simple pole at $z = n\pi = 0$ where $n = 0, \pm1, \pm2, \ldots..$

Write, $f(z) = \frac{\varphi(z)}{\psi(z)} = \frac{1}{\sin z}$

Then $\text{Res}(z=0) = \left[\frac{1}{\psi'(z)}\right]_{z=0} = \left[\frac{1}{\cos z}\right]_{z=0} = 1$.

Question: 10) Determine pole and residue at each pole of the function f(z) = cot z.

Solution:- Given, $f(z) = \cot z = \frac{\cos z}{\sin z} = \frac{\varphi(z)}{\psi(z)}$

The pole of the function f(z) is given by

$\sin z = 0$

$z = n\pi$ where, $n = 0, \pm1, \pm2, \ldots..$

The function has simple pole at $z = n\pi = 0$ where, $n = 0, \pm1, \pm2, \ldots..$

Write, $f(z) = \frac{\varphi(z)}{\psi(z)} = \frac{\cos z}{\sin z}$

Then, $\text{Res}(z=0) = \left[\frac{1}{\psi'(z)}\right]_{z=0} = \left[\frac{\cos z}{\cos z}\right]_{z=0} = 1$

Question: 11) Find the pole and residue of the function $\frac{z}{\sin z}$.

Solution:- Let f(z) = $\frac{z}{\sin z} = \frac{\varphi(z)}{\psi(z)}$

The pole of the function is given by,

$\sin z = 0$

z = nπ where, n = 0, ±1, ±2,.....

The function has simple pole at z = nπ = 0 where n = 0, ±1, ±2,.....

Then, $\text{Res}(z = n\pi) = [\frac{1}{\psi'(z)}]_{z=0} = [\frac{z}{\cos z}]_{z=0} = \frac{n\pi}{\cos n\pi} = \frac{n\pi}{(-1)^n}$

Hence the pole of f(z) is $n\pi$ and residue is $\frac{n\pi}{(-1)^n}$.

Question: 12) Find the residue of the function $\frac{z^3}{(z-1)^2\,(z+3)}$.

Solution:- Let f(z) = $\frac{z^3}{(z-1)^2\,(z+3)}$

The pole of f(z) is given by,

$(z-1)^2\,(z+3) = 0$

z = 1,1 and z = -3

$\text{Res}(z = -3) = \lim_{z\to -3}(z+3)\,f(z) = \lim_{z\to -3}(z+3)\frac{z^3}{(z-1)^2\,(z+3)} = \lim_{z\to -3}\frac{z^3}{(z-1)^2} = -\frac{27}{16}.$

$\text{Res}(z = 1) = \lim_{z\to 1}\frac{1}{(2-1)}\{\frac{d^{2-1}}{dz^{2-1}}(z-1)^2\frac{z^3}{(z-1)^2\,(z+3)}\} = \lim_{z\to 1}\frac{1}{1}\{\frac{d}{dz}\frac{z^3}{(z+3)}\}$

$= \lim_{z\to 1}\frac{1}{1}\{\frac{d}{dz}\frac{z^3}{(z+3)}\} = \lim_{z\to 1}\frac{1}{1}\{\frac{(z+3)\,3z^2-z^3}{(z+3)^2}\} = \frac{11}{16}.$

∴ Residue of f(z) has double pole is $\frac{11}{16}$ and simple pole is z = -3 is $-\frac{27}{16}$.

Question: 13) Determine the residue of the function f(z) = $\frac{z^2}{(z+1)^2\,(z-2)}$ at its double pole.

Solution:- Given, f(z) = $\frac{z^2}{(z+1)^2\,(z-2)}$

The pole of f(z) is given by

$(z+1)^2\,(z-2) = 0$

z = -1, -1, 2

$\text{Res}(z = -1) = \lim_{z\to -1}\frac{1}{(2-1)!}\{\frac{d}{dz}\frac{(z+1)^2\cdot z^2}{(z+1)^2\,(z-2)}\} = \lim_{z\to -1}\frac{1}{1}\{\frac{d}{dz}\frac{z^2}{(z-2)}\}$

$$= \lim_{z\to -1} \frac{1}{1} \{ \frac{(z-2)2z - z^2 \cdot 1}{(z-2)^2} \} = \frac{-3*(-2)-1}{9} = \frac{5}{9}.$$

Question: 14) Determine the residue of $\frac{1}{(z^2+1)^3}$ at z = I .

Solution:- Let $f(z) = \frac{1}{(z^2+1)^3}$

The pole of f(z) is given by,

$(z^2 + 1)^3 = 0$

$z^2 = -1$

$z = \pm I$

$$\text{Res}(z = i) = \lim_{z\to i} \frac{1}{(3-1)!} \{ \frac{d^2}{dz^2} \frac{(z-i)^3 \cdot 1}{(z^2+1)^3} \} = \lim_{z\to i} \frac{1}{2} \{ \frac{d^2}{dz^2} \frac{1}{(z+i)^3} \}$$

$$= \lim_{z\to i} \frac{1}{2} \{ \frac{3*4}{(z+i)^5} \} = \frac{1}{2} \{ \frac{12}{(z+i)^5} \} = \frac{3}{16i} = \frac{-3i}{16}$$

∴ Residue of f(z) at z = i is $\frac{-3i}{16}$.

Question: 15) Find the residue of $\frac{z+1}{z^2 (z-3)}$.

Solution:- Let $f(z) = \frac{z+1}{z^2 (z-3)}$

The pole of f(z) is given by,

$z^2 (z-3) = 0$

$z^2 = 0$ and $(z-3) = 0$

$z = 0$ and $z = 3$

$$\text{Res}(z = 3) = \lim_{z\to 3}(z-3) f(z) = \lim_{z\to 3}(z-3) \frac{z+1}{z^2 (z-3)} = \lim_{z\to 3} \frac{z+1}{z^2} = \frac{4}{9}.$$

$$\text{Res}(z = 0) = \lim_{z\to 0} \frac{1}{(2-1)!} \{ \frac{d}{dz} (z-0)^2 \frac{z+1}{z^2 (z-3)} \} = \lim_{z\to 0} \frac{1}{1} \{ \frac{d}{dz} \frac{z^2 (z+1)}{z^2 (z-3)} \}$$

$$= \lim_{z\to 0} [\frac{(z+3) \cdot 1 - (z+1) \cdot 1}{(z-3)^2} = \frac{-3-1}{9} = \frac{-4}{9}.$$

Question: 16) Find the residue of $f(z) = \frac{z e^z}{(z-a)^2}$ at its pole.

Solution:- Given, $f(z) = \frac{z e^z}{(z-a)^3}$

The pole of f(z) is given by,

$(z - a)^3 = 0$

z = a is a 3rd order pole.

Put z – a = t

Then, $f(z) = \frac{z e^z}{(z-a)^3} = \frac{(a+t)\, e^{a+t}}{t^3} = (\frac{a}{t^3} + \frac{1}{t^2})\, e^{a+t}$

$= e^a\, ((\frac{a}{t^3} + \frac{1}{t^2})\, e^t = e^a \left(\frac{a}{t^3} + \frac{1}{t^2}\right)[\,1 + \frac{t}{1!} + \frac{t^2}{2!} + \cdots]$

$= e^a\, [\left(\frac{a}{t^3} + \frac{a}{t^2} + \frac{a}{2t} + \frac{1}{t^2} + \frac{1}{t} + \frac{1}{2} + \cdots]\right) = e^a\, [\,\frac{1}{2} + (\frac{a}{2} + 1\,)\frac{1}{t} + (\,a + 1)\frac{1}{t^2} + a\frac{1}{t^3} + \ldots]$

∴ coefficient of $\frac{1}{t} = (\frac{a}{2} + 1\,)\, e^a$

Res(z = a) $= (\frac{a}{2} + 1\,)\, e^a$.

EXERCISE:-

1. Find the residue at $\frac{z^3}{(z-1)^4\,(z-2)\,(z-3)}$ at a pole of order 4. Ans: $\frac{101}{16}$

2.Find the order of each pole and residue of $\frac{1-2z}{z\,(z-1)(z-2)}$. Ans: Simple pole at z = 0, 1, 2 and Residue $\frac{1}{2}$, 1, $\frac{-3}{2}$ respectively.

3. Find the residue of $\frac{z^3}{(z-2)\,(z-3)}$. Ans: 27, -8

4. Find the residue of $\frac{1}{(z^2-a^2)^2}$ at z = ia. Ans: $\frac{-i}{4a^3}$

5. Find the residue of $\frac{1}{z\,(e^z-1)}$ at its poles. Ans: $\frac{-1}{2}$

6.Find the residue of $\frac{1}{z^2\,(z-i)}$ at z = I . Ans: -1

CAUCHY'S RESIDUE THEOREM

Theorem: If f(z) is analytic function within and on a closed contour, except at finite poles $z_1, z_2, z_3 \ldots\ldots z_n$ within C then $\int_C f(z)dz = 2\pi i \sum_{r=1}^{n} \text{Res}\,(z = z_0) = 2\pi i$ (sum of residues at the poles within C) .

Proof:- Consider $C_1, C_2, C_3 \ldots\ldots C_n$ be the non- intersecting circles with the center at $a_1, a_2, a_3 \ldots\ldots a_n$ respectively. The radii of circles are so small at they lie entirely within the closed curve C, as show in fig(4).

f(z) is analytic within the annulus bounded by these circles and the circle C.

Aptly Cauchy's theorem ,

$$\int_C f(z)dz = \int_{C_1} f(z)dz + \int_{C_2} f(z)dz + \int_{C_3} f(z)dz + \ldots\ldots + \int_{C_n} f(z)dz$$

$\{ \therefore$ we know that $\int_C f(z)dz = 2\pi i \,\text{Res}(z = z_0) \}$

$$\int_C f(z)dz = 2\pi i \,\text{Res}(z = z_1) + 2\pi i \,\text{Res}(z = z_2) + 2\pi i \,\text{Res}(z = z_n)$$

$$= 2\pi i \,[\,\text{Res}(z = z_1) + \text{Res}(z = z_2) + \text{Res}(z = z_n)\,]$$

$$\boldsymbol{\int_C f(z)dz = 2\pi i \sum_{r=1}^{n} \text{Res}\,(z = z_0)} .$$

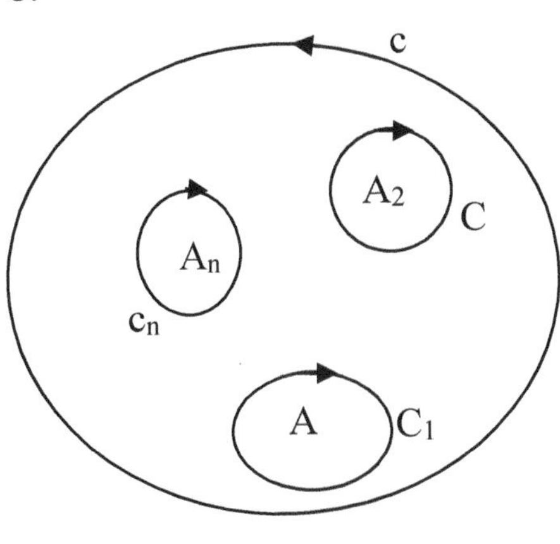

Fig(4)

Question: 1) Evaluate $\int_C \frac{1-2z\,dz}{z\,(z-1)(z-2)}$ where C is the circle $|z| = 1.5$.

Solution:- Let $I = \int_C \frac{1-2z\,dz}{z\,(z-1)(z-2)}$ and $f(z) = \frac{1-2z}{z\,(z-1)(z-2)}$

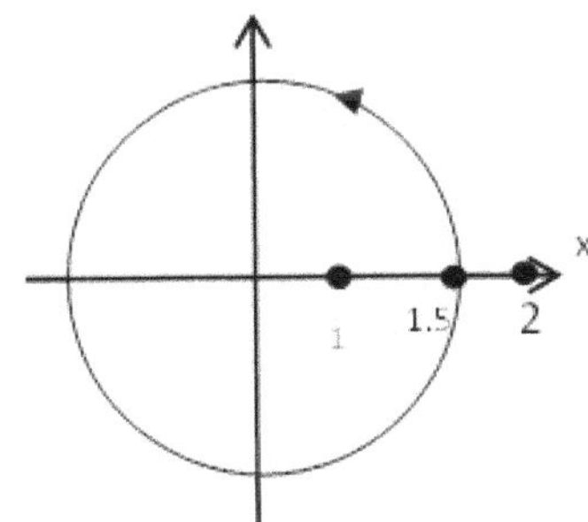

The pole of the integral is given by

$$z\,(z-1)(z-2) = 0$$

$$z = 0,\ 1,\ 2$$

Draw a circle $|z| = 1.5$ having centre (0, 0) & radius r = 1.5 .

The circle C is enclosed the poles at z = 0 and z = 1 and z = 2 is outside.

$$\text{Res}(z = 0) = \lim_{z\to 0}(z-0)\, f(z) = \lim_{z\to 0}(z-0)\,\frac{1-2z}{z\,(z-1)(z-2)}$$

$$= \frac{1}{-1*(-2)} = \frac{1}{2}$$

$$\text{Res}(z = 1) = \lim_{z\to 1}(z-1)\, f(z) = \lim_{z\to 1}(z-1)\,\frac{1-2z}{z\,(z-1)(z-2)} = \frac{1-2}{1*(1-2)} = 1$$

By Cauchy's Integral formula,

$$I = \int_C f(z)dz = 2\pi i\ [\,\text{Res}(z = 0) + \text{Res}(z = 1)\,]$$

$$= 2\pi i\,(\tfrac{1}{2} + 1) = \boldsymbol{3\pi i} .$$

Question: 2) Evaluate the following integral using residue theorem $\frac{4-3z}{z(z-1)(z-2)}$, where circle $|z| = \frac{3}{2}$.

Solution:- Let $I = \int_C \frac{4-3z\ dz}{z(z-1)(z-2)}$ and $f(z) = \frac{4-3z}{z(z-1)(z-2)}$

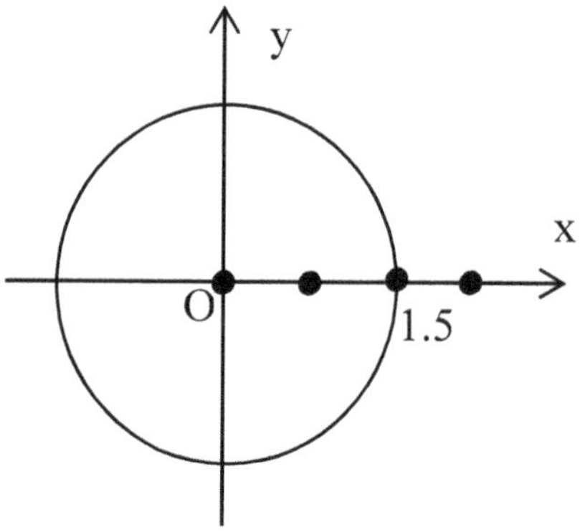

The pole of the function are given by,

$z(z-1)(z-2) = 0$

$z = 0, 1, 2$

Draw a circle $|z| = \frac{3}{2}$ having center (0, 0) and radius $r = \frac{3}{2}$.

The circle enclosed the poles at z = 0 and z = 1 and

the pole z = 2 lies outside.

$$\text{Res}(z=0) = \lim_{z\to 0}(z-0)\, f(z)$$

$$= \lim_{z\to 0}(z-0)\frac{4-3z}{z(z-1)(z-2)}$$

$$= \lim_{z\to 0}\left(\frac{4-3z}{(z-1)(z-2)}\right)$$

$$= \frac{4}{-1*(-2)} = \mathbf{2}$$

$$\text{Res}(z=1) = \lim_{z\to 1}(z-1)\, f(z) = \lim_{z\to 1}(z-1)\frac{4-3z}{z(z-1)(z-2)}$$

$$= \lim_{z\to 1}\left(\frac{4-3z}{z(z-2)}\right) = \frac{4-3}{1*(1-2)} = -1$$

By Cauchy's Integral formula ,

$$I = \int_C f(z)dz = 2\pi i\ [\text{Res}(z=0) + \text{Res}(z=1)]$$

$$= 2\pi i\,(2-1) = \mathbf{2\pi i}.$$

Question:3) Evaluate the following integral using residue theorem $\int_C \frac{1+z\ dz}{z(2-z)}$ where, C is the circle $|z| = 1$

Solution:- Let $I = \int_C \frac{4+z\ dz}{z(2-z)}$ and $f(z) = \frac{1+z}{z(2-z)}$

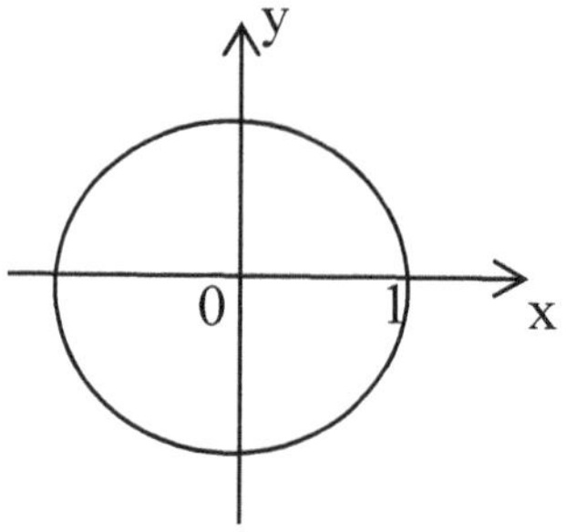

The pole of the f(z) are given by,

$z(2-z) = 0$

$z = 0, 2$

Draw a circle $|z| = 1$ having center (0, 0) and radius = 1.

The circle C enclosed the pole at z = 0 and pole z = 2 lies outside the circle.

By using Cauchy's Integral formula ,

$$I = \int_C f(z)dz = 2\pi i \ [\,Res(z = 0)\,]$$

$$= 2\pi i \lim_{z \to 0}(z - 0)\, f(z) \ = 2\pi i \lim_{z \to 0}(z - 0) \frac{1+z}{z\,(2-z)}$$

$$= 2\pi i \lim_{z \to 0} \frac{1+z}{(2-z)} = 2\pi i * \frac{1}{2} = \pi i \,.$$

Question: 4) Evaluate the following complex integration $\int_C \frac{z-1}{(z+1)^2\,(z-2)}$ dz.

where, C is the circle $|z - 1| = 2$.

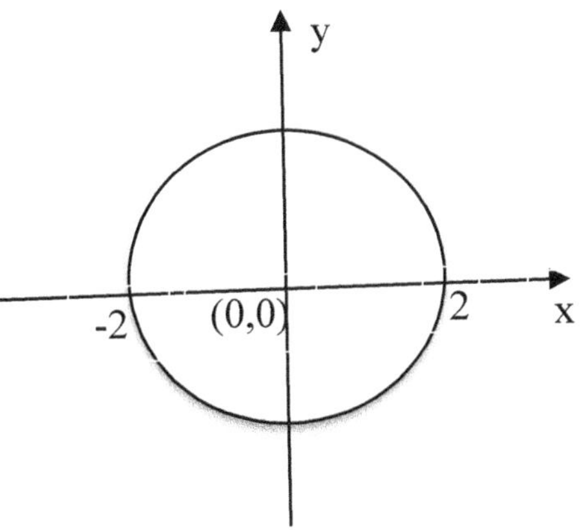

Solution:- Let $I = \int_C \frac{z-1}{(z+1)^2\,(z-2)}$ dz and $f(z) = \frac{z-1}{(z+1)^2\,(z-2)}$

The pole of the function are given by

$$(z + 1)^2 \ (z - 2) = 0$$

$$z = -1, -1, 2$$

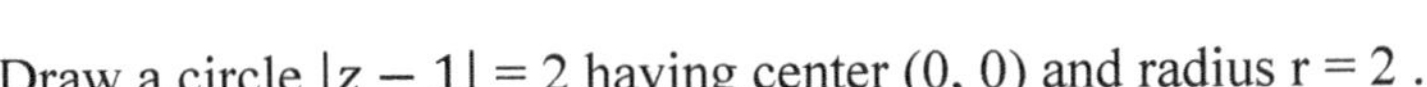
Draw a circle $|z - 1| = 2$ having center (0, 0) and radius r = 2 .

The circle enclosed the pole at z = -1 and the pole z = 2 lies outside the circle.

$$Res(z = -1) = \lim_{z \to -1} \frac{1}{(2-1)!} \{\frac{d}{dz}(z+1)^2 \frac{z-1}{(z+1)^2\,(z-2)}\}$$

$$= \lim_{z \to -1} \frac{d}{dz} \frac{z-1}{(z-2)} = \lim_{z \to -1} \frac{(z-2)\cdot 1 - (z-1)\cdot 1}{(z-2)^2}$$

$$= \frac{-3-(-2)}{9} = \frac{-1}{9}$$

By Cauchy's Integral formula

$$I = \int_C f(z)dz = 2\pi i \ [\,Res(z = -1)\,] = \frac{-2\pi i}{9} \,.$$

Question: 5) Evaluate the complex integral $\int_C \frac{\sin z}{z^6} dz$ where C is the circle $|z| = 2$.

Solution:- Let $I = \int_C \frac{\sin z}{z^6} dz$ and $f(z) = \frac{\sin z}{z^6}$

The pole of the f(z) is given by

$$z^6 = 0$$

$$z = 0$$

$$f(z) = \frac{\sin z}{z^6} = \frac{1}{z^6}[\,z - \frac{z^3}{3!} + \frac{z^5}{5!} - \frac{z^7}{7!} + \ldots\ldots] = \frac{1}{z^5} - \frac{1}{3!\,z^3} + \frac{1}{5!\,z} - \frac{z}{7!} + \ldots\ldots$$

Coefficient of $\frac{1}{z} = \frac{1}{5!}$

Res(z = 0) = Coefficient of $\frac{1}{z} = \frac{1}{5!}$

By Cauchy's Integral formula ,

$$I = \int_C f(z)dz = 2\pi i \; [\,Res(z = 0)\,] = \frac{2\pi i}{5!} = \frac{\pi i}{60}.$$

Question: 6) Determine the pole of the following function and residue at each pole

$f(z) = \frac{z^2}{(z-1)^2\,(z+2)}$ and hence evaluate $\int_C \frac{z^2}{(z-1)^2\,(z+2)}\,dz$ where C is $|z| = 3$.

Solution:- Let $I = \int_C \frac{z^2}{(z-1)^2\,(z+2)}\,dz$ and $f(z) = \frac{z^2}{(z-1)^2\,(z+2)}$

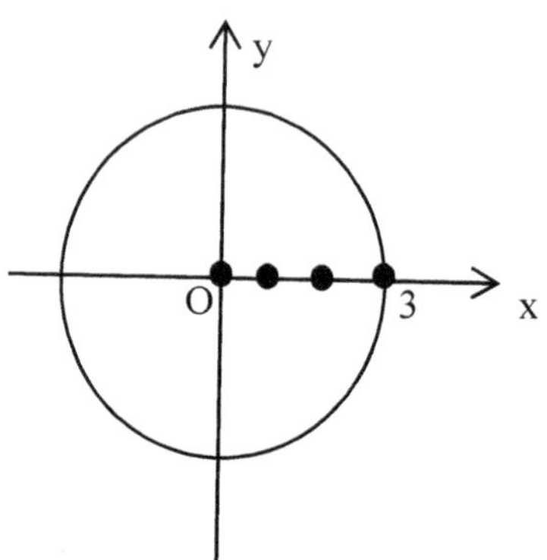

The pole of f(z) is given by

$$(z - 1)^2\,(z + 2) = 0$$

$$z = 1, 1, -2$$

Draw a circle $|z| = 3$ having center (0, 0) and radius r = 3 .

The circle is enclosed pole z = 1 and z = -2

$$Res(z = -2) = \lim_{z\to -2}(z + 2)\,f(z) = \lim_{z\to -2}(z + 2)\,\frac{z^2}{(z-1)^2\,(z+2)}$$

$$= \frac{(-2)^2}{(-2-1)^2} = \frac{4}{9}$$

$$Res(z = 1) = \lim_{z\to 1}\frac{1}{(2-1)!}\{\frac{d}{dz}(z - 1)\,f(z)$$

$$= \lim_{z\to 1}\frac{1}{1!}\{\frac{d}{dz}\frac{(z-1)^2 z^2}{(z-1)^2\,(z+2)}\}$$

$$= \lim_{z\to 1}\{\frac{d}{dz}\frac{z^2}{(z+2)}\}$$

$$= \lim_{z\to 1}\{\frac{(z+2)\,2z - z^2}{(z+2)^2}\}$$

$$= \frac{(3*2)-1}{9} = \frac{5}{9}$$

By Cauchy's Integral formula ,

$$I = \int_C f(z)dz = 2\pi i \; [\,Res(z = 1) + Res(z = -2)\,] = 2\pi i\,[\frac{5}{9} + \frac{4}{9}] = \mathbf{2\pi i}.$$

Question: **7)** Evaluate by the concept of complex residues $\int_C \frac{1}{(z-1)\,(z+1)}\,dz$

where C is a circle $|z| = 3$.

Solution:- Let $I = \int_C \frac{1}{(z-1)\,(z+1)}\,dz$ and $f(z) = \frac{1}{(z-1)\,(z+1)}$

The pole of the f(z) is given by,

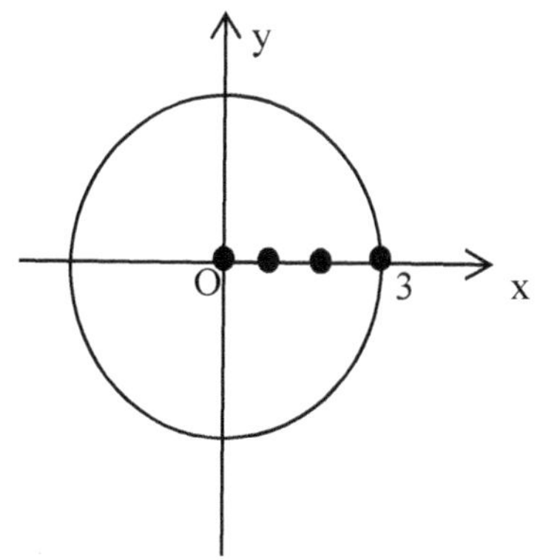

$$z\,(z-1)\,(z+1) = 0$$

$$z = 1, -1$$

Draw a circle $|z| = 3$ having center (0, 0) and radius r = 3.

The circle is enclosed pole z = 1 and z = -1

$$\text{Res}(z = 1) = \lim_{z\to 1}(z-1)\, f(z)$$

$$= \lim_{z\to 1}(z-1)\frac{1}{(z-1)\,(z+1)}$$

$$= \lim_{z\to 1}\frac{1}{(z+1)} = \frac{1}{2}$$

$$\text{Res}(z = -1) = \lim_{z\to -1}(z+1)\, f(z) = \lim_{z\to -1}(z+1)\frac{1}{(z-1)\,(z+1)}$$

$$= \lim_{z\to -1}\frac{1}{(z-1)} = -\frac{1}{2}$$

By Cauchy's Integral formula,

$$I = \int_C f(z)dz = 2\pi i\ [\text{Res}(z = 1) + \text{Res}(z = -1)]$$

$$= 2\pi i\left[\frac{1}{2} + \frac{-1}{2}\right] = \mathbf{0}.$$

Question: 8) Find the complex integration $\int_C \frac{1}{(z^2+1)\,(z-4)}\,dz$ where C is a circle $|z| = 3$.

Solution:- Let $I = \int_C \frac{1}{(z^2+1)\,(z-4)}\,dz$ and $f(z) = \frac{1}{(z^2+1)\,(z-4)}$

The pole of f(z) is given by,

$$(z^2+1)\,(z-4) = 0$$

$$z = \pm\, i, 4$$

Draw a circle $|z| = 3$ having center (0, 0) and radius r = 3.

The pole $z = \pm i$ lies inside the circle and z = 4 lies outside the circle.

$$\text{Res}(z = i) = \lim_{z\to i}(z-i)\, f(z) = \lim_{z\to 1}(z-i)\frac{1}{(z^2+1)\,(z-4)}$$

$$= \lim_{z\to i}\frac{1}{(z+i)\,(z-4)} = \frac{1}{2i\,(i-4)}$$

$$\text{Res}(z = -i) = \lim_{z\to -i}(z+i)\, f(z) = \lim_{z\to -i}(z+i)\frac{1}{(z-i)\,(z-4)}$$

$$= \lim_{z\to -i}\frac{1}{(z-i)\,(z-4)} = \frac{1}{2i\,(i+4)}$$

By Cauchy's Integral formula,

$$I = \int_C f(z)dz = 2\pi i \ [\,Res(z = i\,) + Res(z = -i)\,]$$

$$= 2\pi i \ [\frac{1}{2i\,(i-4)} + \frac{1}{2i\,(i+4)}] = \frac{-2\pi i}{17}.$$

Question: 9) Find the complex integration $\int_C \frac{e^z}{z\,(z-1)^2} dz$ where C is the circle $|z| = 2$.

Solution:- Let $I = \int_C \frac{e^z}{z\,(z-1)^2} dz$ and $f(z) = \frac{e^z}{z\,(z-1)^2}$

The pole of f(z) is given by,

$z\,(z-1)^2 = 0$

$z = 0, 1, 1$

Draw a circle $|z| = 2$ having center (0, 0) and radius r = 2 .

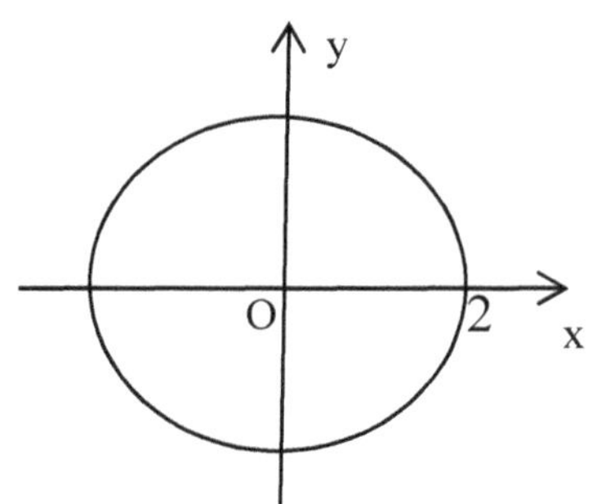

The circle is enclosed pole z = 0 and z = 1

$$Res(z = 0) = \lim_{z\to 0}(z - 0)\,f(z)$$

$$= \lim_{z\to 0}(z)\,\frac{e^z}{z\,(z-1)^2}$$

$$= \lim_{z\to 0}\frac{e^z}{(z-1)^2}$$

$$= \frac{e^0}{(0-1)^2} = -1$$

$$Res(z = 1) = \lim_{z\to 1}(z - 1)\,f(z) = \lim_{z\to 1}(z - 1)\,\frac{e^z}{z\,(z-1)^2}$$

$$= \lim_{z\to 1}(\frac{e^z}{z\,(z-1)}) = 0$$

By Cauchy's Integral formula,

$$I = \int_C f(z)dz = 2\pi i \ [\,Res(z = 0\,) + Res(z = 1)\,] = 2\pi i\,(\,1) = \mathbf{2\pi i}\,.$$

Question: 10) Evaluate $\int_C \frac{1}{\sin hz} dz$ where C is the circle $|z| = 2$.

Solution:- Let $I = \int_C \frac{1}{\sin hz} dz$ and $f(z) = \frac{1}{\sin hz}$

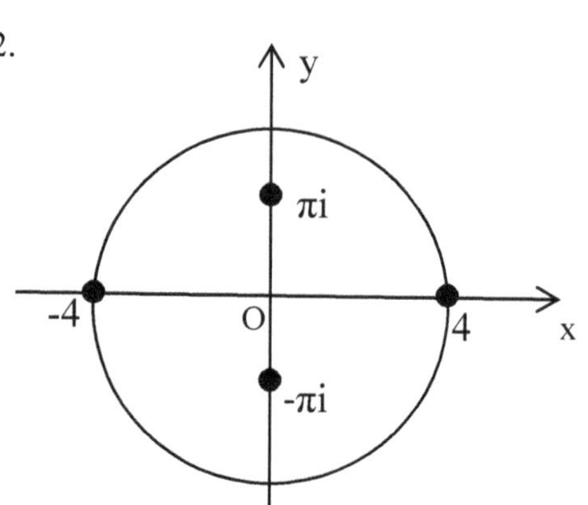

The pole of f(z) is given by,

$\sin hz = 0$

$\sin i\,z = 0$

$z = n\,\pi i$ Where, n = 0, ±1, ±2, …

Draw a circle $|z| = 4$ having center (0, 0) and radius r = 4.

The circle is enclosed pole z = 0 and z = ±πi lies inside the circle.

$$\text{Res}(z=0) = \frac{\varphi(z)}{\psi(z)} = \frac{\varphi(z=0)}{\psi'(z=0)} = \frac{1}{\cos hz} = \frac{1}{\cos h(0)} = 1$$

$$\text{Res}(z=\pi i) = \frac{1}{\cos h(\pi i)} = \frac{1}{\cos i(\pi i)} = \frac{1}{\cos(-\pi)} = -1$$

$$\text{Res}(z=-\pi i) = \frac{1}{\cos h(-\pi i)} = \frac{1}{\cos i(\pi i)} = \frac{1}{\cos(\pi)} = -1$$

By Cauchy's Integral formula,

$$I = \int_C f(z)dz = 2\pi i\ [\text{Res}(z=0) + \text{Res}(z=\pi i) + \text{Res}(z=-\pi i)]$$

$$= 2\pi i\ [1 - 1 - 1] = \mathbf{-2\pi i}.$$

Question: 11) Evaluate the complex integral $\int_C \frac{1}{\cos hz} dz$ where C is the $|z| = 2$.

Solution:- Let $I = \int_C \frac{1}{\cos hz} dz$ and $f(z) = \frac{1}{\cos hz} = \frac{1}{\frac{e^z + e^{-z}}{2}} = \frac{2e^z}{e^{2z}+1}$

The pole of f(z) is given by

$$e^{2z} + 1 = 0$$

$$(e^z + i)(e^z - i) = 0$$

$$e^z = \pm i$$

$$e^z = e^{\pm\frac{\pi i}{2}}$$

$$z = \pm\frac{\pi i}{2}$$

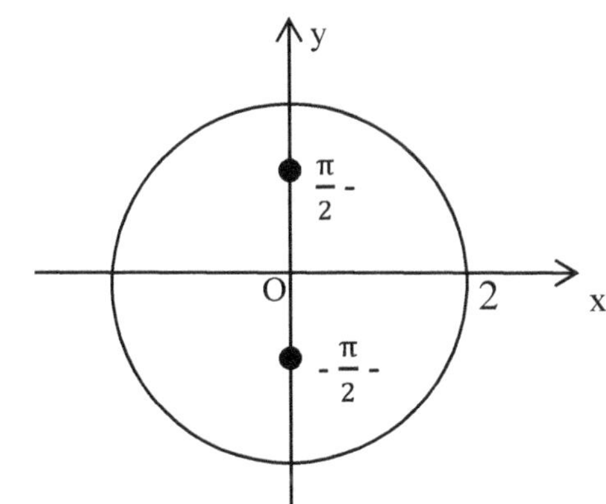

Draw a circle $|z| = 2$ having center (0, 0) and radius r = 2 .

The circle is enclosed pole $z = \pm\frac{\pi i}{2}$ lies inside the circle.

$$\therefore\ \text{Res}\left(z=\frac{\pi i}{2}\right) = \frac{\varphi(z)}{\psi(z)} = \frac{\varphi(z=\frac{\pi i}{2})}{\psi'\left(z=\frac{\pi i}{2}\right)} = \frac{2e^z}{2e^{2z}} = -i$$

$$\text{Res}\left(z=-\frac{\pi i}{2}\right) = \frac{\varphi(z)}{\psi(z)} = \frac{\varphi(z=-\frac{\pi i}{2})}{\psi'\left(z=-\frac{\pi i}{2}\right)} = \frac{2e^z}{2e^{2z}} = \frac{1}{e^z} = i$$

By Cauchy's Integral formula,

$$I = \int_C f(z)dz = 2\pi i\ [\text{Res}(z=\tfrac{\pi i}{2}) + \text{Res}(z=-\tfrac{\pi i}{2})] = 2\pi i\ [-i + i] = \mathbf{0}$$

EXERCISE:-

1. Evaluate the complex integral $\int_C \frac{\cot hz}{z-i} dz$ where C is the circle $|z| = 2$. Ans: $2\Pi i\,(i + \cot hi)$

2. Evaluate $\int_C \frac{1}{z \sin z} dz$ where C is a circle about at origin. Ans: 0

3. Find $\int_C \frac{1}{z^2 \sin hz} dz$ where C is the circle $|z - 1| = 2$. Ans: $\frac{\pi i}{3}$

4. Evaluate $\int_C z\, e^{\frac{1}{z}} dz$ around a unit circle . Ans: Πi

5. Find the Values of $\int_C z^4\, e^{\frac{1}{z}} dz$ where C is a circle $|z| = 1$. Ans: $\frac{\pi i}{60}$

6. Using residual theorem find $\int_C \frac{e^{zt}}{z^2 (z^2 + 2z + 2)} dz$ where C is a circle $|z| = 3$. Ans: $\frac{t-1}{2} + \frac{e^{-t}}{2} \cos t$

7. Determine the pole of the function and residue at each pole $f(z) = \int_C \frac{z^2}{(z-1)^2 (z+2)} dz$ and hence evaluate $\int_C \frac{z^2}{(z-1)^2 (z+2)} dz$ where C, $|z| = 3$. Ans: $2\Pi i$

1). EVALUATION OF INTEGRAL $\int_0^{2\pi} (\cos\theta + \sin\theta)\, d\theta$

$\Rightarrow$ Where, f(cos θ, sin θ) is a rotational function of cos θ and sin θ .

Consider unit circle $|z| = 1$

$$z = e^{i\theta}$$

$$dz = i\, e^{i\theta}\, d\theta$$

$$\Rightarrow \quad d\theta = \frac{dz}{i\, e^{i\theta}}$$

$$\sin\theta = \frac{e^{i\theta} - e^{-i\theta}}{2i} = \frac{1}{2i}\left[z - \frac{1}{z} \right]$$

$$\cos\theta = \frac{e^{i\theta} + e^{-i\theta}}{2} = \frac{1}{2}\left[z + \frac{1}{z} \right]$$

Convert the given integrand into a function of z.

Apply Cauchy's residue theorem to evaluate the integral.

2). EVALUATION OF IMPROPER DEFINITE INTEGRAL $\int_{-\infty}^{\infty} \frac{f_1(x)}{f_2(x)}\, dx$.

$\Rightarrow$Where, $f_1(x)$ and $f_2(x)$ are polynomial in x.

Such a integral can be reduced to contour integral if , i) $f_2(x)$ has no real roots. ii) the degree of $f_2(x)$ is greater than that of $f_1(x)$ by at least two.

Procedure:- Let $f(x) = \frac{f_1(x)}{f_2(x)}$

Consider $\int_C f(z)\, dz$

Where, C is a curve, consisting of upper half C_R of the circle $|z| = R$ and part of the real axis from –R to +R.

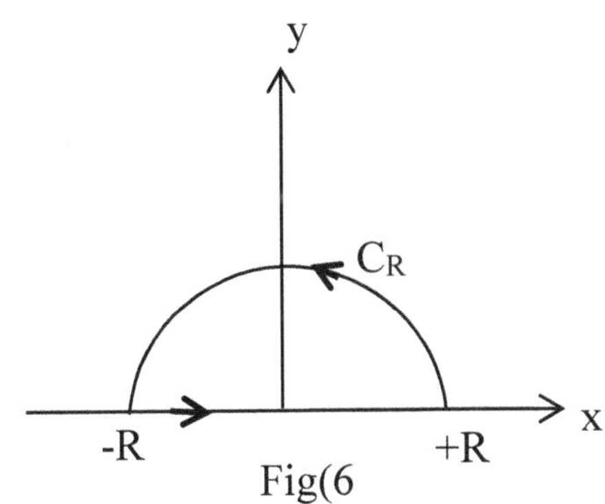

Fig(6

If there is no pole of real axis, the circle $|z| = R$, which is arbitrary can be taken such that there is no singularity on its circumference C_R in the upper half of the plane but possibly same pole indicate contour C specified above.

Using Cauchy's residue theorem, we have

$\int_C f(z)\, dz = 2\pi i$ [sum of the residues of f(z) at the poles within C]

i.e. $\int_{-R}^{R} f(x)\, dx + \int_{-C_R} f(z)\, dz = 2\pi i$ [sum of the residues within C]

$$\int_{-R}^{R} f(x)\, dx = -\int_{C_R} f(z)\, dz + 2\pi i \text{ [sum of the residues within C]}$$

$$\lim_{R\to\infty}\int_{-R}^{R} f(x)\, dx = \lim_{R\to\infty}\int_{C_R} f(z)\, dz + 2\pi i \text{ [sum of the residues within C]}$$

Now, $\lim_{R\to\infty}\int_{C_R} f(z)\, dz = \int_0^{\pi} f(R\cdot e^{i\theta})\, Ri\, e^{i\theta}\, d\theta$

Thus above equation reduces to

$$\int_{-\infty}^{\infty} f(x)\, dx = 2\pi i \text{ [sum of the residues within C].}$$

Question: 1) Find the integral $\int_0^{2\pi} \frac{1}{5-3\cos\theta}\, d\theta$.

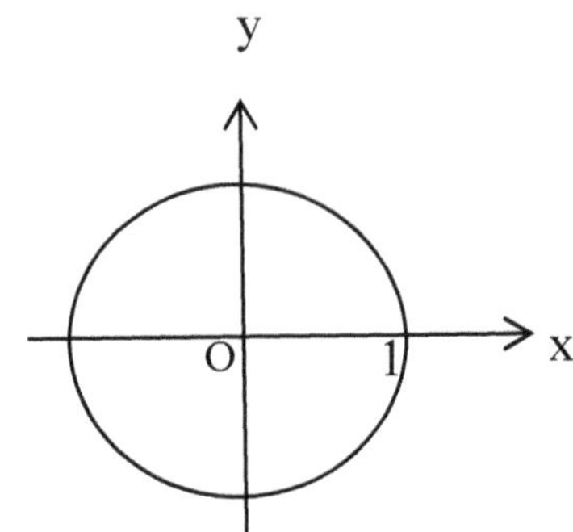

Solution:- Given, $I = \int_0^{2\pi} \frac{1}{5-3\cos\theta}\, d\theta$

$z = e^{i\theta}$

$dz = i\, e^{i\theta}\, d\theta$

$\Rightarrow d\theta = \frac{dz}{i\, e^{i\theta}}$

$\cos\theta = \frac{e^{i\theta}+e^{-i\theta}}{2}$

$$\int_0^{2\pi} \frac{1}{5-3\cos\theta}\, d\theta = \int_0^{2\pi} \frac{1}{5-3\left(\frac{e^{i\theta}+e^{-i\theta}}{2}\right)}\, d\theta = \int_0^{2\pi} \frac{2}{10-3\left(e^{i\theta}+e^{-i\theta}\right)}\, d\theta$$

$$\int_C \frac{2}{10-3z-\frac{3}{z})}\, \frac{dz}{iz} = \frac{1}{i}\int_C \frac{2\, dz}{10z-3z^2-3}$$ where, C is the unit circle.

$$= -\frac{2}{i}\int_C \frac{dz}{3z^2-10z+3} = 2i\int_C \frac{dz}{(3z-1)(z-3)}$$

The pole of integrand is given by,

$(3z-1)(z-3) = 0$

$z = 3, \frac{1}{3}$.

The pole at $z = \frac{1}{3}$ lies inside the circle and $z = 3$ lies outside the circle.

$$\therefore \text{Residue } (z = \tfrac{1}{3}) = \lim_{z\to\frac{1}{3}} (z-\tfrac{1}{3})\, f(z) = \lim_{z\to\frac{1}{3}} (z-\tfrac{1}{3})\, \frac{2i}{(3z-1)(z-3)} = \lim_{z\to\frac{1}{3}} \frac{2i}{3(z-3)}$$

$$= \lim_{z\to\frac{1}{3}} \frac{2i}{3\left(\frac{1}{3}-3\right)} = \frac{-i}{4}$$

Hence by Cauchy's residue theorem,

$$I = 2\pi i\ [\operatorname{Res}(z = \tfrac{1}{3})] = 2\pi i\, (\tfrac{-i}{4}) = \frac{\pi}{2}$$

$$\therefore 2i\int_C \frac{dz}{(3z-1)(z-3)} = \frac{\pi}{2}.$$

Question:2) Use residue calculus to evaluate $\int_0^{2\pi} \frac{1}{5-4\sin\theta} d\theta$.

Solution:- Let I = $\int_0^{2\pi} \frac{1}{5-4\sin\theta} d\theta$

$z = e^{i\theta}$

$dz = i e^{i\theta} d\theta$

$\Rightarrow d\theta = \frac{dz}{i e^{i\theta}}$

$\sin\theta = \frac{e^{i\theta} - e^{-i\theta}}{2i}$

$$\int_0^{2\pi} \frac{1}{5-4\sin\theta} d\theta = \int_0^{2\pi} \frac{1}{5-4\left(\frac{e^{i\theta}-e^{-i\theta}}{2i}\right)} d\theta = \int_0^{2\pi} \frac{1}{5+2i\,(e^{i\theta}+e^{-i\theta})} d\theta$$

$$= \int_C \frac{1}{5+2iz-\frac{2i}{z})} \frac{dz}{iz} = \int_C \frac{dz}{5iz-2z^2+2}$$ where, C is the unit circle.

The pole of integrand is given by,

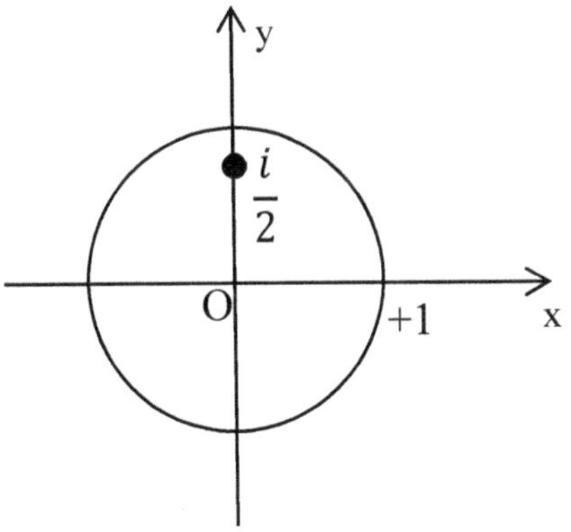

$5iz - 2z^2 + 2 = 0$

$z = \frac{-5i \pm \sqrt{-25+16}}{-4}$

$z = \frac{-5i+3i}{-4}$

$z = 2i, \frac{i}{2}$

The pole at $z = \frac{i}{2}$ lies inside the circle.

$\therefore$ Residue $(z = \frac{i}{2}) = \lim_{z\to\frac{i}{2}} (z - \frac{i}{2})\, f(z) = \lim_{z\to\frac{i}{2}} (z - \frac{i}{2}) \frac{1}{(2z-i)(-z+2i)}$

$= \lim_{z\to\frac{i}{2}} (z - \frac{i}{2}) \frac{1}{2(-z+2i)} = \frac{1}{3i}$

Hence by Cauchy's residue theorem,

$I = 2\pi i\ [\text{Res}(z = \frac{i}{2})] = 2\pi i\, (\frac{1}{3i}) = \frac{2\pi}{3}$

$\therefore \int_0^{2\pi} \frac{1}{5-3\cos\theta} d\theta = \frac{2\pi}{3}$.

Question: 3) Evaluate $\int_0^{\pi} \frac{1}{3+2\cos\theta} d\theta$.

Solution:- Let I = $\int_0^{\pi} \frac{1}{3+2\cos\theta} = \frac{1}{2}\int_0^{2\pi} \frac{1}{3+2\cos\theta}$

Since $e^{i\theta} = z$

$dz = ie^{i\theta} d\theta \quad \Rightarrow d\theta = \frac{dz}{iz}$

$\cos\theta = \frac{e^{i\theta}+e^{-i\theta}}{2} = \frac{1}{2}\left[z+\frac{1}{z}\right]$

$I = \frac{1}{2}\int_C \frac{1}{3+2\frac{1}{2}\left[z+\frac{1}{z}\right]}\frac{dz}{iz} = \frac{1}{2}\int_C \frac{dz}{iz\left[3+z+\frac{1}{z}\right]} = \frac{1}{2i}\int_C \frac{dz}{z^2+3z+1}$

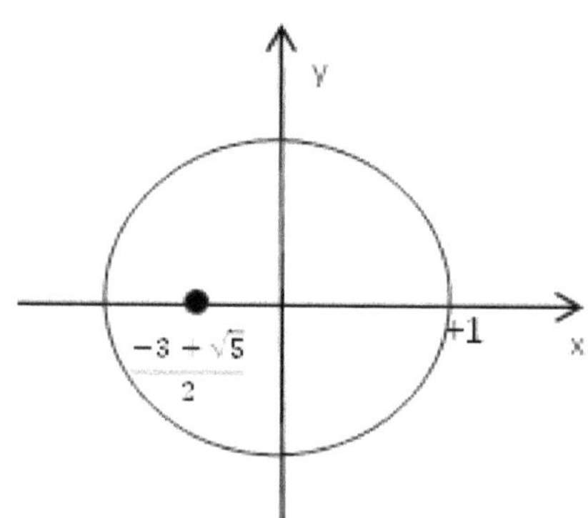

Pole of the integral is given by

$z^2+3z+1=0$

$z = \frac{-3z\pm\sqrt{9-4}}{2} = \frac{-3\pm\sqrt{5}}{2}.$

The pole at $z = \frac{-3+\sqrt{5}}{2}$ lies inside the circle

$\text{Res}\left(z = \frac{-3+\sqrt{5}}{2}\right) = \lim_{z\to\frac{-3+\sqrt{5}}{2}}\left[z-\frac{-3+\sqrt{5}}{2}\right]\times f(z) = \lim_{z\to\frac{-3+\sqrt{5}}{2}} \frac{\left[z-\frac{-3+\sqrt{5}}{2}\right]\times 1}{\left[z-\frac{-3+\sqrt{5}}{2}\right]\left[z-\frac{-3-\sqrt{5}}{2}\right]} = \frac{1}{\sqrt{5}}$

Hence by Cauchy integral form

$I = 2\pi i Res\left(z = \frac{-3+}{2}\ \frac{-3\pm\sqrt{5}}{2}\frac{=}{5}\times\frac{2\pi i}{2i} = \frac{\pi}{\sqrt{5}}.\right.$

Question: 4) Use the complex variable technique to find the value of integral $\int_0^{2\pi}\frac{d\theta}{2+\cos\theta}$.

Solution:- Let $I = \int_0^{2\pi}\frac{d\theta}{2+\cos\theta}$

Since $z = e^{i\theta}$

$dz = ie^{i\theta}d\theta \Rightarrow d\theta = \frac{dz}{iz}$

$\cos\theta = \frac{e^{i\theta}+e^{-i\theta}}{2} = \frac{1}{2}\left[z+\frac{1}{z}\right]$

$I = \int_C \frac{1}{2+\frac{1}{2}\left[z+\frac{1}{z}\right]}\frac{dz}{iz} = \int_C \frac{2dz}{iz\left[4+z+\frac{1}{z}\right]} = \frac{2}{i}\int\frac{dz}{z^2+4z+1}$

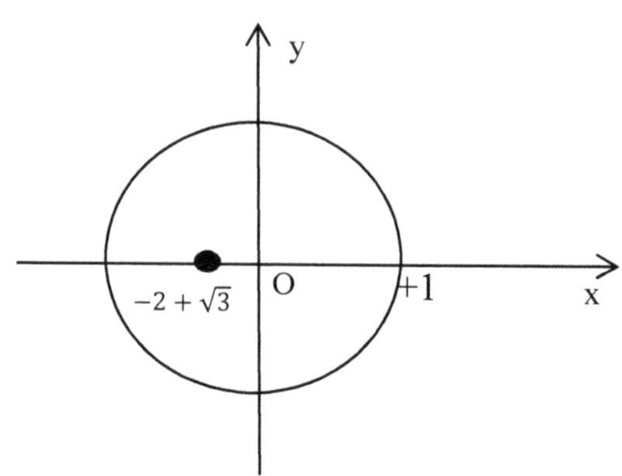

The pole of the integral are given by

$z^2+4z+1=0$

$z = \frac{-4\pm\sqrt{16-4}}{2} = -2\pm\sqrt{3}$

The pole at $z = -2\pm\sqrt{3}$ lies inside the circle

$\text{Res}(z=-2+\sqrt{3}) = \lim_{z\to-2+\sqrt{3}}(z+2-\sqrt{3})\,f(z) = \lim_{z\to-2+\sqrt{3}}\frac{(z+2-\sqrt{3})}{(z+2-\sqrt{3})(z+2+\sqrt{3})}\cdot\frac{2}{i} = \frac{1}{\sqrt{3}i}$

By Cauchy's integral form

$I = 2\pi i Res(z = -2+\sqrt{3}) = 2\pi i\times\frac{1}{\sqrt{3}i} = \frac{2\pi}{\sqrt{3}}.$

Question: 5) Evaluate $\int_0^{2\pi} \frac{\cos 2\theta}{5+4\cos\theta} d\theta$ by using contour integration .

Let , $I = \int_0^{2\pi} \frac{\cos 2\theta}{5+4\cos\theta} d\theta$

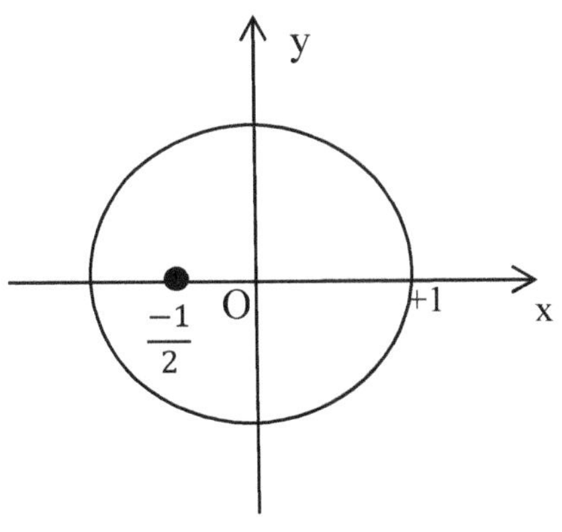

$z = e^{i\theta}$

$dz = ie^{i\theta} d\theta \Rightarrow d\theta = \frac{dz}{iz}$

$\cos 2\theta = \frac{e^{2i\theta}+e^{-2\theta}}{2} = \frac{1}{2}\left[z^2 + \frac{1}{z^2}\right]$

$I =$ real part of $\int_0^{2\pi} \frac{\cos 2\theta + i\sin 2\theta}{5+4\cos\theta} d\theta$

$=$ real part of $\int_c \frac{z^2}{5+4.\frac{1}{2}\left[z+\frac{1}{z}\right]} . \frac{dz}{iz}$

$=$ real part of $\int_c \frac{z^2 dz}{(2z^2+5z+2)i}$

$=$ real part of $\int_c \frac{-iz^2 dz}{2z^2+5z+2}$ $=$ real part of $\int_c \frac{-iz^2 dz}{(2z+1)(z+2)}$

The poles of given integral are given by

$(2z+1)(z+2) = 0$

$\Rightarrow z = -2, \frac{-1}{2}$

The pole at $z = -\frac{1}{2}$ lies inside the circle

$\text{Res}\left(z = -\frac{1}{2}\right) = \lim_{z\to -\frac{1}{2}} \left(z+\frac{1}{2}\right) f(z) = \lim_{z\to -\frac{1}{2}} \left(z+\frac{1}{2}\right) . \frac{-iz^2}{(2z+1)(z+2)} = \frac{-i}{12}$

By Cauchy's integral theorem

$I = 2\pi i Res\left(z = -\frac{1}{2}\right) = 2\pi i . \left(\frac{-i}{12}\right) = \frac{\pi}{6}$.

Question: 6) Evaluate $\int_0^{\theta} \frac{\cos mx}{(x^2+1)}$ dx .

Solution:- Let , $I = \int_0^{\theta} \frac{\cos mx}{(x^2+1)}$ dx

Where, $f(z) = \frac{\cos mx}{(x^2+1)} = \frac{e^{imz}}{z^2+1}$ taken around the closed countor C consisting of the upper half of a large circle $|z| = R$ and the real axis from –R to +R.

The pole of f(z) are given by

$z^2 + 1 = 0$

$z^2 = -1$

$z = \pm i$

The pole z= i lies inside the circle

$$\text{Res}(z = i) = \lim_{z\to i}(z - i)f(z) = \lim_{z\to i}\frac{(z-i)e^{imz}}{(z^2+1)} = \lim_{z\to i}\frac{e^{imz}}{z+i} = \frac{e^{-m}}{2i}$$

Hence by Cauchy's residue theorem,

$$I == 2\pi i Res(z = i) = 2\pi i.\frac{e^{-m}}{2i} = \pi e^{-m}.$$

Question: 7) Use contour integration to evaluate the real integral $\int_0^{\infty}\frac{1}{(1+z^2)^3}$ dx .

Solution:- Let $I = \int_0^{\infty}\frac{1}{(1+z^2)^3}$ dx and $f(z) = \frac{1}{(1+z^2)^3}$

Taken around closed contour consisting of real and upper half C_R of a large semi-circle $|z| = R$

The pole of f(z) are given by,

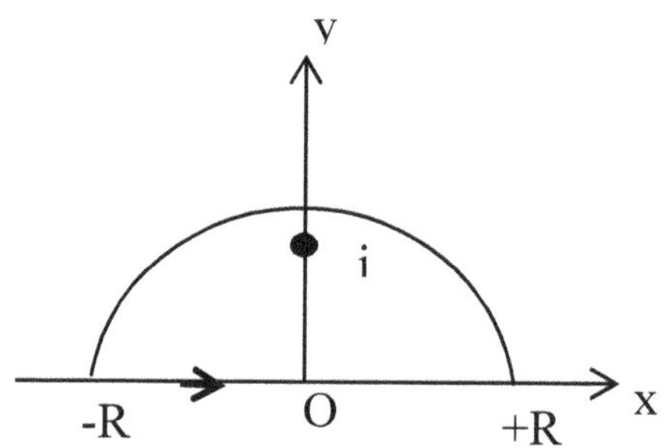

$$(1+ z^2)^3 = 0$$

$$(z^2 - i^2)^3 = 0$$

$$(z+i)^3 (z-i)^3 = 0$$

$z = \pm i$ pole of order 3

The pole at z = i lies inside the circle.

$$\text{Res}(z = i) = \lim_{z\to i}\frac{1}{(3-1)!}\{\frac{d^2}{dz^2}(z-i)^2\frac{1}{(1+z^2)^3}\}$$

$$= \lim_{z\to i}\frac{1}{2!}\{\frac{d^2}{dz^2}\frac{1}{(z+1)^3}\} = \frac{3}{16i}$$

Hence by Cauchy's Integral theorem

$$\mathbf{I = 2\pi i Res(z = i) = 2\pi i.\left(\frac{3}{16i}\right) = \frac{3\pi}{8}}$$

Question: 8) Using complex variable technique evaluate the integral $\int_{-\infty}^{+\infty}\frac{1}{(x^4+1)}$dx.

Solution:- Let $I = \int_{-\infty}^{+\infty}\frac{1}{(x^4+1)}$dx and $f(z) = \frac{1}{(z^4+1)}$

Taken around the closed contour consisting of real axis and upper half C_R of a large semi-circle $|z| = R$.

The pole of f(z) is given by,

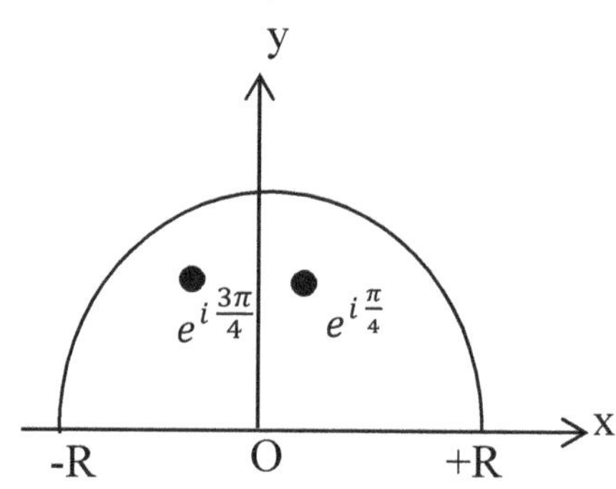

$$(z^4 + 1) = 0$$

$$z^4 = -1 = \cos\pi + i\sin\pi$$

$$= \cos(2n+1)\pi + i\sin(2n+1)\pi$$

$z = \cos(2n+1)\frac{\pi}{4} + i\sin(2n+1)\frac{\pi}{4}$

If $n = 0$, $\quad z = \cos\frac{\pi}{4} + i\sin\frac{\pi}{4} = e^{i\frac{\pi}{4}}$

If $n = 1$, $\quad z = \cos\frac{3\pi}{4} + i\sin\frac{3\pi}{4} = e^{i\frac{3\pi}{4}}$

If $n = 2$, $\quad z = \cos\frac{5\pi}{4} + i\sin\frac{5\pi}{4} = e^{i\frac{5\pi}{4}}$

If $n = 3$, $\quad z = \cos\frac{7\pi}{4} + i\sin\frac{7\pi}{4} = e^{i\frac{7\pi}{4}}$

The pole $z = e^{i\frac{\pi}{4}}$ and $z = e^{i\frac{3\pi}{4}}$ lies inside the circle.

$$\text{Res}(z = e^{i\frac{\pi}{4}}) = \frac{\varphi(z)}{\psi(z)} = \frac{\varphi(z=e^{i\frac{\pi}{4}})}{\psi'\left(z=e^{i\frac{\pi}{4}}\right)} = \frac{1}{4z^3} = \frac{1}{4e^{i\frac{3\pi}{4}}}$$

$$= \frac{e^{-i\frac{3\pi}{4}}}{4} = \frac{1}{4}[\ \cos\frac{3\pi}{4} + i\sin\frac{3\pi}{4}\ ] = \frac{1}{4}[-\frac{1}{\sqrt{2}} - \frac{i}{\sqrt{2}}]$$

$$\text{Res}(z = e^{i\frac{3\pi}{4}}) = \frac{\varphi(z)}{\psi(z)} = \frac{\varphi(z=e^{i\frac{3\pi}{4}})}{\psi'\left(z=e^{i\frac{3\pi}{4}}\right)} = \frac{1}{4z^3} = \frac{1}{4e^{i\frac{9\pi}{4}}} = \frac{e^{-i\frac{9\pi}{4}}}{4}$$

$$= \frac{1}{4}[\ \cos\frac{9\pi}{4} + i\sin\frac{9\pi}{4}\ ] = \frac{1}{4}[\frac{1}{\sqrt{2}} - \frac{i}{\sqrt{2}}]$$

Hence by Cauchy's Integral theorem

$$I = 2\pi i[\ \text{Res}\left(z = e^{i\frac{\pi}{4}}\right) + \text{Res}\left(z = e^{i\frac{3\pi}{4}}\right)$$

$$= 2\pi i.\left(\frac{1}{4}\left[-\frac{1}{\sqrt{2}} - \frac{i}{\sqrt{2}}\right] + \frac{1}{4}\left[\frac{1}{\sqrt{2}} - \frac{i}{\sqrt{2}}\right.\right) = \frac{\pi}{\sqrt{2}}.$$

Question: 9) Evaluate $\int_0^\infty \frac{1}{(x^6+1)}dx$.

Solution:- Let $I = \int_0^\infty \frac{1}{(x^6+1)}dx$ and $f(z) = \frac{1}{(z^6+1)}$ taken around the closed contour consisting of real axis and upper half C_R of a large semi-circle $|z| = R$.

The pole of f(z) are given by,

$z^6 + 1 = 0$

$z^6 = -1 = \cos\pi + i\sin\pi$

$= \cos\left(\frac{\pi}{6}\right) + i\sin\left(\frac{\pi}{6}\right)$

$= \cos(2n+1)\pi + i\sin(2n+1)\pi$

$z = \cos(2n+1)\frac{\pi}{6} + i\sin(2n+1)\frac{\pi}{6} = e^{i(2n+1)\frac{\pi}{6}}$

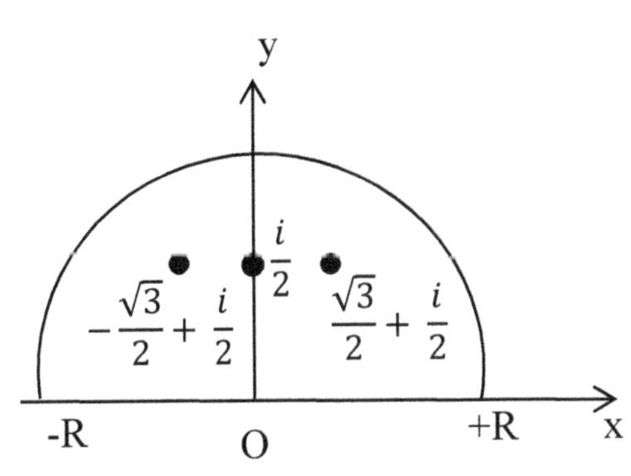

If $n = 0$, $\quad z = \cos\frac{\pi}{6} + i\sin\frac{\pi}{6} = e^{i\frac{\pi}{6}} = \frac{\sqrt{3}}{2} + \frac{i}{2}$

If n = 1, $z = \cos\frac{\pi}{2} + i\sin\frac{\pi}{2} = e^{i\frac{3\pi}{6}} = i$

If n = 2, $z = \cos\frac{5\pi}{6} + i\sin\frac{5\pi}{6} = e^{i\frac{5\pi}{6}} = -\frac{\sqrt{3}}{2} + \frac{i}{2}$

If n = 3, $z = \cos\frac{7\pi}{6} + i\sin\frac{7\pi}{6} = e^{i\frac{7\pi}{6}} = -\frac{\sqrt{3}}{2} - \frac{i}{2}$

If n = 4, $z = \cos\frac{9\pi}{6} + i\sin\frac{9\pi}{6} = e^{i\frac{9\pi}{6}} = -i$

The pole $z = e^{i\frac{\pi}{6}}, e^{i\frac{3\pi}{6}}, e^{i\frac{5\pi}{6}}$ lies inside the circle.

$$\text{Res}(z = e^{i\frac{\pi}{6}}) = \lim_{z \to e^{i\frac{\pi}{6}}} \frac{1}{6z^5} = \frac{e^{-i\frac{5\pi}{6}}}{6}$$

$$\text{Res}(z = e^{i\frac{\pi}{2}}) = \lim_{z \to e^{i\frac{\pi}{2}}} \frac{1}{6z^5} = \frac{e^{-i\frac{5\pi}{2}}}{6}$$

$$\text{Res}(z = e^{i\frac{5\pi}{6}}) = \lim_{z \to e^{i\frac{5\pi}{6}}} \frac{1}{6z^5} = \frac{e^{-i\frac{25\pi}{6}}}{6}$$

Hence by Cauchy's Integral theorem

$$I = 2\pi i\left[\text{Res}\left(z = e^{i\frac{\pi}{6}}\right) + \text{Res}\left(z = e^{i\frac{3\pi}{6}}\right) + \text{Res}\left(z = e^{i\frac{5\pi}{6}}\right)\right]$$

$$= 2\pi i.\left[\frac{e^{-i\frac{5\pi}{6}}}{6} + \frac{e^{-i\frac{5\pi}{2}}}{6} + \frac{e^{-i\frac{25\pi}{6}}}{6}\right] = \frac{2\pi i}{6}.\frac{-i}{3}$$

$$\int_{-\infty}^{\infty} \frac{1}{(x^6+1)}dx. = \frac{2\pi}{3}$$

$$\int_{0}^{\infty} \frac{1}{(x^6+1)}dx. = \frac{\pi}{3}.$$

Question: 10) Evaluate $\int_0^{\infty} \frac{\cos a x}{(x^2 + b^2)^2}dx$, a > 0, b > 0.

Solution:- $I = \int_0^{\infty} \frac{\cos a x}{(x^2 + b^2)^2}dx = \int_C f(z)\, dz$

Where $f(z) = \frac{\cos a z}{(z^2 + b^2)^2}$ taken around the closed contour consisting of real axis and upper half C_R of a large semi-circle $|z| = R$.

The pole of f(z) are given by,

$(z^2 + b^2)^2 = 0$

$z = \pm ib$

The pole z = ib lies inside the circle.

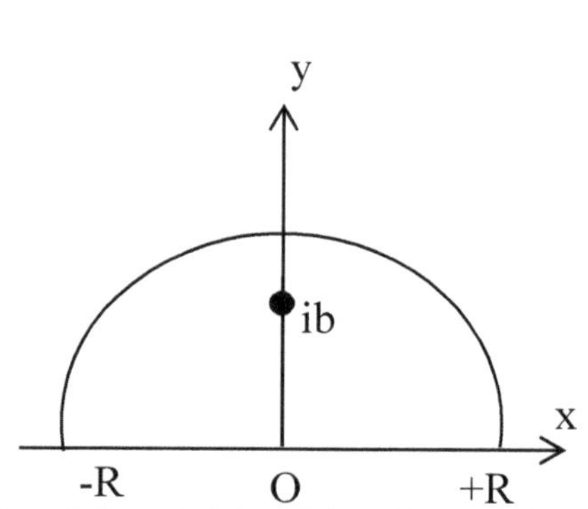

$$\text{Res}(z = ib) = \lim_{z\to ib} \{\frac{d}{dz}(z-ib)^2 \frac{\cos a z}{(z^2+b^2)^2}\}$$

$$= \lim_{z\to ib} \{\frac{d}{dz}(z-ib)^2 \frac{e^{iaz}}{(z^2+b^2)^2}\}$$

$$= \lim_{z\to ib} \{\frac{d}{dz}\frac{e^{iaz}}{(z+ib)^2}\} = \lim_{z\to ib} \{\frac{(z+ib)^2\, ia\, e^{iaz} - e^{iaz}\, 2(z+ib)}{(z+ib)^4}\} = \frac{(1+ab)\, e^{-ab}}{4i\ b^3}$$

By Cauchy's Integral theorem

$$I = 2\pi i[\text{Res}(z = ib)] = 2\pi i \frac{(1+ab)\, e^{-ab}}{4i\ b^3}$$

$$= \frac{1}{2} 2\pi i \frac{(1+ab)\, e^{-ab}}{4i\ b^3}$$

$$\int_0^\infty \frac{\cos a x}{(x^2+b^2)^2} dx = \frac{\pi (1+ab)\, e^{-ab}}{4 b^3}$$

EXERCISES:-

1. Evaluate $\int_0^\infty \frac{\cos 2x}{(x^2+9)^2(x^2+16)} dx.$ Ans: $\frac{\pi}{196}[\frac{31 e^{-6}}{27} + \frac{e^{-6}}{2}]$

2. Evaluate $\int_0^\infty \frac{\sin mx}{x} dx.$ Ans: $\frac{\pi}{2}$

3. Prove that $\int_0^\infty \frac{x^{a-1}}{1+x} dx = \frac{\pi}{\sin \pi a}$ and $\int_0^\infty \frac{x^{a-1}}{1+x} dx = \pi\cot \pi a.$

4. Prove that $a \geq b \geq 0$, then $\int_0^\infty \frac{\cos 2ax - \cos 2bx}{x^2} dx = \pi(b-a).$

5. Evaluate $\int_0^\infty \frac{\cos 3x}{(x^2+1)(x^2+4)} dx.$ Ans: $\frac{\pi}{2}[\frac{e^{-3}}{3} + \frac{e^{-6}}{6}]$

6. Evaluate $\int_{-\infty}^{+\infty} \frac{x^2\, dx}{(x+1)(x^2+4)}.$ Ans: $\frac{\pi}{3}$

7. Evaluate $\int_0^\pi \frac{\cos 3\theta}{5-4\cos\theta} d\theta.$ Ans: $\frac{\pi}{12}$

8. Evaluate $\int_0^{2\pi} \frac{1}{a+b\sin\theta} d\theta$ if $a > |b|$ Ans: $\frac{2\pi}{\sqrt{a^2}\ \sqrt{b^2}}$

9. Evaluate $\int_0^{2\pi} \frac{1}{1-2p\sin\theta+p^2} d\theta$ where $p < 1$ Ans: $\frac{2\pi}{1-p^2}$

10. Evaluate $\int_0^{2\pi} \frac{1}{5+4\sin\theta} d\theta.$ Ans: $\frac{8\pi}{3}$

Unit III : SOLUTION OF ALGEBRAIC,TRANSCENDENTAL EQUATION ,FINITE DIFFERENCES AND NEWTON FORMULAE

BASICS OF EQUATION :

The most challenging problem nowadays is to find root of any given equation. i.e. $f(x) = 0$

Consider a function with degree 'n' as

$f_n(x) = a_0x^n + a_1x^{n-1} + \cdots + a_n$ this polynomial will contain 'n' roots.

$f_n(x) = a_0x^n + a_1x^{n-1} + \cdots + a_n$ this function is known as **polynomial function.**

TRANSCENDENTAL EQUATIONS :

Suppose an equation contains single variable 'x' and a particular constant 'c' which takes a form as $f(x) + c = 0$

If $f(x)$ involve functions such as trigonometric, logarithmic, exponential etc. then such equation is known as transcendental equation.

Ex:

- $f(x) = logx - 75$
- $f(x) = cos^3x - 4x + 5$

This Chapter involves study of numerical methods for the solution of $f(x) = 0$ where $f(x)$ can be algebraic, transcendental or combination of both.

BISECTION METHOD

This method is based on a theorem that if a function $f(x)$ is continuous between a and b and $f(a)$ and $f(b)$ have opposite signs then there exists at least one number ε such that $f(\varepsilon) = 0$

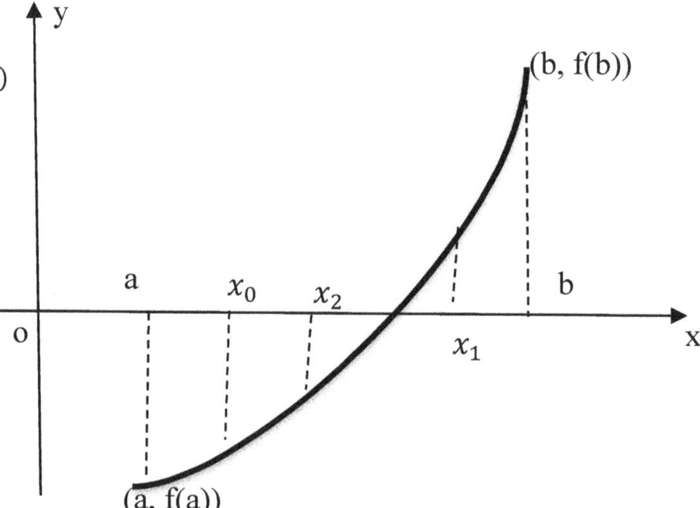

Fig: Graphical representation of Bisection method

Steps:

- To find the root of $f(x) = 0$ choose two number a and b such that $f(a)$ and $f(b)$

have opposite signs.

- Root lies between a and b and first approximation is given by $x_0 = \frac{a+b}{2}$
- If $f(x_0) = 0$ the x_0 is the root of given equation
- If $f(x_0) \neq 0$ then root will be between
- **Case I:** either x_0 *and* a if $f(x_0)$ and $f(a)$ has opposite signs
- **Case II**: x_0*and* b if $f(x_0)$ and $f(b)$ has opposite signs
- Thus, next approximation will be either $x_1 = \frac{x_0+a}{2}$ or $x_1 = \frac{x_0+b}{2}$
- On Repeating the procedure till $f(x) = 0$ we get the approximated roots

Example 1: find the root of the equation $x^3 + x - 1 = 0$ corrected up to **three** decimal places.

Solution: Let $f(x) = x^3 + x - 1 = 0$ ...(1)

Let, a=0, $f(a) = f(0) = -1$ (Negative)

and b=1, $f(b) = f(1) = 1$ (Positive)

Hence the root of given equation lies **between 0 and 1**

$$x_0 = \frac{0+1}{2} = 0.5$$

$f(x_0) = f(0.5) = -0.375$ (Negative), Hence Root lies between **0.5 and 1**

$$x_1 = \frac{0.5+1}{2} = 0.75$$

$f(x_1) = f(0.75) = 0.1719$ (Positive), Hence root lies between **0.5 and 0.75**

$$x_2 = \frac{0.5+0.75}{2} = 0.625$$

$f(x_2) = f(0.625) = -0.1308$ (Negative), Hence root lies between **0.625 and 0.75**

$$x_3 = \frac{0.625+0.75}{2} = 0.6875$$

$f(x_3) = f(0.6875) = 0.0124$ (Positive), Hence root lies between **0.6875 and 0.625**

$$x_4 = \frac{0.6875+0.625}{2} = 0.6562$$

$f(x_4) = f(0.6562) = -0.0612$ (Negative), Hence root lies between **0.6875 and 0.6562**

$$x_5 = \frac{0.6875+0.6562}{2} = 0.6718$$

$f(x_5) = f(0.6718) = -0.0250$ (Negative), Hence root lies between **0.6875 and 0.6718**

$$x_6 = \frac{0.6875+0.6718}{2} = 0.6796$$

$f(x_6) = f(0.6796) = -0.0065$ (Negative), Hence root lies between **0.6875 and 0.6796**

$$x_7 = \frac{0.6875+0.6796}{2} = 0.6835$$

$f(x_7) = f(0.6835) = 0.00028$ (Positive), Hence root lies between **0.6835 and 0.6796**

$$x_8 = \frac{0.6835+0.6796}{2} = 0.6815$$

$f(x_8) = f(0.6815) = -0.0019$ (Negative), Hence root lies between **0.6835 and 0.6815**

$$x_9 = \frac{0.6835+0.6815}{2} = \mathbf{0.6825}$$

$f(x_9) = f(0.6825) = 0.000412$ (Positive), Hence root lies between **0.6815 and 0.6825**

$$x_{10} = \frac{0.6815+0.6825}{2} = \mathbf{0.6820}$$

$f(x_{10}) = f(0.6820) = -0.00078$ (Negative), Hence root lies between **0.6825 and 0.6820**

$$x_{11} = \frac{0.6825+0.6820}{2} = \mathbf{0.6822}$$

Thus $\boldsymbol{x} = \mathbf{0.6822}$ is the root of given equation approximated up to 3 decimal places

Example 2: Find the root of the equation $f(x) = x^3 + x^2 + x + 7 = 0$ corrected up to **second** decimal places

Solution: Let $f(x) = x^3 + x^2 + x + 7 =$ ...(1)

To find a and b such that $f(a) and\ f(b)$ has opposite signs

Put $x = 1$ in equation 1, $f(1) = 10$

Put $x = 2$ in equation 1, $f(2) = 21$

Put $x = 0$ in equation 1, $f(0) = 7$

Put $x = -1$ in equation 1, $f(-1) = 6$

Put $x = -2$ in equation 1, $\boldsymbol{f(-2) = 1}$

Put $x = -3$ in equation 1, $\boldsymbol{f(-3) = -14}$

Thus for $x = -2\ and\ x = -3\ we\ get\ f(-2) and\ f(-3)$ with opposite signs

Hence, Root lies between **-2 and -3**

Let a= -2 and b= -3

$$x_0 = \frac{-2-3}{2} = -2.5$$

$f(-2.5) = -4.875$ (Negative) Hence, Root lies between **-2 and -2.5**

$$x_1 = \frac{-2-2.5}{2} = -2.25$$

$f(-2.25) = -1.5781$ (Negative) Hence, Root lies between **-2 and -2.25**

$$x_2 = \frac{-2-2.25}{2} = -2.125$$

$f(-2.125) = -0.2050$ (Negative) Hence, Root lies between **-2 and -2.125**

$$x_3 = \frac{-2-2.125}{2} = -2.0625$$

$f(-2.0625) = 0.4177$ (Positive) Hence Root lies between **-2.0625 and -2.125**

$$x_4 = \frac{-2.0625-2.125}{2} = -2.09375$$

$f(-2.09375) = 0.1114$ (Positive) Hence, Root lies between **-2.125 and -2.09375**

$$x_5 = \frac{-2.125-2.09375}{2} = -2.1093$$

$f(-2.1093) = -0.044$ (Negative) Hence, Root lies between **-2.09375 and -2.1093**

$$x_6 = \frac{-2.09375-2.1093}{2} = -2.1015$$

$f(-2.1015) = 0.0339$ (Positive) Hence, Root lies between **-2.1093 and -2.1015**

$$x_7 = \frac{-2.1093-2.1015}{2} = -2.1054$$

Thus $\boldsymbol{x} = \mathbf{-2.1054}$ is the root of given equation approximated up to second decimal place.

Example 3: Find the root of the equation $f(x) = 4e^{-x}sinx - 1 = 0$ lying between 0 and 0.5 corrected up to three decimal places.

Solution: Let, $f(x) = 4e^{-x}sinx - 1 = 0$ ...(1)

Since, it is given that root lies between 0 and 0.5

Therefore let $a = 0\ and\ b = 0.5$

$\boldsymbol{f(0) = -1}$ **(Negative)** $\boldsymbol{f(0.5) = 0.163145}$ **(Positive)**

$$x_0 = \frac{0+0.5}{2} = 0.25$$

$f(0.25) = -0.2292$ (Negative) Hence, Root lies between **0.25 and 0.5**

$$x_1 = \frac{0.5+0.25}{2} = 0.375$$

$f(0.375) = 0.00694$ (Positive) Hence, Root lies between **0.25 and 0.375**

$$x_2 = \frac{0.25+0.375}{2} = 0.3125$$

$f(0.3125) = -0.1002$ (Negative) Hence, Root lies between **0.375 and 0.3125**

$$x_3 = \frac{0.375+0.3125}{2} = 0.343$$

$f(0.343) = -0.0441$ (Negative) Hence, Root lies between **0.375 and 0.343**

$$x_4 = \frac{0.375+0.343}{2} = 0.359$$

$f(0.359) = -0.018$ (Negative) Hence, Root lies between **0.375 and 0.359**

$$x_5 = \frac{0.375+0.359}{2} = 0.367$$

$f(0.367) = -0.00536$ (Negative) Hence, Root lies between **0.375 and 0.367**

$$x_6 = \frac{0.375+0.367}{2} = 0.371$$

$f(0.371) = 0.000069$ (Positive) Hence, Root lies between **0.367 and 0.371**

$$x_7 = \frac{0.367+0.371}{2} = 0.369$$

$f(0.369) = -2.45$ (Negative) Hence, Root lies between **0.371 and 0.369**

$$x_8 = \frac{0.371+0.369}{2} = 0.370$$

$f(0.370) = -8.79$ (Negative) Hence, Root lies between **0.371 and 0.370**

$$x_9 = \frac{0.371+0.370}{2} = 0.3705$$

Thus $\boldsymbol{x = 0.3705}$ is the root of given equation corrected up to three decimal places.

FALSE POSITION / REGULAR FALSI METHOD

To Find the root of $f(x) = 0$, Let $a \; and \; b$ be two numbers such that $f(a) and f(b)$ are of opposite signs. Then the root of this equation lies between a and b.

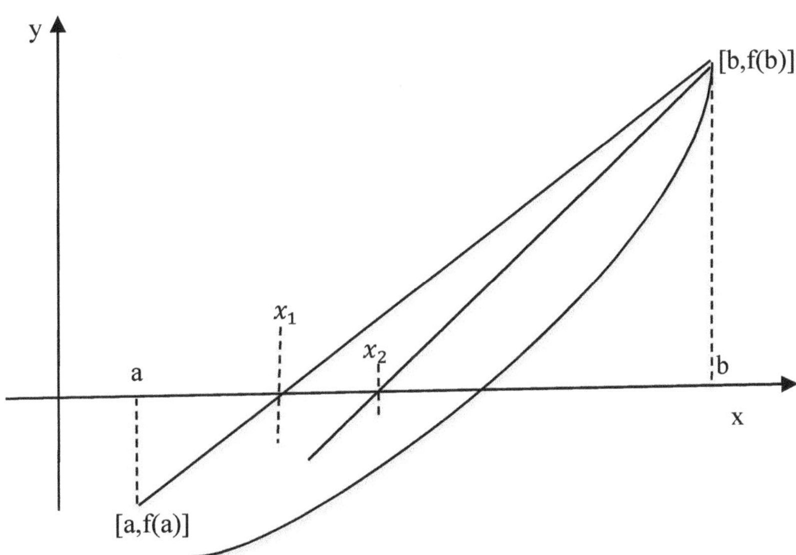

Fig; Graphical representation of Regular Falsi Method

Thus if $(a, f[a]) and \; (b, f[b])$ are two points then equation of chord joining these two points is given by

$$\frac{y - f(a)}{f(b) - f(a)} = \frac{x - a}{b - a}$$

The point of intersection of this chord with x-axis gives us the approximate root of $f(x) = 0$

Thus, for y=0 we can obtain the first approximation as

$$\boldsymbol{x_1 = \frac{af(b) - bf(a)}{f(b) - f(a)}}$$

Steps:

- Find a and b such that $f(a) and \; f(b)$ are of opposite signs
- Find first approximation as $\boldsymbol{x_1 = \frac{af(b)-bf(a)}{f(b)-f(a)}}$
- Check $f(x_1)$

3. if $f(x_1) and\ f(a)$ are of opposite signs then root lies between $x_1\ and\ a$

Hence x_2 will be obtained by replacing b by x_1

4. if $f(x_1) and\ f(b)$ are of opposite signs then root lies between $x_1\ and\ b$

Hence x_2 will be obtained by replacing a by x_1

- Continuing in this way one can obtain the approximated root of given equations corrected up to certain decimal places

Example 1: Find the root of the equation $f(x) = x^3 - 2x - 5 = 0$ corrected up to second decimal place

Solution: Let, $f(x) = x^3 - 2x - 5 = 0$ ...(1)

To find: a and b

Put x=0 in equation (1) $f(0) = -5$

Put x=1 in equation (1) $f(1) = -6$

Put x=2 in equation (1) $f(2) = -1$

Put x=3 in equation (1) $f(3) = 16$

Thus, for x=2 and x=3 values of $f(2) and\ f(3)$ are positive and negative respectively

Hence, Root lies **between 2 and 3**

$$x_1 = \frac{af(b) - bf(a)}{f(b) - f(a)}$$

$$x_1 = \frac{(2)*(16)-(3)(-1)}{16-(-1)} = 2.05882$$

$f(2.05882) = -0.3908$ (Negative) Hence, Root lies between **2.05882 and 3**

$$x_2 = \frac{2.05882*16-3*(-0.3908)}{16-(-0.3908)} = 2.08126$$

$f(2.08126) = -0.1472$ (Negative) Hence, Root lies between **2.08126 and 3**

$$x_3 = \frac{2.8126*16-3*(-0.1472)}{16-(-0.1472)} = 2.0886$$

$f(2.0886) = -0.0662$ (Negative) Hence, Root lies between **2.0886 and 3**

$$x_4 = \frac{2.0886*16-3*(-0.662)}{16-(-0.0662)} = 2.0929$$

$f(2.0929) = -0.0184$ (Negative) Hence, Root lies **between 2.0929 and 3**

$$x_5 = \frac{2.0926*16-3*(-0.0184)}{16-(-0.0184)} = 2.0936$$

Thus $x = \mathbf{2.0936}$ is the root of given equation approximated up to second decimal place.

Example 2: The equation $2x = log_{10}x + 7$ has a root between 3 and 4. Find the root corrected up to three decimal places

Solution: Let, $f(x) = 2x - log_{10}x - 7 = 0$ ...(1)

Given that the root lies between 3 and 4

Therefore, $f(3) = -1.47712$ (Negative) and $f(4) = 0.39794$ (Positive)

$$x_1 = \frac{3*(0.39794)-4*(-1.47112)}{0.39794-(-1.147112)} = 3.78777$$

$f(3.78777) = -0.0028436$ (Negative) Hence, Root lies between **3.78777 and 4**

$$x_2 = \frac{3.78777*(0.39794)-4*(-0.0028436)}{0.39794-(-0.0028436)} = 3.78927$$

$f(3.78927) = -0.00001551$ (Negative) Hence, Root lies between **3.78927 and 4**

$$x_3 = \frac{3.78927*(0.39794)-4*(-0.00001551)}{0.39794-(-0.00001551)} = 3.7892$$

$f(3.7892) = -0.0001475$ (Negative) Hence, Root lies between **3.7892 and 4**

Thus $x = \mathbf{3.7892}$ is the root of given equation approximated up to third decimal place.

SECANT METHOD

Secant method is another method for finding the roots of the equation$f(x)$ =0 which is a resemblance of regular falsi method.

Steps:

1.Find a and b such that $f(a) and\ f(b)$ are of opposite signs

2.Then first approximation x_0 is given by $x_0 = \frac{af(b)-bf(a)}{f(b)-f(a)}$

3.In general, if $x_0 = a\ and\ x_1 = b$ then general formula for approximation is of following type

$$x_{n+1} = \frac{x_{n-1}f(x_n) - x_n f(x_{n-1})}{f(x_n) - f(x_{n-1})}$$

Example 1: Find the root of the equation $f(x) = 4(x - sinx) - 1$ corrected up to third decimal places.

Solution: Let $f(x) = 4(x - sinx) - 1 = 0$ ...(1)

To find: a and b

Put x=0 in equation (1), $f(0) = -1$

Put x=1 in equation (1), $f(1) = -0.3658$

Put x=2 in equation (1), $f(2) = 3.3628$

Therefore $f(1) = -0.3658$ (Negative) and $f(2) = 3.3628$ (Positive)

Hence the root of the given equation lies between 1 and 2

So, a=1=x_0 and b=2=x_1

We have,

$$x_{n+1} = \frac{x_{n-1}f(x_n) - x_n f(x_{n-1})}{f(x_n) - f(x_{n-1})}$$

Substituting n=1 in above equation we get

$$x_2 = \frac{x_0 f(x_1) - x_1 f(x_0)}{f(x_1) - f(x_0)}$$

First approximation

$$x_2 = \frac{1 * (3.3628) - 2 * (-0.3658)}{3.3628 - (-0.3658)}$$

$$x_2 = 1.098$$

$f(1.098) = -0.1691$

$$x_3 = \frac{x_1 f(x_2) - x_2 f(x_1)}{f(x_2) - f(x_1)}$$

$$x_3 = \frac{2 * (-0.1691) - 1.098(3.3628)}{(-0.1691) - 3.3628}$$

$$x_3 = 1.1411$$

$f(1.411) = -3.0719$

$$x_4 = \frac{x_2 f(x_3) - x_3 f(x_2)}{f(x_3) - f(x_2)}$$

$$x_4 = \frac{1.098 * (-3.0719) - 1.411 * (-0.1691)}{(-3.0719) - (-0.1619)}$$

$$x_4 = 1.0797$$

$f(1.0797) = -3.2084$

$$\boldsymbol{x_5} = \frac{\boldsymbol{x_3 f(x_4) - x_4 f(x_3)}}{\boldsymbol{f(x_4) - f(x_3)}}$$

$$x_5 = \frac{1.1411 * (-3.2084) - 1.0797 * (-3.0719)}{(-3.2084) - (-3.0719)}$$

$$x_5 = 1.3817$$

$f(1.3817) = 0.5981$

$$\boldsymbol{x_6} = \frac{\boldsymbol{x_4 f(x_5) - x_5 f(x_4)}}{\boldsymbol{f(x_5) - f(x_4)}}$$

$$x_6 = \frac{1.0797 * 0.5981 - 1.3817 * (-3.2084)}{0.5981 - (-3.2084)}$$

$$x_6 = 1.3342$$

$f(1.3342) = 0.4482$

$$\boldsymbol{x_7} = \frac{\boldsymbol{x_5 f(x_6) - x_6 f(x_5)}}{\boldsymbol{f(x_6) - f(x_5)}}$$

$$x_7 = \frac{1.3817 * (0.4482) - 1.3342 * (0.5981)}{0.4482 - 0.5981}$$

$$x_7 = 1.3456$$

$f(1.3456) = 0.4833$

$$\boldsymbol{x_8} = \frac{\boldsymbol{x_6 f(x_7) - x_7 f(x_6)}}{\boldsymbol{f(x_7) - f(x_6)}}$$

$$x_8 = \frac{1.3342 * 0.4833 - 1.3456 * 0.4482}{0.4833 - 0.4482}$$

$$x_8 = 1.1886$$

$f(1.1886) = 0.04300$

$$\boldsymbol{x_9 = \frac{x_7 f(x_8) - x_8 f(x_7)}{f(x_8) - f(x_7)}}$$

$$x_9 = \frac{1.3456 * 0.04300 - 1.1866 * 0.4833}{0.04300 - 0.4833}$$

$$x_9 = 1.1710$$

$f(1.1710) = 0.0005611$

$$\boldsymbol{x_{10} = \frac{x_8 f(x_9) - x_9 f(x_8)}{f(x_9) - f(x_8)}}$$

$$x_{10} = \frac{1.1886 * 0.0005611 - 1.1710 * 0.04300}{0.0005611 - 0.04300}$$

$$\boldsymbol{x_{10} = 1.1712}$$

Thus $\boldsymbol{x = 1.1712}$ is the root of given equation approximated upto second decimal place

Example 2: Find the root of the equation $f(x) = xe^x - 1 = 0$ corrected up to second decimal place.

Solution: Let, $f(x) = xe^x - 1 = 0$ ...(1)

To Find: a and b

Put x=0 in equation (1), $f(0) = -1$ (Negative)

Put x=1 in equation 1, $f(1) = 1.7182$ (Postive)

Thus, the root lies between 0 and 1

We have,

$$\boldsymbol{x_{n+1} = \frac{x_{n-1} f(x_n) - x_n f(x_{n-1})}{f(x_n) - f(x_{n-1})}}$$

Substituting n=1 in above equation we get

$$x_2 = \frac{x_0 f(x_1) - x_1 f(x_0)}{f(x_1) - f(x_0)}$$

$$x_2 = \frac{0 * 1.7182 - 1(-1)}{1.7182 - (-1)}$$

$$x_2 = 0.3678$$

$f(0.3678) = -0.4685$

$$\boldsymbol{x_3 = \frac{x_1 f(x_2) - x_2 f(x_1)}{f(x_2) - f(x_1)}}$$

$$x_3 = \frac{1 * (-0.4685) - 0.3678 * 1.7182}{-0.4685 - 1.1782}$$

$$x_3 = 0.5032$$

$f(0.5032) = -0.1676$

$$\boldsymbol{x_4 = \frac{x_2 f(x_3) - x_3 f(x_2)}{f(x_3) - f(x_2)}}$$

$$x_4 = \frac{0.3678 * (-0.1676) - 0.5032 * (-0.4685)}{(-0.1676) - (-0.4685)}$$

$$x_4 = 0.5786$$

$f(0.5786) = 0.0319$

$$\boldsymbol{x_5 = \frac{x_3 f(x_4) - x_4 f(x_3)}{f(x_4) - f(x_3)}}$$

$$\boldsymbol{x_5} = \frac{0.5032 * (0.0319) - 0.5786 * (-0.1676)}{0.0319 - (-0.1676)}$$

$$x_5 = 0.5665$$

$f(0.5665) = -0.0000169$

$$\boldsymbol{x_6 = \frac{x_4 f(x_5) - x_5 f(x_4)}{f(x_5) - f(x_4)}}$$

$$x_6 = \frac{0.5786 * (-0.0000169) - 0.5665 * 0.0319}{-0.0000169 - 0.0319}$$

$$x_6 = 0.5671$$

Thus $x = 0.5671$ is the root of the given equation corrected up to second decimal place

ITERATION METHOD

As discussed in previous methods like Bisection method, Regular Falsie method and Secant Method we used to require two initial approximations like a and b such that $f(a) and f(b)$ should be of opposite signs. But in case of of iteration method and Newton Raphson method we require only single approximation.

Steps:

1.Suppose if the given function is $f(x) = 0$

2.Express the function as $\phi(x) = 0$ which can be done in many ways.

3.If x_0 is the approximated root then chose $\phi(x)$ such that $|\phi'(x_0)| < 1$

4.Thus, successive approximations of the root of given equation are given by

$$\boldsymbol{x_{n+1} = \phi(x_n) \qquad n = 0, 1, 2, 3 \ldots \ldots}$$

Example 1: Find the root of the equation $f(x) = 2x - 3 - cosx$ in the interval $[\frac{3}{2}, \frac{\pi}{2}]$

Solution: Let $f(x) = 2x - 3 - cosx$ ...(1)

It is given that root lies between $\frac{3}{2}$ and $\frac{\pi}{2}$ so Let $x_0 = 1$ be the initial approximation.

Now we have to express the given function $f(x)$ in some $\phi(x)$ form which satisfies the condition $|\phi'(x_0)| < 1$

Thus, $2x - 3 - cosx = 0$

$2x = cosx + 3$

$x = \frac{cosx+3}{2}$

Therefore, $\phi(x) = \frac{cosx+3}{2}$

Now, $\phi'(x) = \frac{-sinx}{2}$

$$|\phi'(x_0)| = \frac{sinx_0}{2} = \frac{sin1}{2} = 0.42 < 1$$

Which satisfies the condition.

Thus, successive approximations of the root of given equation are given by

$$x_{n+1} = \phi(x_n) \qquad n = 0, 1, 2, 3 \ldots\ldots \text{ with } \phi(x) = \frac{cosx+3}{2}$$

$$x_0 = 1$$

$$x_1 = \frac{1}{2}[cos(x_0) + 3] = \frac{1}{2}[cos(1) + 3] = 1.7701$$

$$x_2 = \frac{1}{2}[cos(x_1) + 3] = \frac{1}{2}[cos(1.7701) + 3] = 1.4010$$

$$x_3 = \frac{1}{2}[cos(x_2) + 3] = \frac{1}{2}[cos(1.4010) + 3] = 1.5844$$

$$x_4 = \frac{1}{2}[cos(x_3) + 3] = \frac{1}{2}[cos(1.5844) + 3] = 1.4931$$

$$x_5 = \frac{1}{2}[cos(x_4) + 3] = \frac{1}{2}[cos(1.4931) + 3] = 1.5388$$

$$x_6 = \frac{1}{2}[cos(x_5) + 3] = \frac{1}{2}[cos(1.5388) + 3] = 1.5159$$

$$x_7 = \frac{1}{2}[cos(x_6) + 3] = \frac{1}{2}[cos(1.5159) + 3] = 1.5254$$

$$x_8 = \frac{1}{2}[cos(x_7) + 3] = \frac{1}{2}[cos(1.5254) + 3] = 1.5226$$

$$x_9 = \frac{1}{2}[cos(x_8) + 3] = \frac{1}{2}[cos(1.5226) + 3] = 1.5240$$

$$x_{10} = \frac{1}{2}[cos(x_9) + 3] = \frac{1}{2}[cos(1.5240) + 3] = 1.5233$$

$$x_{11} = \frac{1}{2}[cos(x_{10}) + 3] = \frac{1}{2}[cos(1.5233) + 3] = 1.5237$$

Thus $x = 1.5237$ is the root of the given equation approximated up to third decimal place.

Example 2: Find the root of the equation $f(x) = x^3 - 9x + 1$ corrected up to third decimal places.

Solution: Let $f(x) = x^3 - 9x + 1 = 0$ ...(1)

Put $x = 2$ in equation (1), $f(2) = -9$ (Negative)

Put $x = 3$ in equation (1), $f(3) = 1$ (Positive)

Hence root lies between 2 and 3, Hence initial approximation can be taken in between 2 and 3.

Let $x_0 = 2.65$ be the initial approximation.

Now we have to express the given function $f(x)$ in some $\phi(x)$ form which satisfies the condition $|\phi'(x_0)| < 1$

Case I: $x^3 - 9x + 1 = 0$

$x(x^2 - 9) + 1 = 0$

$x = \frac{-1}{(x^2-9)} = \frac{1}{9-x^2}$

$$\boldsymbol{\phi(x) = \frac{1}{9 - x^2}}$$

$\phi'(x) = \frac{2x}{(9 - x^2)^2}$

At $x = x_0 = 2.65$

$$\phi'(x_0) = \frac{2x_0}{(9 - {x_0}^2)^2} = \frac{2 * 2.65}{((9 - (2.65)^2)^2} = \mathbf{1.355 > 1}$$

Therefore, $\boldsymbol{\phi(x)} = \frac{1}{9-x^2}$ This form is not allowed

Case II: $x^3 = 9x - 1$

$x = (9x - 1)^{\frac{1}{3}}$

$\phi(x) = (9x - 1)^{\frac{1}{3}}$

$$\boldsymbol{\phi'(x) = \frac{3}{(9x - 1)^{\frac{2}{3}}}}$$

$$\phi'(x_0) = \frac{3}{(9x_0 - 1)^{\frac{2}{3}}} = \frac{3}{(9 * 2.65 - 1)^{\frac{2}{3}}} = \mathbf{0.3725 < 1}$$

Therefore $\boldsymbol{\phi}$**(x)=(9x – 1)**$^{\frac{1}{3}}$ this form is allowed

Thus, successive approximations of the root of given equation are given by

$$\boldsymbol{x_{n+1} = \phi(x_n)} \qquad \boldsymbol{n = 0, 1, 2, 3 \ldots\ldots} \text{ with } \boldsymbol{\phi(x)=(9x - 1)^{\frac{1}{3}}}$$

$$\boldsymbol{x_0 = 2.65}$$

$$\boldsymbol{x_1} = (9x_0 - 1)^{\frac{1}{3}} = (9 * 2.65 - 1)^{\frac{1}{3}} = \mathbf{2.8376}$$

$$\boldsymbol{x_2} = (9x_1 - 1)^{\frac{1}{3}} = (9 * 2.8376 - 1)^{\frac{1}{3}} = \mathbf{2.9059}$$

$$\boldsymbol{x_3} = (9x_2 - 1)^{\frac{1}{3}} = (9 * 2.9059 - 1)^{\frac{1}{3}} = \mathbf{2.9299}$$

$$\boldsymbol{x_4} = (9x_3 - 1)^{\frac{1}{3}} = (9 * 2.9299 - 1)^{\frac{1}{3}} = \mathbf{2.9383}$$

$$\boldsymbol{x_5} = (9x_4 - 1)^{\frac{1}{3}} = (9 * 2.9983 - 1)^{\frac{1}{3}} = \mathbf{2.9412}$$

$$\boldsymbol{x_6} = (9x_5 - 1)^{\frac{1}{3}} = (9 * 2.9412 - 1)^{\frac{1}{3}} = \mathbf{2.9422}$$

$$\boldsymbol{x_7} = (9x_6 - 1)^{\frac{1}{3}} = (9 * 2.9422 - 1)^{\frac{1}{3}} = \mathbf{2.9426}$$

$$\boldsymbol{x_8} = (9x_7 - 1)^{\frac{1}{3}} = (9 * 2.9426 - 1)^{\frac{1}{3}} = \mathbf{2.9427}$$

Thus $\boldsymbol{x} = \mathbf{2.9427}$ is the root of the given equation approximated up to third decimal place.

Example 3: Find the root the equation $f(x) = 5x^3 - 20x + 3$ approximated up to third decimal place.

Solution: Let, $f(x) = 5x^3 - 20x + 3$ ...(1)

Put $x = 0$ in equation 1, $f(0) = 3$ (Positive)

Put $x = 1$ in equation 1, $f(1) = 12$ (Negative)

Hence root lies between 0 and 1, Hence initial approximation can be taken in between 0 and 1.

Let $x_0 = 0.5$ be the initial approximation.

Now we have to express the given function $f(x)$ in some $\phi(x)$ form which satisfies the condition $|\phi'(x_0)| < 1$

$5x^3 - 20x + 3=0$

$20x = 5x^3 + 3$

$x = \frac{5x^3 + 3}{20}$

$$\phi(x)=\frac{5x^3+3}{20}, \phi'(x) = \frac{15x^2}{20}$$

$$\phi'(x_0) = \frac{15{x_0}^2}{20} = \frac{15 * (0.5)^2}{20} = 0.1875 < 1$$

Thus $\phi(x)=\frac{5x^3+3}{20}$ this from is allowed.

Thus, successive approximations of the root of given equation are given by

$$x_{n+1} = \phi(x_n) \qquad n = 0, 1, 2, 3 \ldots\ldots \text{ with } \phi(x)=\frac{5x^3+3}{20}$$

$$x_0 = 0.5$$

$$x_1 = \frac{5(x_0)^3 + 3}{20} = \frac{5(0.5)^3 + 3}{20} = 0.18125$$

$$x_2 = \frac{5(x_1)^3 + 3}{20} = \frac{5(0.18125)^3 + 3}{20} = 0.15148$$

$$x_3 = \frac{5(x_2)^3 + 3}{20} = \frac{5(0.15148)^3 + 3}{20} = 0.15086$$

$$x_4 = \frac{5(x_3)^3 + 3}{20} = \frac{5(0.15086)^3 + 3}{20} = 0.15085$$

$$x_5 = \frac{5(x_4)^3 + 3}{20} = \frac{5(0.15085)^3 + 3}{20} = \mathbf{0.150858}$$

Thus $\boldsymbol{x} = \mathbf{0.1508}$ is the root of the given equation approximated up to third decimal place

NEWTON RAPHSON METHOD

Let, x_0 be approximate root of the equation $f(x) = 0$ and suppose $x_1 = x_0 + h$ be its corrected root.

Then $$f(x_0 + h) = 0$$

By Using Taylors Series Expansion, we have

$$f(x_0) + hf'(x_0) + \frac{h^2}{2!}f''(x_0) + \cdots \ldots = 0$$

On Neglecting high derivative terms we get,

$$f(x_0) + hf'(x_0) = 0$$

$$h = -\frac{f(x_0)}{f'(x_0)}$$

$$x_1 = x_0 - \frac{f(x_0)}{f'(x_0)}$$

Thus, for successive approximation we get

$$\boldsymbol{x_{n+1} = x_n - \frac{f(x_n)}{f'(x_n)}}$$

Steps:

1.Find initial root x_0 such that it is closer to the original root

2.Find $f(x_0)$ and $f'(x_0)$

3.First approximate root will be given by (n=1)

$$\boldsymbol{x_1 = x_0 - \frac{f(x_0)}{f'(x_0)}}$$

4.Thus, one can find the root with this approximation.

Example 1: Find the root of the equation $f(x) = sinx - \frac{x}{2}$ which lies between $\frac{\pi}{2}$ and π corrected upto third decimal place.

Solution: Let $f(x) = sinx - \frac{x}{2} = 0$ ... (1)

Since the root lies between $\frac{\pi}{2}$ and π ,we can take initial root in between these values.

$f(x) = sinx - \frac{x}{2}$ and $f'(x) = cosx - \frac{1}{2}$

We have,

$$x_{n+1} = x_n - \frac{f(x_n)}{f'(x_n)}$$

First approximate root will be given by n=0

$$x_1 = x_0 - \frac{f(x_0)}{f'(x_0)}$$

$f(x_0) = sinx_0 - \frac{x_0}{2} = sin\frac{\pi}{2} - \frac{\pi}{4} = \mathbf{0.2146}$

$f'(x_0) = cosx_0 - \frac{1}{2} = cos\frac{\pi}{2}\frac{1}{2} = -\mathbf{0.5}$

$$x_1 = \frac{\pi}{2} - \frac{0.2146}{(-0.5)} = 2$$

$$x_2 = x_1 - \frac{f(x_1)}{f'(x_1)}$$

$f(x_1) = sinx_1 - \frac{x_1}{2} = sin2 - \frac{2}{2} = -\mathbf{0.0907}$

$f'(x_1) = cosx_1 - \frac{1}{2} = cos2 - \frac{1}{2}$=**-0.9161**

$$x_2 = 2 - \frac{(-0.0907)}{(-0.9161)} = 1.9010$$

$$x_3 = x_2 - \frac{f(x_2)}{f'(x_2)}$$

$f(x_2) = sinx_2 - \frac{x_2}{2} = sin(1.9010) - \frac{1.9010}{2} = -0.00452$

$f'(x_2) = cosx_2 - \frac{1}{2} = cos(1.9010) - \frac{1}{2} = -0.8242$

$$x_3 = 1.9010 - \frac{(-0.00452)}{(-0.8242)} = 1.8955$$

$$x_4 = x_3 - \frac{f(x_3)}{f'(x_3)}$$

$f(x_3) = sinx_3 - \frac{x_3}{2} = sin(1.8955) - \frac{1.8955}{2} = -0.000004695$

$f'(x_3) = cosx_3 - \frac{1}{2} = cos(1.8955) - \frac{1}{2} = -0.8190$

$$x_4 = 1.8955 - \frac{-0.000004695}{-0.8190} = 1.8954$$

Thus $x = 1.8954$ is the root of given equation corrected up to third decimal place.

Example 2: Find the root of the equation $f(x) = x^3 - 3x + 1$ corrected up to fourth decimal place.

Solution: Let $f(x) = x^3 - 3x + 1 = 0$ ...(1)

Put $x = 0$ in equation 1, $f(0) = 1$ (Positive)

Put $x = 1$ in equation 1, $f(1) = -1$ (Negative)

Hence root lies between 0 and 1, so initial approximation can be taken in between 0 and 1

Let $x_0 = 0.3$ be initial approximation

$$f(x) = x^3 - 3x + 1$$

$$f'(x) = 3x^2 - 3$$

We have,

$$x_{n+1} = x_n - \frac{f(x_n)}{f'(x_n)}$$

First approximate root will be given by n=0

$$x_1 = x_0 - \frac{f(x_0)}{f'(x_0)}$$

$f(x_0) = x_0{}^3 - 3x_0 + 1 = (0.3)^3 - 3 * 0.3 + 1 = 0.12$

$f'(x_0) = 3x_0{}^2 - 3 = 3(0.3)^2 - 3 = -2.73$

$$x_1 = 0.3 - \frac{0.127}{-2.73} = 0.34652$$

$$x_2 = x_1 - \frac{f(x_1)}{f'(x_1)}$$

$$f(x_1) = x_1{}^3 - 3x_1 + 1 = (0.34652)^3 - 3(0.34562) + 1 = 2.0487 * 10^{-3}$$

$f'(x_1) = 3x_1{}^2 - 3 = 3(0.34652)^2 - 3 = -2.6397$

$$x_2 = 0.34652 - \frac{2.0487 * 10^{-3}}{-2.6397} = 0.34729$$

$$`f(x_2) = x_2{}^3 - 3x_2 + 1 = (0.34729)^3 - 3 * (0.34729) + 1 = 1.67 * 10^{-5}$$

$f'(x_2) = 3x_2{}^2 - 3 = 3(0.34729) - 3 = -2.6381$

$$x_3 = 0.34729 - \frac{1.67 * 10^{-5}}{-2.6381} = 0.3472$$

Thus $\boldsymbol{x} = \mathbf{0.3472}$ is the root of the given equation corrected up to fourth decimal place.

Example 3: Find the root of the equation $f(x) = sinx - 1 + x = 0$ corrected upto three **decimal places.**

Solution: Let $f(x) = sinx - 1 + x = 0$ ...(1)

Put $x = 0$ in equation(1). $f(0) = -1$ (Negative)

Put $x = 1$ in equation (1), $f(1) = 0.8414$ (Positive)

Hence the root lies between 0 and 1 so we can take the first approximation in between 0 and 1

Let $x_0 = 0$ be initial approximation.

$$\boldsymbol{f(x) = sinx - 1 + x}$$

$$\boldsymbol{f'(x) = cosx + 1}$$

We have,

$$\boldsymbol{x_{n+1} = x_n - \frac{f(x_n)}{f'(x_n)}}$$

First approximate root will be given by n=0

$$x_1 = x_0 - \frac{f(x_0)}{f'(x_0)}$$

$f(x_0) = sinx_0 - 1 + x_0 = \sin(0) - 1 + 0 = -1$

$f'(x_0) = cosx_0 + 1 = \cos(0) + 1 = 2$

$$x_1 = 0 - \frac{-1}{2} = 0.5$$

$$x_2 = x_1 - \frac{f(x_1)}{f'(x_1)}$$

$f(x_1) = sinx_1 - 1 + x_1 = \sin(0.5) - 1 + 0.5 = -0.0205$

$f'(x_1) = cosx_1 + 1$ =cos (0.5) +1=1.8775

$$x_2 = 0.5 - \frac{-0.0205}{1.8775} = 0.5109$$

$$x_3 = x_2 - \frac{f(x_2)}{f'(x_2)}$$

$f(x_2) = sinx_2 - 1 + x_2 = \sin(0.5109) - 1 + 0.5109 = -0.000137$

$f'(x_2) = cosx_2 + 1 = \cos(0.5109) + 1 = 1.8723$

$$x_3 = 0.5109 - \frac{-0.000137}{1.8723} = 0.51097$$

Thus $x = \mathbf{0.51097}$ is the root of the given equation coreected upto four decimal places.

Exercise:

Find the root of following equations using different methods.

1). $xe^x - 1 = 0$ 2). $x^{\sin(2)} - 4 - 0$ 3). $e^x = \cot x$ 4). $5x^3 - 20x + 3 = 0$

5). $xe^{-2x} = \frac{1}{2} sinx$ 6). $4(x - sinx) = 1$ 7. $sinx = 10(x - 1)$ 8). $e^x = x^2$

9). $x + logx = 2$ 10). $x^3 - x - 4$ 11). $sinx = \frac{x}{2}$ 12). $x^4 + x^2 - 80 = 0$

13). $x - cosx = 0$

FINITE DIFFERENCES

Suppose we have an equation$y = f(x)$ which says for every value of x there is a value for y.

So, such values can be expressed in a tabular form as follows

x	$y = f(x)$
x_0	y_0
x_1	y_1
x_2	y_2
x_3	y_3
x_4	y_4
x_n	y_n

Here

x_0 *and* x_n are initial and final values respectively. Thus, the process of finding any y value in between x_0 *and* x_n is called as interpolation.

If the values of x are equally spaced then there are three ways to find the y value corresponding to any x value in-between x_0 *and* x_n.

1.Forward Difference

2.Backward Difference

3.Central Difference.

1.Forward Difference Table:

x	y	Δ	Δ^2	Δ^3	Δ^4
x_0	y_0				
		$\Delta y_0{=}y_1 - y_0$			
x_1	y_1		$\Delta^2 y_0 = \Delta y_1 - \Delta y_0$		
		$\Delta y_1 = y_2 - y_1$		$\Delta^3 y_0 = \Delta^2 y_1 - \Delta^2 y_0$	
x_2	y_2		$\Delta^2 y_1 = \Delta y_2 - \Delta y_1$		$\Delta^4 y_0 = \Delta^3 y_1 - \Delta^3 y_0$
		$\Delta y_2 = y_3 - y_2$		$\Delta^3 y_1 = \Delta^2 y_2 - \Delta^2 y_1$	
x_3	y_3		$\Delta^2 y_2 = \Delta y_3 - \Delta y_2$		
		$\Delta y_3{=}y_4 - y_3$			
x_4	y_4				

2.Backward Difference Table:

x	y	∇	∇^2	∇^3	∇^4
x_0	y_0				
		$\nabla y_0 = y_1 - y_0$			
x_1	y_1		$\nabla y_0 = \nabla y_1 - \nabla y_0$		
		$\nabla y_1 = y_2 - y_1$		$\nabla^3 y_0 = \nabla^2 y_1 - \nabla^2 y_0$	
x_2	y_2		$\nabla^2 y_1 = \nabla y_2 - \nabla y_1$		$\nabla y_0 = \nabla^3 y_1 - v^3 y_0$
		$\nabla y_2 = y_3 - y_2$		$\nabla^3 y_1 = \nabla^2 y_2 - \nabla^2 y_1$	
x_3	y_3		$\nabla^2 y_2 = \nabla y_3 - \nabla y_2$		
		$\nabla y_3 = y_4 - y_3$			
x_4	y_4				

NEWTONS FORMULAE

Newtons Forward Difference Formula:

$$y_n(x) = y_0 + P\Delta y_0 + \frac{P(P-1)}{2!}\Delta^2 y_0 + \frac{P(P-1)(P-2)}{3!}\Delta^3 y_0 + \cdots + \frac{P(P-1)(P-2)\ldots P(P-1)(P-2)..(P-n+1)}{n!}\Delta^n y_0$$

Where $P = \frac{x-x_0}{h}$

And $x_0 = start\ value\ and\ h = difference\ in\ x\ value$

Newtons Backward Difference Formula:

$$y_n(x) = y_n + P\nabla y_n + \frac{P(P+1)}{2!}\nabla^2 y_n + \frac{P(P+1)(P+2)}{3!}\nabla^3 y_n + \cdots + \frac{P(P+1)(P+2)\ldots(P+n-1)}{n!}\nabla^n y_n$$

$$where\ P = \frac{x - x_n}{h}$$

Example1) The table gives that the value for tan x as

x	y= tan x
0.10	0.1003
0.15	0.1527
0.20	0.2027
0.25	0.2553
0.30	0.3093

Find a) tan (0.12)

b) tan (0.26)

Solution –

x	y	Δ	Δ^2	Δ^3	Δ^4
0.10	0.1003				
		0.0508			
0.15	0.1511		0.0008		
		0.0516		0.0002	
0.20	0.2027		0.0010		0.0002
		0.0526		0.0004	
0.25	0.2553		0.0014		
		0.0540			
0.30	0.3093				

1. To find x = 0.12, We have $x_0 = 0.10$

Here h = $x_1 - x_0 = 0.15 - 0.10 = 0.05$

P $= \frac{x-x_0}{h} = \frac{(0.12-0.10)}{0.05} = 0.4$

By Newton's forward difference formula

$$y_n(x) = y_0 + P\Delta y_0 + \frac{P(P-1)}{2!}\Delta^2 y_0 + \frac{P(P-1)(P-2)}{3!}\Delta^3 y_0 + \cdots + \frac{P(P-1)(P-2)\ldots P(P-1)(P-2)..(P-n+1)}{n!}\Delta^n y_0$$

$$y_n(0.12) = 0.1003 + 0.4 \times 0.0508 + \frac{0.4(0.4-1)}{2!} \times 0.0008 + \frac{0.4(0.4-1)(0.4-2)}{3!} \times 0.0002 + \frac{0.4(0.4-1)(0.4-2)(0.4-3))}{4!} \times 0.0002$$

$y_n(0.12) = 0.1003 + 0.2032 + (-9.6 \times 10^{-5}) + 1.28 \times 10^{-5} + (-8.32 \times 10^{-6})$

$y_n(0.12) = 0.1205$

x	y	Δ	Δ^2	Δ^3	Δ^4
0.10	0.1003				
		0.0508			
0.15	0.1511		0.0008		
		0.0516		0.0002	
0.20	0.2027		0.0010		0.0002
		0.0526		0.0004	
0.25	0.2553		0.0014		
		0.0540			
0.30	0.3093				

2. To find x = 0.26, We have x_n = 0.30

$P = \frac{x-x_n}{h} = \frac{(0.26-0.30)}{0.05}$ = -0.8

By Newton's Backward difference formula

$$y_n(x) = y_n + P\nabla y_n + \frac{P(P+1)}{2!}\nabla^2 y_n + \frac{P(P+1)(P+2)}{3!}\nabla^3 y_n + \dots + \frac{P(P+1)(P+2)\dots(P+n-1)}{n!}\nabla^n y_n$$

$$y_n(0.26) = 0.3093 + (-0.8) \times (0.0540) + \frac{-0.8(-0.8+1)}{2!} \times 0.0014 + \frac{-0.8(-0.8+1)(-0.8+2)}{3!} \times 0.0004 + \frac{-0.8(-0.8+1)(-0.8+2)(-0.8+3)}{4!} \times 0.0002$$

$y_n(0.26)$ = 0.3093 + (-0.0432) + (-1.12 × 10^{-4}) + (-1.28 × 10^{-5}) +(−3.52 × 10^{-6})

$y_n(0.26)$ = 0.2659

Example 2. Population of the town were as under

Year	Population
1921	46
1931	66
1941	81
1951	93
1961	101

Estimate population in year 1955.

Solution -

x(Years)	y(population)	Δ	Δ^2	Δ^3	Δ^4
1921	46				
		20			
1931	66		−5		
		15		2	
1941	81		−3		−3
		12		−1	
1951	93		−4		
		8			
1961	101				

3. To find x = 1955, We have x_n = 1961

Here h = x_1- x_0 = $1931 - 1921 = 1$

$P = \frac{x-x_n}{h} = \frac{(1955-1961)}{10} = -0.6$

By Newton's Backward difference formula

$$y_n(x) = y_n + P\nabla y_n + \frac{P(P+1)}{2!}\nabla^2 y_n + \frac{P(P+1)(P+2)}{3!}\nabla^3 y_n + \cdots + \frac{P(P+1)(P+2)\ldots(P+n-1)}{n!}\nabla^n y_n$$

$$y_n(1955) = 101 + (-0.6)\times 8 + \frac{-0.6(-0.6+1)}{2!}\times(-4) + \frac{-0.6(-0.6+1)(-0.6+2)}{3!}\times(-1) + \frac{-0.6(-0.6+1)(-0.6+2)(-0.6+3)}{4!}\times(-3)$$

=101 + (-4.8) + 0.48 + 0.056 + 0.1008

= 96.83

Example 3) The following values are taken from the table of cube

x	$y = x^3$
6.1	226.981
6.2	238.328
6.3	250.047
6.4	262.441
6.5	274.625
6.6	287.496
6.7	300.763

Find $(6.36)^3$ *and* $(6.61)^3$

Solution – The forward difference table is

x	$y = x^3$	Δ	Δ^2	Δ^3	Δ^4	Δ^5	Δ^6
6.1	226.981						
		11.347					
6.2	238.328		0.372				
		11.719		0.006			
6.3	250.047		0.378		0.000		
		12.097		0.006		0.000	
6.4	262.144		0.384		0.000		0.000
		12.481		0.006		0.000	
6.5	274.625		0.390		0.000		
		12.871		0.006			
6.6	287.496		0.396				
		13.267					
6.7	300.763						

4. To find x = 0.12, We have x_0 = 0.10

Here h = x_1- x_0 = 6.2 – 6.1=0.1

P= $\frac{x-x_0}{h}$ = $\frac{(6.36-6.1)}{0.1}$ = 2.6

By Newton's forward difference formula

$$y_n(x) = y_0 + P\Delta y_0 + \frac{P(P-1)}{2!}\Delta^2 y_0 + \frac{P(P-1)(P-2)}{3!}\Delta^3 y_0 + \cdots + \frac{P(P-1)(P-2)\ldots P(P-1)(P-2)..(P-n+1)}{n!}\Delta^n y_0$$

$$y_n(6.36) = 226.981 + (2.6)(11.347) + \frac{2.6(2.6-1)}{2!} \times 0.372 + \frac{2.6(2.6-1)(2.6-2)}{3!} \times 0.006$$

= 226.981 + 29.5022 + 0.77376 + 0.002496

= 257.2595

The backward difference table is

x	$y = x^3$	Δ	Δ^2	Δ^3	Δ^4	Δ^5	Δ^6
6.1	226.981						
		11.347					
6.2	238.328		0.372				
		11.719		0.006			
6.3	250.047		0.378		0.000		
		12.097		0.006		0.000	
6.4	262.144		0.384		0.000		0.000
		12.481		0.006		0.000	
6.5	274.625		0.390		0.000		
		12.871		0.006			
6.6	287.496		0.396				
		13.267					
6.7	300.763						

5. To find x = 6.61, We have x_n = 6.7

Here h = x_1- x_0 = 6.2 - 6.1 = 0.1

$P = \frac{x-x_n}{h} = \frac{(6.61-6.7)}{0.1} = -0.9$

By Newton's Backward difference formula

$$y_n(x) = y_n + P\nabla y_n + \frac{P(P+1)}{2!}\nabla^2 y_n + \frac{P(P+1)(P+2)}{3!}\nabla^3 y_n + \cdots + \frac{P(P+1)(P+2)\ldots(P+n-1)}{n!}\nabla^n y_n$$

$$y_n(6.61) = 300.763 + (-0.9) \times (13.267) + \frac{-0.9(-0.9+1)}{2!} \times 0.396 + \frac{-0.9(-0.9+1)(-0.9+2)}{3!} \times 0.006$$

= 300.763 – 11.9403 – 0.01782- 0.000099

= 288.805

Example 4) From the following table of values of x and $f(x)$, determine (i) $f(0.23)$ (ii) $f(0.29)$

x	$f(x)$
0.20	1.6596
0.22	1.6698
0.24	1.6804
0.26	1.6912
0.28	1.7024
0.30	1.7139

Solution : The Forword difference table is

x	$f(x)$	Δ	Δ^2	Δ^3	Δ^4	Δ^5
0.20	0.6596					
		0.0102				
0.22	1.6698		0.0004			
		0.0106		-0.0002		
0.24	1.6804		0.0002		0.0004	
		0.0108		0.0002		-0.0007
0.26	1.6912		0.0004		-0.0003	
		0.0112		-0.0001		
0.28	1.7024		0.0003			
		0.0115				
0.30	1.7139					

6. To find x = 0.23, We have $x_0 = 0.20$

Here h = x_1- x_0 = 0.22 – 0.20=0.02

P= $\frac{x-x_0}{h} = \frac{(0.23-0.20)}{0.02}$ =1.5

By Newton's forward difference formula

$$y_n(x) = y_0 + P\Delta y_0 + \frac{P(P-1)}{2!}\Delta^2 y_0 + \frac{P(P-1)(P-2)}{3!}\Delta^3 y_0 + \cdots + \frac{P(P-1)(P-2)\ldots P(P-1)(P-2)..(P-n+1)}{n!}\Delta^n y_0$$

$$y_n(0.23) = 1.6596 + (1.5)(0.0102) + \frac{1.5(1.5-1)}{2!} \times 0.0004 + \frac{1.5(1.5-1)(1.5-2)}{3!} \times (-0.0002)$$
$$+ \frac{1.5(1.5-1)(1.5-2)(1.5-3)}{4!} \times 0.0004$$
$$+ \frac{1.5(1.5-1)(1.5-2)(1.5-3)(1.5-4)}{5!} \times (-0.0007)$$

= 1.6596 + 0.0153 + 0.00015 + 0.0000125 + 0.000009375 + 0.0000082034 = 1.6751

The backward difference table is

x	$f(x)$	Δ	Δ^2	Δ^3	Δ^4	Δ^5
0.20	0.6596					
		0.0102				
0.22	1.6698		0.0004			
		0.0106		-0.0002		
0.24	1.6804		0.0002		0.0004	
		0.0108		0.0002		-0.0007
0.26	1.6912		0.0004		-0.0003	
		0.0112		-0.0001		
0.28	1.7024		0.0003			
		0.0115				
0.30	1.7139					

7. To find x = 0.29, We have x_n = 0.30

Here h = x_1 - x_0 = 0.22-0.20 = 0.02

$P = \frac{x-x_n}{h} = \frac{(0.29-0.30)}{0.02} = -0.5$

By Newton's Backward difference formula

$$y_n(x) = y_n + P\nabla y_n + \frac{P(P+1)}{2!}\nabla^2 y_n + \frac{P(P+1)(P+2)}{3!}\nabla^3 y_n + \cdots + \frac{P(P+1)(P+2)\ldots(P+n-1)}{n!}\nabla^n y_n$$

$$y_n(0.29) = 1.7139 + (-0.5) \times (0.0115) + \frac{-0.5(-0.5+1)}{2!} \times 0.0003 + \frac{-0.5(-0.5+1)(-0.5+2)}{3!} \times (-0.0001)$$
$$+ \frac{-0.5(-0.5+1)(-0.5+2)(-0.5+3)}{4!} \times (-0.0003)$$
$$+ \frac{-0.5(-0.5+1)(-0.5+2)(-0.5+3)(-0.5+4)}{5!} \times (-0.0007)$$

= 1.7139 - 0.00575 - 0.0000375 + 0.0000117188 + 0.0000019141= 1.7081

UNIT IV : LAGRANGES INTERPOLATION,NUMERICAL INTEGRATION AND SOLUTION OF ODE

LAGRANGES INTERPOLATION

As Discuss earlier, we have solved the tabular form of certain equation with equally spaced 'x' values with the help of Newtons Forword and Backward difference formulae. But this does not work with certainly if the values of 'x' are unequally spaced, so for this case we use Lagrange's interpolation formulae.

x	y
x_1	y_1
x_2	y_2
x_3	y_3
x_4	y_4

Here $x_1 - x_0 \neq x_2 - x_1 \neq x_3 - x_2$

Special Case

The spacing in particular cases of 'x' values can also be same.

Formula:

$$y_n(x) = \frac{y_1(x-x_2)(x-x_2)(x-x_2)}{(x_1-x_2)(x_1-x_3)(x_1-x_4)} + \frac{y_2(x-x_1)(x-x_3)(x-x_4)}{(x_2-x_1)(x_2-x_3)(x_2-x_4)}$$

$$+ \frac{y_3(x-x_1)(x-x_2)(x-x_4)}{(x_3-x_1)(x_3-x_3)(x_3-x_4)} + \frac{y_4(x-x_1)(x-x_2)(x-x_3)}{(x_4-x_1)(x_4-x_2)(x_4-x_3)}$$

Example No. 1

The function $y = \sin x$ is tabulated as

x	$y = \sin x$
0	0
$\frac{\pi}{4}$	0.70711
$\frac{\pi}{2}$	1.0

Find $\sin\left(\frac{\pi}{6}\right)$

Solution:

By Lagrange's Interpolation Formulae:

$$y_n(x) = \frac{y_1(x-x_2)\,(x-x_2)(x-x_2)}{(x_1-x_2)(x_1-x_3)(x_1-x_4)} + \frac{y_2(x-x_1)(x-x_3)(x-x_4)}{(x_2-x_1)(x_2-x_3)(x_2-x_4)}$$

$$+ \frac{y_3(x-x_1)(x-x_2)(x-x_4)}{(x_3-x_1)(x_3-x_3)(x_3-x_4)} + \frac{y_4(x-x_1)(x-x_2)(x-x_3)}{(x_4-x_1)(x_4-x_2)(x_4-x_3)}$$

$$\sin\frac{\pi}{6} = \frac{0\left(\frac{\pi}{6}-0\right)\left(\frac{\pi}{6}-\frac{\pi}{2}\right)}{\left(0-\frac{\pi}{6}\right)\left(0-\frac{\pi}{2}\right)} + \frac{0.70711\left(\frac{\pi}{6}-0\right)\left(\frac{\pi}{6}-\frac{\pi}{2}\right)}{\left(\frac{\pi}{4}-0\right)\left(\frac{\pi}{4}-\frac{\pi}{2}\right)} + \frac{1.0\left(\frac{\pi}{6}-0\right)\left(\frac{\pi}{6}-\frac{\pi}{4}\right)}{\left(\frac{\pi}{2}-0\right)\left(\frac{\pi}{2}-\frac{\pi}{4}\right)}$$

$$\sin\frac{\pi}{6} = 0 + \frac{\pi\times 0.70711\left(\frac{1}{6}-0\right)\left(\frac{1}{6}-\frac{1}{2}\right)}{\pi\left(\frac{1}{4}-0\right)\left(\frac{1}{4}-\frac{1}{2}\right)} + \frac{\pi\times 1.0\left(\frac{1}{6}\right)\left(\frac{1}{6}-\frac{1}{4}\right)}{\pi\left(\frac{1}{2}\right)\left(\frac{1}{2}-\frac{1}{4}\right)}$$

$\sin\frac{\pi}{6} = 0 + 0.62854 + (-0.11111)$

$\sin\frac{\pi}{6} \cong 0.51742$

Example 2 : Using Lagrange's Interpolation , Find $l_n(2.7)$

x	$y = l_n(2.7)$
2	0.69315
2.5	0.91629
3.0	1.09861

Solution

Using Lagrange's Interpolation Formulae

$$y_n(x) = \frac{y_1(x-x_2)(x-x_2)(x-x_2)}{(x_1-x_2)(x_1-x_3)(x_1-x_4)} + \frac{y_2(x-x_1)(x-x_3)(x-x_4)}{(x_2-x_1)(x_2-x_3)(x_2-x_4)}$$

$$+ \frac{y_3(x-x_1)(x-x_2)(x-x_4)}{(x_3-x_1)(x_3-x_3)(x_3-x_4)} + \frac{y_4(x-x_1)(x-x_2)(x-x_3)}{(x_4-x_1)(x_4-x_2)(x_4-x_3)}$$

$$y_n(2.7) = \frac{0.69315(2.7-2.5)\,(2.7-3.0)}{(2-2.5)(2-3.0)} + \frac{0.91629(2.7-2)(2.7-3.0)}{(2.5-3.0)(2.5-2)}$$

$$+ \frac{1.09861(2.7-2)(2.7-2.5)}{(3.0-2)(3.0-2.5)}$$

= - 0.08317 + 0.769681 + 0.30761

= 0.99411

NUMERICAL INTEGRATION

As seen in previous section we have been dealing with values of x and y in tabular form with $y = f(x)$ i.e. to every value of x we were given a value of y. The spacing of x can be either be equal or unequal.

Let $(x_0, y_0), (x_1, y_1) \dots (x_n, y_n)$ be a data set of points of $y = f(x)$. The we have

$$I=\int_a^b y\,dx=\int_a^b f(x)\,dx \qquad ...(1)$$

Now I, Let the interval [a, b] be divided into 'n' equal subintervals such that

$$a = x_0 < x_1 < x_2 < \cdots \dots \dots \dots \dots < x_n = b$$

With $x_n = x_0 + nh$

Thus $h = \frac{x_n - x_0}{n}$

$$I=\int_{x_0}^{x_n} y\,dx \qquad ...(2)$$

Approximating y With the help of Newtons Forward Difference Formula equation 2 becomes

$$I=\int_{x_0}^{x_n}[y_0 + P\Delta y_0 + \frac{P(P-1)}{2!}\Delta^2 y_0 + \frac{P(P-1)(P-2)}{3!}\Delta^3 y_0 + \cdots]dx \qquad ...(3)$$

$$\text{Also, } p = \frac{x - x_0}{h}$$

$$hp = x - x_0$$

$$diferentiating$$

$$hdp = dx$$

$$I=\int_0^n[y_0 + P\Delta y_0 + \frac{P(P-1)}{2!}\Delta^2 y_0 + \frac{P(P-1)(P-2)}{3!}\Delta^3 y_0 + \cdots]hdp \qquad ....(4)$$

$$I=h[y_0.P + \frac{P^2}{2}\Delta y_0 + \frac{\frac{P^3}{3}-\frac{P^2}{2}}{2}\Delta^2 y_0 + \cdots \dots ....]_0^n$$

$$I = h[ny_0 + \frac{n^2}{2}\Delta y_0 + \frac{\frac{n^3}{3}-\frac{n^2}{2}}{2}\Delta^2 y_0 + \cdots]$$

$$I = nh[y_0 + \frac{n}{2}\Delta y_0 + \frac{\frac{n^2}{3}-\frac{n}{2}}{2}\Delta^2 y_0 + \cdots]$$

$$\boldsymbol{I = nh[y_0 + \frac{n}{2}\Delta y_0 + \frac{n(2n-3)}{12}\Delta^2 y_0 + \cdots.]} \qquad \textbf{...(4)}$$

Equation no (5) Represents a General Formula Where n can take different values and can be used to derive different integration formulae.

Trapezoidal Rule:

Put n=1 in equation (5). So, all the terms having differences greater than 1 becomes zero

So, the intervals will be $[x_0, x_1]$, $[x_1, x_2]$, ... $[x_{n-1}, x_n]$

$$I = h\left[y_0 + \frac{1}{2}\Delta y_0\right]$$

$$I = h\left[y_0 + \frac{1}{2}(y_1 - y_0)]\right]$$

$$I = \frac{h}{2}[y_0 + y_1)]$$

$$I = \int_{x_0}^{x_n} y\,dx = \frac{h}{2}[y_0 + y_1)]$$

Similarly

$$I = \int_{x_1}^{x_2} y\,dx = \frac{h}{2}[y_1 + y_2)]$$

And so, on

Combining all such terms we get,

$$\boldsymbol{I = \int_{x_0}^{x_n} y\,dx = \frac{h}{2}[y_0 + 2(y_1 + y_0 + \cdots + y_{n-1}) + y_n]}$$

This equation is known as Trapezoidal Rule.

Simspsons $\frac{1}{3}$ Rule

We have $\boldsymbol{I = nh[y_0 + \frac{n}{2}\Delta y_0 + \frac{n(2n-3)}{12}\Delta^2 y_0 + \cdots]}$

Put n=2 in above equation no (5)thus the intervals will be$[x_0, x_2]$, $[x_2, x_4]$, ... $[x_{n-2}, x_n]$

Thus $I = \int_{x_0}^{x_2} y\,dx = 2h[y_0 + \Delta y_0 + \frac{1}{6}\Delta^2 y_0 + \cdots]$

Where $\Delta y_0 = y_1 - y_0$, $\Delta^2 y_0 = \Delta y_1 - \Delta y_0$

$$I = \int_{x_0}^{x_2} y\,dx = \frac{h}{3}[y_0 + 4y_1 + y_2 + \cdots]$$

Similarly for interval $[x_2, x_4]$

$$I = \int_{x_2}^{x_4} y\,dx = \frac{h}{3}[y_2 + 4y_3 + y_4 + \cdots]$$

Combining all these we get

$$I = \int_{x_0}^{x_n} y\,dx = \frac{h}{3}[y_0 + 4(y_1 + y_3 + y_5 + \cdots + y_{n-1}) + 2(y_2 + y_4 + y_6 + .. + y_{n-2}) + y_n]$$

Which is Known as Simpsons $\frac{1}{3}$ Rule

Simpsons $\frac{3}{8}$ Rule

We have $\quad I = nh[y_0 + \frac{n}{2}\Delta y_0 + \frac{n(2n-3)}{12}\Delta^2 y_0 + \cdots]$

Put n=3 in above equation no (5) thus the intervals will be$[x_0, x_3]$, $[x_3, x_6]$, ... $[x_{n-3}, x_n]$

We get $I = \int_{x_0}^{x_3} y\,dx = 3h[y_0 + \frac{3}{2}\Delta y_0 + \frac{3}{4}\Delta^2 y_0 + \cdots]$

$$I = \int_{x_0}^{x_3} y\,dx = \frac{3h}{8}[y_0 + 3y_1 + 3y_2 + y_3]$$

Similarly for the interval $[x_3, x_6]$,

$$I = \int_{x_3}^{x_6} y\,dx = \frac{3h}{8}[y_3 + 3y_4 + 3y_5 + y_6]$$

Combining all such terms we get

$$I = \int_{x_0}^{x_n} y\,dx = \frac{3h}{8}[y_0 + 3y_1 + 3y_2 + 2y_3 + 3y_4 + 3y_5 + 2y_6 + .. + 2y_{n-3} + 3y_{n-2} + 3y_{n-1} + 3y_n]$$

Which is known as Simpsons 3/8 Rule

Example 1: From the following Table, Find the area bounded by the curve along x-axis from $x = 7.47 \text{ to } x = 7.52$ using Trapezoidal and Simpsons $\frac{1}{3}$ rule.

x	$y = f(x)$
7.47	1.93
7.48	1.95
7.49	1.98
7.50	2.01
7.51	2.03
7.52	2.06

Solution: Let $I \int_{x_0}^{x_n} f(x)dx$ ...(1)

x		$y = f(x)$	
7.47	x_0	1.93	y_0
7.48	x_1	1.95	y_1
7.49	x_2	1.98	y_2
7.50	x_3	2.01	y_3
7.51	x_4	2.03	y_4
7.52	x_5	2.03	y_5

Therefore $I \int_{x_0}^{x_5} f(x)dx$ . ... (2)

We have $h = \frac{x_n - x_0}{n} = \frac{7.52-7.47}{5} = 0.01$

A.By Trapezoidal rule

$$\boldsymbol{I = \int_{x_0}^{x_n} y\, dx = \frac{h}{2}[y_0 + 2(y_1 + y_0 + \cdots + y_{n-1}) + y_n]}$$

$$\boldsymbol{I = \int_{x_0}^{x_5} y\, dx = \frac{h}{2}[y_0 + 2(y_1 + y_2 + y_3 + y_4) + y_5]}$$

$$I = \int_{7.47}^{7.52} y\, dx = \frac{0.01}{2}[1.93 + 2(1.95 + 1.98 + 2.01 + 2.03) + 2.06]$$

I =0.00965

B.By Simpsons $\frac{1}{3}$ *Rule*

$$\boldsymbol{I = \int_{x_0}^{x_n} y\, dx = \frac{h}{3}[y_0 + 4(y_1 + y_3 + y_5 + \cdots + y_{n-1}) + 2(y_2 + y_4 + y_6 + .. + y_{n-2}) + y_n]}$$

$$I = \int_{7.47}^{7.52} y\, dx = \frac{h}{3}[y_0 + 4(y_1 + y_3) + 2(y_2 + y_4) + y_5]$$

$$I = \int_{7.47}^{7.52} y\, dx = \frac{0.01}{3}[1.93 + 4(1.95 + 2.01) + 2(1.98 + 2.03) + 2.06]$$

$I = 0.09283$

Example 2: Evaluate $I = \int_0^1 \frac{1}{1+x}\, dx$ using Trapezoidal and Simpsons Rule.

Solution: Let $I = \int_0^1 \frac{1}{1+x}\, dx$ ...(1)

We have $\boldsymbol{h} = \frac{\boldsymbol{x_n - x_0}}{\boldsymbol{n}}$

From equation 1, x_0=0, $x_n = 1$

$h = \frac{1-0}{2} = \frac{1}{2} = 0.5$

x		$f(x)$	
0	x_0	1	y_0
0.5	x_1	0.6666	y_1
1	x_2	0.5	y_2

A.By Trapezoidal rule

$$\boldsymbol{I = \int_{x_0}^{x_n} y\, dx = \frac{h}{2}[y_0 + 2(y_1 + y_2 + \cdots + y_{n-1}) + y_n]}$$

$$I = \int_0^1 \frac{1}{1+x}\, dx = \frac{0.5}{2}[1 + 2(0.6666) + 0.5]$$

I = 0.7083

B. By Simpsons $\frac{1}{3}$ *Rule*

$$\boldsymbol{I = \int_{x_0}^{x_n} y\, dx = \frac{h}{3}[y_0 + 4(y_1 + y_3 + y_5 + \cdots + y_{n-1}) + 2(y_2 + y_4 + y_6 + .. + y_{n-2}) + y_n]}$$

$$I = \int_0^1 \frac{1}{1+x}\, dx = \frac{0.5}{3}[1 + 4(0.6666) + 0.5]$$

$I = 0.6944$

Example 3: Apply Trapezoidal Rule to the integral $I = \int_0^1 \sqrt{(1-x^2}\, dx$ with 5 subintervals

Solution: Let $I = \int_0^1 \sqrt{(1-x^2)}\, dx$ ...(1)

We have $\boldsymbol{h} = \frac{x_n - x_0}{n}$

$$h = \frac{1-0}{5} = 0.2$$

x		$f(x)$	
0	x_0	1	y_0
0.2	x_1	0.9797	y_1
0.4	x_2	0.9165	y_2
0.6	x_3	0.8	y_3
0.8	x_4	0.6	y_4
1	x_5	0	y_5

1. **By Trapezoidal rule**

$$\boldsymbol{I = \int_{x_0}^{x_n} y\, dx = \frac{h}{2}[y_0 + 2(y_1 + y_2 + \cdots + y_{n-1}) + y_n]}$$

$$\boldsymbol{I} = \int_0^1 \sqrt{(1-x^2)}\, dx = \frac{0.2}{2}[1 + 2(0.9797 + 0.9165 + 0.8 + 0.6) + 0]$$

$I = 0.7592$

B. By Simpsons $\frac{3}{8}$ Rule

$$\boldsymbol{I = \int_{x_0}^{x_n} y\,dx = \frac{3h}{8}[y_0 + 3y_1 + 3y_2 + 2y_3 + 3y_4 + 3y_5 + 2y_6 + .. + 2y_{n-3} + 3y_{n-2} + 3y_{n-1} + 3y_n]}$$

$$I = \int_0^1 \sqrt{(1-x^2)}\,dx = \frac{3*0.2}{8}[1 + 3*(0.9797 + 0.9165 + 0.6) + 2*0.8)]$$

Example 4: Evaluate $\int_0^{\pi} t\,sint\,dt$ using trapezoidal and Simpsons Rule.

Solution: Let $I = \int_0^{\pi} t\,sint\,dt$ ...(1)

We have $\boldsymbol{h = \frac{x_n - x_0}{n}}$

$$h = \frac{\pi - 0}{4} = \frac{\pi}{4}$$

x		$f(x)$	
0	x_0	0	y_0
$\frac{\pi}{4}$	x_1	0.5553	y_1
$\frac{\pi}{2}$	x_2	1.5707	y_2
$\frac{3\pi}{4}$	x_3	1.6608	y_3
Π	x_4	0	y_4

$$\boldsymbol{I = \int_{x_0}^{x_n} y\,dx = \frac{h}{2}[y_0 + 2(y_1 + y_2 + \cdots + y_{n-1}) + y_n]}$$

$$I = \int_0^t t\,sint\,dt = \frac{\frac{\pi}{4}}{2}[0 + 2(0.5553 + 1.5707 + 1.6608) + 0]$$

***I* =2.9741**

B. By Simpsons $\frac{1}{3}$ *Rule*

$$\boldsymbol{I = \int_{x_0}^{x_n} y\,dx = \frac{h}{3}[y_0 + 4(y_1 + y_3 + y_5 + \cdots + y_{n-1}) + 2(y_2 + y_4 + y_6 + .. + y_{n-2}) + y_n]}$$

$$I = \int_0^t t\,sint\,dt = \frac{\frac{\pi}{4}}{3}(0+4(0.5553+1.6608) +2(1.5707)+0)$$

I=3.1431

Exercise :

1) Evaluate $\int_{\frac{1}{2}}^{1} \frac{dx}{x}$ by Trapezoidal and Simpsons rule dividing into 4 parts.

2) Using Trapezoidal rule find $\int_0^6 f(x)dx$ from the following data

x	0	1	2	3	4	5	6
$f(x)$	1.56	3.64	4.62	5.12	7.05	9.22	10.44

3) Using Trapezoidal rule and Simpsons rule evaluate $\int_0^{3.14} sinxdx$ dividing into 6 parts.

4) Using Simpsons rule and diving into 4 parts evaluate $\int_0^1 xe^x dx$.

5) Evaluate $\int_0^2 e^x dx$ Using Simpsons rule $h = 1$ and $h = 0.5$

6) Apply Simpsons $\frac{3}{8}$ rule to the following data

x	0	0.25	0.50	0.75	1.0	1.25	1.50	1.75	2.0
$f(x)$	1.000	1.284	1.649	2.117	2.718	3.490	4.482	5.755	7.389

7) Evaluate $\sqrt{155}$ using Lagrange's Interpolation Formula from the following table

x	$y = \sqrt{x}$
150	12.247
152	12.329
154	12.410
156	12.490

8) Find Cubic polynomial which approximates the following data using Lagrange's interpolation formula

x	f(x)
-2	-12
-1	-8
2	3
3	5

EULERS METHOD

Suppose we have a differential equation $\frac{dy}{dx} = f(x, y)$ such that $y(x_0) = y_0$ as an initial condition and we have to find $y(x_n) = y_n$

Then one can use Eulers method for solution of this differential equation with formula as

$$\boldsymbol{y_n = y(x_n) = y_{n-1} + hf(x_{n-1}, y_{n-1})} \quad \text{...(1)}$$

Were, $h = x_n - x_{n-1}$

$$x_n = x_0 + nh$$

Put $n = 1$ in equation 1

$$y_1 = y_0 + hf(x_0, y_0)$$

Put $n = 2$ in equation 2

$$y_2 = y_1 + hf(x_1, y_1)$$

And so on.

Example 1: Find $y(2.2)$ using Eulers Method from the equation $\frac{dy}{dx} = -xy^2$ with $y(2) = 1$.

Solution: Let $\frac{dy}{dx} = -xy^2 = f(x, y)$

Thus $\quad f(x, y) = -xy^2 \quad$ ...(1)

Also, we have $y(x_0) = y_0 \quad$ ...(2)

Given that $y(2) = 1 \quad$ ...(3)

On comparing equation 2 and 3 we get

$$x_0 = 2 \; and \; y_0 = 1$$

We have $h = \frac{x_n - x_0}{n}$

$$h = \frac{2.2 - 2}{4} = \frac{0.2}{4} = 0.05$$

Now, $x_1 = x_0 + nh = 2 + 1 * 0.05$=2.05

$x_2 = x_0 + nh = 2 + 2 * 0.05$=2.10

$x_3 = x_0 + nh = 2 + 3 * 0.05$=2.15

$x_4 = x_0 + nh = 2 + 4 * 0.05$=2.2

By Euler method we have

$$\boldsymbol{y_n = y(x_n) = y_{n-1} + hf(x_{n-1}, y_{n-1})}$$

For $\boldsymbol{n = 1}$

$$y_1 = y(x_1) = y_0 + hf(x_0, y_0)$$

We have $y_0 = 1$ $x_0 = 2$, $f(x_0, y_0) = -x_0 {y_0}^2 = -(2 * (1)^2) = -2$

$$y_1 = 1 + 0.05 * (-2) = 0.9$$

For n =2

$$y_2 = y(x_2) = y_1 + hf(x_1, y_1)$$

We have $x_1 = 2.05, y_1 = 0.9, h = 0.05, f(x_1, y_1) = -x_1{y_1}^2 = -2.05 * (0.9)^2 = -1.6605$

$$y_2 = 0.9 + 0.05 * (-1.6605) = 0.8169$$

For n =3

$$y_3 = y(x_3) = y_2 + hf(x_2, y_2)$$

We have

$$x_2 = 2.10 \ , y_2 = 0.8169, h = 0.05, f(x_2, y_2) = -x_2{y_2}^2 = -2.10 * (0.8169)^2 = -1.4013$$

$$y_3 = 0.8169 + 0.05(-1.4013) = 0.7468$$

For n =4

$$y_4 = y_3 + hf(x_3, y_3)$$

We have

$$x_3 = 2.15 \ , y_3 = 0.7468 \ , h = 0.05 \ , f(x_3, y_3) = -x_3{y_3}^2 = -2.15 * (0.7468)^2 = -1.1990$$

$$y_4 = 0.7468 + 0.05(-1.1990) = 0.6868$$

Thus, value of $y(2.2)$ for the given differential equations is 0.6868

Example 2: Find $y(0.04)$ using Eulers Method from the equation $\frac{dy}{dx} = -y$ with $y(0) = 1$.

Solution: Let $\frac{dy}{dx} = -y = f(x, y)$

Thus $\quad f(x, y) = -y$ ...(1)

Also, we have $y(x_0) = y_0$ ...(2)

Given that $y(0) = 1$ ...(3)

On comparing equation 2 and 3 we get

$$x_0 = 0 \ and \ y_0 = 1$$

We have $h = \frac{x_n - x_0}{n}$

$$h = \frac{0.04 - 0}{4} = \frac{0.04}{4} = 0.01$$

$x_1 = x_0 + nh = 0 + 1 * 0.01 = 0.01$

$x_2 = x_0 + nh = 0 + 2 * 0.01 = 0.02$

$x_3 = x_0 + nh = 0 + 3 * 0.01$=0.03

$x_4 = x_0 + nh = 0 + 4 * 0.01$=0.04

By Euler method we have

$$\boldsymbol{y_n = y(x_n) = y_{n-1} + hf(x_{n-1}, y_{n-1})}$$

For $n = 1$

$$y_1 = y(x_1) = y_0 + hf(x_0, y_0)$$

We have $x_0 = 0$, $y_0 = 1$,h=0.01, $f(x_0, y_0) = -y_0 = -(1) = -1$

$$y_1 = 0 + 0.01 * (-1) = 0.99$$

For $n = 2$

$$y_2 = y_1 + hf(x_1, y_1)$$

We have $x_1 = 0.01$, $y_1 = 0.99$,h=0.01, $f(x_1, y_1) = -y_1 = -(0.99) = -0.99$

$$y_2 = 0.99 + 0.01 * (-0.99) = 0.9801$$

For $n = 3$

$$y_3 = y_2 + hf(x_2, y_2)$$

We have $x_2 = 0.02$, $y_2 = 0.9801$,h=0.01, $f(x_2, y_2) = -y_2 = -(0.9801) = -0.9801$

$$y_3 = 0.9801 + 0.01 * (-0.9801) = 0.9703$$

For $n = 4$

$$y_4 = y_3 + hf(x_3, y_3)$$

We have $x_3 = 0.03$, $y_3 = 0.9703$,h=0.01, $f(x_3, y_3) = -y_3 = -(0.9703) = -0.9703$

$$y_4 = 0.9703 + 0.01 * (-0.9703) = 0.9608$$

Thus, the value of $y(0.04)$ for the given differential equation is 0.9608

Example 3: Find $y(0.1), y(0.2) and\ y(0.3)$ using Eulers Method from the equation $\frac{dy}{dx}$ + 2y=0 with $y(0) = 1$.

Solution: Let $\frac{dy}{dx} = -2y = f(x, y)$

Thus $f(x, y) = -2y$ ...(1)

Also, we have $y(x_0) = y_0$ ...(2)

Given that $y(0) = 1$ ...(3)

On comparing equation 2 and 3 we get

$$x_0 = 0 \text{ and } y_0 = 1$$

Since we have to find $y(0.1), y(0.2) and\ y(0.3)$ therefore clearly $h = 0.1$

$x_1 = x_0 + nh = 0 + 1 * 0.1$=0.1

$x_2 = x_0 + nh = 0 + 2 * 0.1$=0.2

$x_3 = x_0 + nh = 0 + 3 * 0.1$=0.3

By Euler method we have

$$\boldsymbol{y_n = y(x_n) = y_{n-1} + hf(x_{n-1}, y_{n-1})}$$

For $n = 1$

$$y_1 = y_0 + hf(x_0, y_0)$$

We have $x_0 = 0$, $y_0 = 1$,h=0.1, $f(x_0, y_0) = -2y_0 = -(2 * 1) = -2$

$$y_1 = 1 + 0.1 * (-2) = 0.8$$

For $n = 2$

$$y_2 = y_1 + hf(x_1, y_1)$$

We have $x_1 = 0.1$, $y_1 = 0.8$,h=0.1, $f(x_1, y_1) = -2y_1 = -(2 * 0.8) = -0.16$

$$y_2 = 0.8 + 0.1 * (-0.16) = 0.64$$

For $n = 3$

$$y_3 = y_2 + hf(x_2, y_2)$$

We have $x_1 = 0.1$, $y_1 = 0.8$,h=0.1, $f(x_1, y_1) = -2y_1 = -(2 * 0.8) = -0.16$

$$y_2 = 0.8 + 0.1 * (-0.16) = 0.64$$

Exercise:

1) Solve the following differential equation with $h = 0.1$

a) $\frac{dy}{dx} = x + y,\ y(1) = 0$

b) $\frac{dy}{dx} = -y^2,\ y(1) = 1$

2)Solve the differential equation to find $y(0.4)$ given that $\frac{dy}{dx} = x^2 + y^2, y(0) = 1\ with$

$h = 0.1\ and\ h = 0.2$

3)taking $h = 0.2$ Solve the differential equation $\frac{dy}{dx} = x + y^2$ with initial condition $y(1) = 1$

Hence find $y(1.6)$

4) Given that $\frac{dy}{dx} = 2x + cosy$ such that $y(0) = 1$ Use Eulers method to find $y(0.2) with$

$h = 0.1$

RUNGE – KUTTA METHOD

Most of the fundamental and frequently occurring problems in physics and engineering uses differential equation . it can be reduced to the problems of solving differential equation that satisfies certain give conditions. There are various methods to solve such problems out of which one being "Runge-Kutta method". This method was developed by German Mathematician 'Carl Runge' and 'Wilhelm Kutta' and hence named as Runge-Kutta. This method takes two forms 'Second order' and ' Fourth Order' .It is widely used method for solving differential equation.

Suppose we have a differential equation $\frac{dy}{dx} = f(x,y)$ such that $y(x_0) = y_0$ as an initial condition and we have to find $y(x_n) = y_n$

Then For Runge-Kutta second order we have $y_1 = y_0 + \frac{1}{2}(k_1 + k_2)$ ....(1)

with $k_1 = hf_0$ *and* $k_2 = hf(x_0 + h, y_0 + k_1)$

Runge-Kutta fourth order formula is given as $y_1 = y_0 + \frac{1}{6}(k_1 + 2k_2 + 2k_3 + k_4)$

With$k_1 = hf_0$, $k_2 = hf\left(x_0 + \frac{h}{2}, y_0 + \frac{k1}{2}\right)$, $k_3 = hf(x_0 + \frac{h}{2}, y_0 + \frac{k2}{2})$, $k_4 = hf(x_0 + h, y_0 + k_3)$

Example 1: Use second order Runge-Kutta method to approximate the value of y when $x = 1.1$

given that $\frac{dy}{dx} = 3x + y^2$ and $y = 1.2$ when $x = 1$ *and* $h = 0.1$

Solution: Given that $\frac{dy}{dx} = 3x + y^2$ .....(1)

We have $f(x,y) = 3x + y^2$ ......(2)

Also, we have $x_0 = 1$ *and* $y_0 = 1.2$ *and* $h = 0.1$

To find y at $x = 1.1$

Using Runge-Kutta second order we have $y_1 = y_0 + \frac{1}{2}(k_1 + k_2)$ ....(3)

with $k_1 = hf_0$ *and* $k_2 = hf(x_0 + h, y_0 + k_1)$

We have $f(x,y) = 3x + y^2$

There $f_0 = 3x_0 + (y_0)^2 = 3 * 1 + (1.2)^2 = 4.44$

$k_1 = hf_0 = 0.1 * 4.44 = 0.444.$ ......(4)

$$k_2 = hf(x_0 + h, y_0 + k_1)$$

$$we\ have\ f(x,y) = 3x + y^2$$

Therefore

$$f(x_0 + h, y_0 + k_1) = 3(x_0 + h) + (y_0 + k_1)^2 = 3(1 + 0.1) + (1.2 + 0.444)^2 = 6.00$$

$k_2 = hf(x_0 + h, y_0 + k_1) = 0.1 * 6.00 = 0.600$ . . .(5)

Using Runge-Kutta second order we have ,

$$y_1 = y_0 + \frac{1}{2}(k_1 + k_2) = 1.2 + \frac{1}{2}(0.444 + 0.600) = 1.722$$

Thus, value y at x=1.1 is approximated as 1.722 using Runge-Kutta second order method.

Example 2: Use fourth order Runge-Kutta method to approximate the value of y when $x = 0.2$ given that $\frac{dy}{dx} = x + y^2$ and $y = 1$ when $x = 0$ *and* $h = 0.2$

Solution : Given that $\frac{dy}{dx} = x + y^2$ .....(1)

We have $f(x, y) = x + y^2$ ......(2)

Also, we have $x_0 = 0$ *and* $y_0 = 1$ *and* $h = 0.2$

To find y at $x = 0.2$

Using Runge-Kutta fourth order we have $y_1 = y_0 + \frac{1}{6}(k_1 + 2k_2 + 2k_3 + k_4)$ ... (3)

With

$$k_1 = hf_0\,, k_2 = hf\left(x_0 + \frac{h}{2}, y_0 + \frac{k1}{2}\right), k_3 = hf(x_0 + \frac{h}{2}, y_0 + \frac{k2}{2}) ,$$
$$k_4 = hf(x_0 + h, y_0 + k_3)$$

$$f_0 = f(x_0, y_0) = x_0 + (y_0)^2 = 0 + (1)^2 = 1$$

$$k_1 = hf_0 = 0.2 * 1 = 0.2$$

we have $f(x, y) = x + y^2$

Therefore

$$f\left(x_0 + \frac{h}{2}, y_0 + \frac{k_1}{2}\right) = \left(x_0 + \frac{h}{2}\right) + \left(y_0 + \frac{k_1}{2}\right)^2 = \left(0 + \frac{0.2}{2}\right) + \left(1 + \frac{0.2}{2}\right)^2 = 1.31$$

$$, k_2 = hf\left(x_0 + \frac{h}{2}, y_0 + \frac{k1}{2}\right) = 0.2 * 1.31 = 0.262$$

we have $f(x, y) = x + y^2$

Therefore

$$f\left(x_0 + \frac{h}{2}, y_0 + \frac{k_2}{2}\right) = \left(x_0 + \frac{h}{2}\right) + \left(y_0 + \frac{k_2}{2}\right)^2 = \left(0 + \frac{0.2}{2}\right) + \left(1 + \frac{0.262}{2}\right)^2 = 1.3791$$

$k_3 = hf(x_0 + \frac{h}{2}, y_0 + \frac{k2}{2})$= 0.2*1.3791=0.2758

$we\ have\ f(x,y) = x + y^2$

Therefore

$$f(x_0 + h, y_0 + k_3) = (x_0 + h) + (y_0 + k_3) = (0 + 0.2) + (1 + 0.2758)^2 = 1.8276$$

$$k_4 = hf(x_0 + h, y_0 + k_3) = 0.2 * 1.8276 = 0.3754$$

Using Runge-Kutta second order we have

$y_1 = y_0 + \frac{1}{6}(k_1 + 2k_2 + 2k_3 + k_4)$= $1 + \frac{1}{6}(0.2 + 2 * 0.262 + 2 * 0.2758 + 0.3754) = 1.2702$

Thus, value y at x=0.2 is approximated as 1.2702using Runge-Kutta fourth order method.

Example 3: Use fourth order Runge-Kutta method to find $y(0.2)\ and\ y(0.4)$ given that $\frac{dy}{dx} = \frac{y^2 - x^2}{y^2 + x^2}$ and $y(0) = 1$

Solution: Given that $\frac{dy}{dx} = \frac{y^2 - x^2}{y^2 + x^2}$ ...(1)

We have $f(x,y) = \frac{y^2 - x^2}{y^2 + x^2}$ ...(2)

Also, we have $x_0 = 0\ and\ y_0 = 1\ and\ take\ h = 0.2$

Using Runge-Kutta fourth order we have $y_1 = y_0 + \frac{1}{6}(k_1 + 2k_2 + 2k_3 + k_4)$ ... (3)

With $k_1 = hf_0\, , k_2 = hf\left(x_0 + \frac{h}{2}, y_0 + \frac{k1}{2}\right), k_3 = hf(x_0 + \frac{h}{2}, y_0 + \frac{k2}{2})$,

$$k_4 = hf(x_0 + h, y_0 + k_3)$$

$k1 = hf(x_0, y_0)$=$0.2(\frac{{y_0}^2 - {x_0}^2}{{y_0}^2 + {x_0}^2}) = 0.2(\frac{1^2 - 0^2}{1^2 + 0^2}) = 0.2$

$k_2 = hf\left(x_0 + \frac{h}{2}, y_0 + \frac{k1}{2}\right) = 0.2f\left(0 + \frac{0.2}{2}, 1 + \frac{0.2}{2}\right) = 0.2f(0.1,1.1)$= $0.2(\frac{(1.1)^2 - (0.1)^2}{(1.1)^2 + (0.1)^2}) = 0.1967$

$k_3 = hf\left(x_0 + \frac{h}{2}, y_0 + \frac{k2}{2}\right) = 0.2f\left(0 + \frac{0.2}{2}, 1 + \frac{0.1967}{2}\right) = 0.2f(0.1,1.0984) = 0.2\left(\frac{(1.0984)^2 - (0.1)^2}{(1.0984)^2 + (0.1)^2}\right) = 0.1967$

$$k_4 = hf(x_0 + h, y_0 + k_3) = 0.2f(0 + 0.2, 1 + 0.1967) = 0.2f(0.2,1.1967) = 0.2\left(\frac{(1.1967)^2 - (0.1)^2}{(1.1967 + (0.1)^2}\right) = 0.1891$$

$$y_1 = y_0 + \frac{1}{6}(k_1 + 2k_2 + 2k_3 + k_4)$$

$$y(0.2) = 1 + \frac{1}{6}(0.2 + 2(0.1967) + 2(0.1967) + 0.1891) = 1.19598$$

Now in order to compute y(0.4) we have to take $x_0 = 0.2\ y_0 = 1.19598$ and $h = 0.2$

On repeating the above procedure, we obtain $k_1 = 0.189, k_2 = 0.1795, k_3 = 0.1793, k_4 = 0.1997$

we have

$$y_1 = y_0 + \frac{1}{6}(k_1 + 2k_2 + 2k_3 + k_4)$$

$$y(0.4) = 1.19598 + \frac{1}{6}(0.189 + 2(0.1795) + 2(0.1793) + 0.1997) = 1.3804$$

So, the values of y(0.2) and y(0.4) are approximated as $1.19598\ and 1.3804$ respectively using Runge-Kutta fourth order method

---

Exercise:

1) Use Runge-Kutta fourth order method to find $y(0.1)$ Given that $\frac{dy}{dx} = \frac{2xy}{1+x^2}$ and $y(0) = 0$

2) Use Runge-Kutta fourth order method to find $y(0.2)$ Given that $\frac{dy}{dx} = 1 + y^2$ and $y(0) = 0$

3) Use Runge-Kutta fourth order method to find $y(1.2)\ and\ y(1.4)$ Given that $\frac{dy}{dx} = \frac{3x+y}{x+2y}$ and $y(1) = 1$

APPENDIX

PYTHON CODE FOR BISECTION METHOD

```
import math

def f(x):

    return x**3 + x - 1

a = 0

b = 1

tol = 0.001

max_iter = 1000


if f(a) * f(b) >= 0:

    print("Initial values do not bracket the root.")

else:

    for i in range(1, max_iter + 1):

        c = (a + b) / 2

        print(f"Iteration {i}: Root = {c:.3f}")


        if abs(f(c)) < tol:

            print(f"Root found: {c:.3f} (within tolerance {tol})")

            break

        elif f(c) * f(a) < 0:

            b = c

        else:

            a = c


        if i == max_iter:

            print("Root not found within the maximum number of iterations.")
```

PYTHON CODE FOR FALSI POSITION METHOD

```
import math
def f(x):
    return 2*x - math.log10(x) - 7
a = 3
b = 4
tol = 0.001
max_iter = 1000
for i in range(1, max_iter + 1):
    c = (a * f(b) - b * f(a)) / (f(b) - f(a))
    print(f"Iteration {i}: Root = {c:.3f}")

    if abs(f(c)) < tol:
        print(f"Root: {c:.3f}")
        break
    elif f(c) * f(a) < 0:
        b = c
    else:
        a = c

    if i == max_iter:
        print("Root not found within the maximum number of iterations.")
```

PYTHON CODE FOR NEWTON RAPHSON METHOD

```
def f(x):

   return x**3 - 3*x + 1

def df(x):

   return 3*x**2-3

x0 = 0.5

tol =1e-4

max_iter = 100

for i in range(1,max_iter + 1):

   x1 = x0 -f(x0)/df(x0)

   print("iteration {}: Root = {:.4f}". format(i,x1))

   if abs(x1 - x0) < tol:

      print("The root of the given equation is found with tolerance {:.4f} at iteration {}". format(tol, i))

      break

   x0 = x1

else:

      print("Root not found within the maximum number of iterations.")
```

PYTHON CODE FOR TRAPEZOIDAL RULE

```
import math
def func(x):
   return math.sqrt(1-x*x)


def trapezoidal(a,b,n):
   h =(float(b - a )/ n)
   m = n+1
   x=list()
   fx=list()
   i=0
   while i<m:
    x.append(a+i*h)
    fx.append(func(x[i]))
    i=i+1
   for i in range(m):
    print("n = ",i," x = %.6f"%x[i], " y = %.6f"%fx[i])
   sum = func(a) + func(b)
   for i in range (1,n):
      sum = sum + 2 * func (x[i])
   return (float (h / 2) * sum )
a=0
b=1
n=50
print("%.6f"% trapezoidal(a,b,n))
```

PYTHON CODE FOR SIMPSON1/3 RD RULE

```
import math

def func(x):

   return 1/(1+x*x)

def simpsons(a,b,n):

   h=(float(b-a)/n)

   m=n+1

   x=list()

   fx=list()

   i=0

   while i<m:

      x.append(a+i*h)

      fx.append(func(x[i]))

      i=i+1

   for i in range(m):

      print("n=",i,"x=%.6f"%x[i],"y=%.6f" %fx[i])

   sum=func(a)+func(b)

   for i in range(1,n):

      if(i%2==0):

         sum=sum+2*func(x[i])

      else:

         sum=sum+4*func(x[i])

   return(float(h/3)*sum)

a=0

b=1

n=8


print("%.6f"%simpsons(a,b,n))
```

PYTHON CODE FOR SIMPSONS 3/8 RULE

```
import math
def func(x):
   return (float ( math.e**(-x**2)) )
def simpson_( a, b, n ):
   h =(float(b - a )/ n)
   x = []
   fx = []
   m = n+1
   i = 0
   while i<m:
      x.append(a + i * h )
      fx.append (func(x[i]))
      i = i+ 1
   for i in range(m):
      print("n = ", i," x = %.6f"%x[i], " y = %.6f"%fx[i])
   i = 0
   sum = func(a) + func(b)
   for i in range (1,n):
      if ( i % 3 == 0 ):
         sum = sum + 2 * func (x[i])
      else:
         sum = sum + 3 * func ( x[i] )
   return ( (float ( 3 * h ) / 8) * sum )
n = 4
a = 0.2
b = 1.5
integral = simpson_(a, b, n )
print ("Ans = %.6f"%integral)
```

PYTHON CODE FOR RUNGE KUTTA SECOND ORDER

```
def dydx(x,y):
    return y-x


def rungekutta2(dydx, x0, y0,x,h):
    while x0 < x:
        k1 = h* dydx(x0,y0)
        k2 = h* dydx(x0 + h, y0+k1)
        y0 = y0+ (1/2)*(k1+k2)
        x0 = x0+h
        print("k1 =%.4f, k2 =%.4f" % (k1, k2))
    return y0


x0 = 0
y0 = 2
h = 0.1


print("For y(0.1):")
y01 = rungekutta2(dydx, x0, y0, 0.1, h)
print("y(0.1) = %f" % y01)


print("\nFor y(0.2):")
y02 = rungekutta2(dydx, x0, y0,0.2, h)
print("y(0.2) = %f" % y02)
```

PYTHON CODE FOR RUNGE KUTTA FOURTH ORDER METHOD

```
def dydx(x,y):
    return y-x


def rungekutta2(dydx, x0, y0,x,h):
    while x0 < x:
        k1 = h* dydx(x0,y0)
        k2 = h* dydx(x0 + h, y0+k1)
        y0 = y0+ (1/2)*(k1+k2)
        x0 = x0+h
        print("k1 =%.4f, k2 =%.4f" % (k1, k2))
    return y0


x0 = 0
y0 = 2
h = 0.1


print("For y(0.1):")
y01 = rungekutta2(dydx, x0, y0, 0.1, h)
print("y(0.1) = %f" % y01)


print("\nFor y(0.2):")
y02 = rungekutta2(dydx, x0, y0,0.2, h)
print("y(0.2) = %f" % y02)
```

www.ingramcontent.com/pod-product-compliance
Lightning Source LLC
Chambersburg PA
CBHW041732100726
47973CB00011B/184
* 9 7 9 8 8 9 4 9 8 2 9 4 6 *